GREENLIGHT
Yourself

The Street-Smart Guide to the Indie Film Biz

GREENLIGHT YOURSELF
The Street-Smart Guide to the Indie Film Biz

ISBN: 979-8-218-78789-9
First Published Edition

Printed in the USA

Cover Design: Roger Lindley

For filmmaking documents, log on
PROFOUNDSTUDIOS.MEDIA

Published by Point Source Media Management, LLC
Fort Worth, Texas

The personal stories in this book are intended to show how we learned the business, many times the hard way. These stories serve as real-world examples of why this book is so important. Relationships are everything in this industry, so we've chosen to omit details from some stories to protect those colleagues from embarrassment. But we don't mind sharing *our* missteps if it means you can learn from them.

Most of the relationships we've built over the years continue strong; some have naturally drifted away, and a few needed to end. Regardless, we bless everyone on their journey and wish them a prosperous and fulfilling life story.

Table of Contents

Chapter One - The Curious Evolution of Indie Film 1

    A Rising Tide Lifts All Boats 7

Chapter Two - Welcome to the Indie Playground 11

    Myth vs Reality in Indie Film 14

Chapter Three - Common Mistakes of Indie Filmmaking 25

Chapter Four - The Two Most Important Questions 55

Chapter Five - Setting Up Your Film Like a Business 67

    How to Create a Pitch Deck 70

    How to Create a Business Plan 73

    Building Your Financial Strategy 85

    Seed Capital 88

Chapter Six - Marketing Unpacked 93

    Budgeting for Marketing to Build Leverage 94

    The Marketing Stack 98

    Cutting the Trailer 108

    The Key to Key Art 115

    Rolling Out Your Marketing Strategy 118

Chapter Seven - Distribution Decoded 135

    Think Like a Distributor 136

    The Revenue Waterfall 139

    Understanding Licensing 145

    Release Strategies 152

    Navigating the Streaming Ecosystem 161

The Hidden Dangers of Deliverables 170

Chapter Eight - Legalese Made Fun 183

Contracts 101 188

Guild Compliance 201

Permits and Clearances 205

Chapter Nine - So... You Wanna Produce? 213

Rising Above as a Producer 229

Chapter Ten - Building a Sustainable Career in Filmmaking 233

Burnout Stops Here. So Does the Drama 238

Hire Smart, Hire Early 243

Lead Like a Pro 248

Always Be in Learning Mode 250

Careers Are Built, Not Born 254

Chapter Eleven - Mastering In-person Networking 255

Networking Hall of Shame 260

Shift Your Mindset 262

Chapter Twelve - Eyes on the Horizon 265

Recap 265

The Future of Indie Filmmaking 269

The Short-form Storytelling Resurgence 278

International Co-productions 281

Tech Is a Tool, Story Is King 284

The Final Truth 287

Epilogue 293

Appendix 301

To those who dare to create their own path.

Thanks to Frank Snyder for lending his wisdom during the journey of this book.

Introduction
Why listen to us?

A lot of things look easy until you try them. Acting. Stand-up comedy. Starting a business. Parenting. Writing a book (sheesh—this one took forever). And making a movie. Filmmaking is one of those things you look at and say the famous last words, "Well, dang, I could do better than that!" So, you write a script and get your Uncle Fred to pony up the money. Three years later, you're knee-deep in legal documents you don't understand, your distributor is demanding 5.1 surround stems you don't have, and Uncle Fred wants to know when he's getting his money back.

Welcome to the beautiful chaos of filmmaking.

Of course, film is art. But it's also business, including contracts, insurance, logistics, emotional endurance, and a hundred people asking you what time lunch is. And that's before you try to sell it.

Filmmaking looks easy until you try it. Then you realize you're over your head after it's too late to back out. There is no command-Z button to undo the mistakes (or Control Z if you're Windows). Not to mention the countless films that never get made.

If it were easy, everyone would do it.

You might be tempted to skim this book or cherry-pick sections. Don't. You'll miss the full picture. It's structured so that each chapter builds on the last, and if you skip *one sentence*, you'll miss something critical. Every piece matters if you want to understand the full picture of the independent film business.

We've been responsible for millions in indie film financing, producing about 30 features, 20 documentaries, hundreds of commercials, and a handful of TV shows. This business punched us in the mouth more times than we can count. We've navigated shady contracts, nightmare shoots, miracle wins, and agonizing losses and still woke up the next morning ready to do it again.

You shelled out money to buy this book, and now you're reading it, so we can assume you're wanting to understand this wacky business that's about as dysfunctional as a 3 a.m. Vegas wedding. Okay then. Let's dig deep.

Beginning with a fun and slightly painful set of unofficial stats for you:

For every movie we helped to get made, we estimate we were either rejected by or had to reject at least 25 other projects. That's over 600 movies that almost happened… but didn't. They fizzled. Fell apart. Lost steam. Or it just never quite caught fire. These weren't bad ideas, either. Many had momentum; some had money, a cast, and even a start date.

For every movie that *did* get made, we reviewed about 150 scripts or pitch decks, totaling more than 4,500 projects that crossed our desks but didn't proceed.

Getting one movie greenlit takes about 2,000 emails, intros, LinkedIn exchanges, and festival handshakes. Do the math—that's 60,000 professional interactions.

Professional.

We're not even counting the countless cold emails, spammy pitches, and late-night DMs from dreamers with 21 pages of booger-soaked napkin scripts. Those deserve their own chapter.

Despite that, we love this madness. We love the puzzle of putting a movie together. That about-to-run-out-of-daylight moment when the scene finally clicks. And we live to help other filmmakers dodge the landmines we've already stepped on.

But the question of the month is, why does anyone sign up for this insanity? If you can survive twelve-hour days on set with your underwear sticking to you, try to sleep for a couple of hours, and wake up wanting more, that's the hunger legends are made of. Sometimes, the fire in your belly dwindles into the ashes of doubt and anxiety, but proper prep and knowledge will ignite the sky if the spark is kept alive.

Your Place in the Picture

This industry will chew you up, spit you out, and invoice you for the damage. But if you're a doer and not just a dreamer, this book will hand you the blueprint to help you survive the system, beat the odds, and build something meaningful that lasts.

This isn't a manual on framing shots or how to edit. *Greenlight Yourself* is about the side of filmmaking that wrecks most indie films: the business. This book is about money. Myths. Mistakes. Marketing. Contracts. Deliverables. Distribution deals. Strategy. All the unsexy stuff that determines whether your film and your career survive. We'll also dismantle myths you've heard (and maybe believed) about "making it" as a professional filmmaker. We'll certainly encourage you along the way, but we're going to give it to you straight without asking how you feel about it. Thin skins bleed hard in this business.

This is how successful, career-level filmmakers do it. This is how they get things done and why industry influencers return their calls. The contents of this book can easily intimidate you, but as you allow each word to be absorbed, think about how you can assemble a team to tackle the stuff that makes your head hurt. You've heard it before; surround yourself with people smarter than yourself and doors open you can't budge on your own. *Everything in this book* is important, and once you apply these tactics and strategies in your next project, you'll say, "Ah, now I understand."

Every year, indie filmmakers, against the odds, plant seeds that grow into lasting careers rooted in the fertile ground that merges business and art. That's what we're here to help you build.

This is your shortcut to a smarter start or a course correction if you've already taken some hits. Every pro was once in your shoes. It would've sucked a lot less for us if we would've had a book like this.

You're about to gear up with knowledge and learn how to make a film with your eyes wide open. You're about to become dangerous in the most excellent way because, in indie films, dangerously excellent is the pedestal you want to stand on.

It's true; you don't need a film degree to be successful in an indie film career. Some of the most outstanding filmmakers come from commercials, web content, or business backgrounds. If you understand story and how money works, you're ahead of the game, but the trick is knowing how to play your hand.

All that said, if you get just one takeaway from this book, we hope it will be this:

Producing a film, especially a short, with your own money and favors from friends is a priceless education. Do it. Fail, learn, and get better. *But the moment you start using other people's money, even from family, you elevate your involvement to a responsibility, not just learning the process. If you don't understand the grand process of independent filmmaking, trying to produce a film funded with other people's money is reckless.* You're almost *guaranteeing* their money will be wasted. First, gain experience on your dime. Don't gamble with someone else's cash.

Before we dive in, we want to share a bit about ourselves. First up: Kirk.

Get Back on the Bike

By Kirk Roos

My first feature film did NOT make its money back. My late wife, Bryn, and I made an indie film for under $75,000, but we came up short. I felt like a failure. And yet, here I am, decades later, still in the game, making films, and now writing this book because I greenlit myself.

This book is all about adapting a mindset of *greenlighting yourself*. It means putting your own money, sweat, tears, and sanity into a project because no one else is going to do it for you. For the past 30 years, that's what I've done. Over and over. The odds are you'll fail too. Sorry. That's why you "check yourself before you wreck yourself." (Credit to Bryn for that gem.)

I had returned to my hometown of Minot, North Dakota to squeeze in a guest role in a musical at my alma mater. Bryn was in the musical, and the relationship quickly sparked. At the time, I was acting in LA, chasing gigs, and scraping by. I was only home for a few weeks, and we tried to stay "friends first" when I told her I had to go back to LA. But I promised her I would take the relationship very seriously if she moved to California. To my surprise, she did. Immediately. It was great. We started our life together. And right away, she encouraged me to keep chasing my dreams but also to take the reins and pave my own path. She loved talking about "Manifesting" and put a lot of faith in me.

While bouncing around some short films, commercials, and documentaries, as well as musicals and other side hustle work, she confidently told me, "You need to make your own feature film. That's the only way your dreams will come true, by doing it yourself." I was nervous, but she assured me with all her heart that it would change our lives and trajectory. And it did.

We got married, and soon, we were making our first feature film. We pooled all our resources, friends, family, old theatre colleagues, and the entire community. That's a story for another book, but she greatly challenged me, and I'm grateful to this day for that experience. Her dreams were often very lofty and sometimes unrealistic. But her passion and faith steadfastly pushed me forward.

Before our first film, I had just come off a brutal shoot in Yosemite, where I was an actor, and I was also roped into lending them my box truck as a makeshift grip truck. Yosemite is gorgeous. It was a really fun location, sure, and by the way, hiking in Yosemite is the best! But the film nearly collapsed, we weren't paid what we were promised, and the producers had no idea what they were doing. They had money and good intentions but no roadmap. And I thought: "I could do better than that." And she agreed.

So, a year later, we made our first film in our hometown of Minot. Better than Yosemite, but... It failed. We failed. I failed. But we tried again. And again.

And...

Each time I failed, that gut-wrenching feeling came. But each time I got back up, the feeling faded. That's the real secret: Success is *inseparably* dependent on how you rise up after failure. You start asking better questions, building stronger teams, and learning to delegate. You stop wearing all the hats and begin understanding the business. *Film is art, but it's also commerce.* And the marriage of the two is where the magic happens.

I'll never forget the day my daughter learned to ride a bike. She was four years old, wobbling down the sidewalk with me jogging behind her, one hand gently gripping the back of her seat. "Are you still holding on?" She asked with a smile on her face despite her fear. And like any good parent bluffing their way through a rite of passage, I lied. "Yes, sweetie, I got you."

But I'd already let go. She didn't know she was pedaling on her own, gliding forward with her hair blowing back and singing, "I'm doing it! I'm doing it!" It was pure magic—until she turned, saw my empty hands, and panicked. Boom. Crash. Tears. Then laughter. Then, the moment of truth: she got back on. That crash was a baptism. That moment, that messy, glorious recovery, is what *success really looks like.*

I've made documentaries, commercials, short films, features, and quirky little passion projects. I've been the writer, actor, director, driver, editor, fundraiser, and janitor. But the turning point was when I learned to delegate. I took the advice of an agent I had years later, "Be an Executive Producer on a bigger film with more experienced producers. Learn from the top down." I stopped lifting the gear and started lifting the vision. On one project—an indie comedy called *High Road,* directed by Matt Walsh, we improvised the entire film. Literally. Matt is known for being an improv King and founder of *Upright Citizens Brigade.* The movie was entirely improvised. I produced. But with a team. I helped find the money, built the team, and stayed through to the end; focusing on festivals, marketing, and we even got our film promoted on Conan O'Brien and Last Call with Carson Daly.

We also developed a unique touring concept that featured a comedy show preceding screenings. It was wild. And I didn't have to wear all the hats. I just had to wear the right one.

And through all this, I started mentoring others, because producing is about coaching. It's about passing on your scars so others don't get as bloodied. I loved that I could share with new producers, "learn from my mistakes," and "You don't have to do everything. Just choose your lane and go."

Bryn and I greenlit ourselves. We lost money on our first project, but only a year or so later, I became a full-time filmmaker, able to support myself, and I've done it for well over 20 years. Other people started hiring me. Corporations and nonprofits. And it all started with a leap of faith and a failed feature film. But did it start there? Or did it start with Bryn challenging me to take a huge risk?

So, my invitation to you is... *Take the leap.* It's not guaranteed to work, but it'll definitely teach you something. It's your real-world film school. Your spiritual training ground. Your entrepreneurial boot camp. Your bike. And when you fall off—and you will—get back on.

Like my daughter did when she learned to ride a bike, fell off, and got back on again with tears of pain, embarrassment, and... JOY.

That's filmmaking.

This book is full of cliches. You've been warned. Mostly tongue-in-cheek. But they're all true. The real heart of it is this: Create the path you want, but *learn the lessons in this book so you don't have to learn the hard way.* Build the team. Ride the bike. And when you crash—and you will—get back on. Again and again.

One reason I agreed to co-write this book was that I wanted to share our experiences from the inside and discuss some of the things they don't teach in film school. But the real secret sauce is humility.

To me, success is knowing you've failed, admitting it, learning from it, and picking yourself up to do it again. And improving each time. I think back on my late wife and one of our first conversations when she said, "I want you to do this movie and stop chasing everyone else's dreams and praying for a one-liner in a Pepsi commercial. Greenlight *yourself.*" We did. Not I, alone. WE. A team. A community. We built something together. One day at a time. One movie at a time. Good luck y'all!

Swinging Hammers and Building Dreams

By Roger Lindley

Roger v1.0 worked in construction. I grew up with a grandpa, uncles and cousins who worked in the drywall business. My father died when I was seven, and mom moved us around a lot. But all of my high school years were lived in Chetek, Wisconsin, an idealistic tourist town in northwest corner of the state. My favorite high school teacher was Gary Mohr, and we struck up a friendship during my Freshman year that lasts to this day.

One of my favorite subjects in high school was AV. At the time, Chetek High School boasted a quaint audio-visual department that taught basic camera skills (which were mostly film-based at that time) and photography, including film development and printing photos in a darkroom. Mr. Mohr was the photography teacher. He was also a carpenter as a side hustle. During one summer break, Gary hired me to help build a house; an experience unlike anything I had known at the time, as I learned how to construct a home from a pile of lumber stacked in the dirt of what would become the front yard. Gary had a blueprint. From those plans, he measured, and I cut. Gary pointed, and I carried lumber and toted boxes of nails from the truck. As the house progressed, I learned about door cripples (84-1/4 inches tall, as I recall), headers, stringers, top and bottom plates, why 2x4s don't quite add up to 2x4, and why that's important to know when building just about anything that involves lumber. Gary taught me why door frames need to be 3" wider and taller than the door itself and why the bottom plate of a framed wall isn't cut away from the door frame immediately. Framing a house sounds simple enough when a layperson explains it; "That's when you build the structure of the house," but myriad techniques and nuances of the craft of framing are impossible to capture in that statement.

That summer had a lifelong effect on me. It spurred a desire to make a career out of construction, to which my grandfather warned, "Don't be a dummy; get into computers." Not one to listen to sound advice at the time, I worked with anything other than computers. After graduating from high school, I worked a winter as a derrick hand on an oil work over rig in Sidney, Montana. An acquaintance invited me to go with him to Texas where he was going to start a roofing company. With construction still smoldering within my desires and a distinct lack of appreciation for -20-degree weather while tripping pipe, I was stupid enough to follow the dude to Amarillo, Texas.

Amarillo is a great place, don't get me wrong, but the job lasted exactly four months before the guy skipped town in the dark of night and stiffed me for $800 in wages. Yeah, that dude. I felt stranded. But, I fell back on what I knew: drywall. Things started looking up when I landed a job with a respected painting contractor in Amarillo, working on a crew that taped and bedded drywall. Excellent pay, and I was doing what I loved: Building things.

But then came the fateful job when the crew was sent to help remodel the newsroom at the local CBS affiliate, KFDA. It was glorious. I had stars in my eyes, seeing the news set I saw on TV each night, the full-sized studio cameras, and eavesdropping on the chatter that sounded like a foreign language on the camera headsets when I was on break. It relit another spark of passion in me that began in the little AV class back in Chetek. One day, the station's Chief Engineer strolled into the newsroom while I was tromping around on stilts, and we started a conversation. I mentioned that while I enjoyed construction, I had wondered about the idea of working in film and television but didn't know how to get started. It so happened that a position was open for operating the studio cameras during the weekend newscasts. I spoke with the production manager and, to my startled glee, was hired for a part-time position on the spot.

That flowed with a journey of figuring out life with no real plan. A pattern was set after my father's death; my mom moved us around so much that I never had the chance to grow roots. I got used to figuring things out as I went—new towns, new schools, new people. That rootlessness followed me into my career. I didn't know where I was headed, just that I was moving. No roadmap. Just movement. And mistakes.

I left construction and began working full-time at the TV station. I moved up rather quickly. A salesman named John Mott invited me to help him with an industrial video the station was hired to produce for the regional power company that became my introduction to operating a Sony Betacam. A few months passed, and I picked up a few bits of basic production skills here and there. Then, a new general manager came on board who strategized a top-to-bottom re-branding for the station. In my youthful naïveté, I asked him if I could produce the thirty-second image promo. He patted me on the head like a good little puppy dog and said, "Sure, sure, you go do that." Not only did he authorize the promo to air, it won a 10th District American Advertising Federation ADDY that year. That experience evolved into being invited to shoot and edit a documentary that won the Chicago International and American Film and Video Festivals. The fire ignited. I set a new course to learn everything I could, and decided that my career goal would be to direct movies. The problem was I knew nothing about the film industry and didn't know where to learn.

My journey was two steps forward, one back. There are no mentors in the fog. Not healthy ones, anyway.

Over time, however, I became one of the top video producers in Amarillo and launched a successful production company, called Ragtown Media. From there, I was invited to LA by Bradley Dorsey to work on films he was producing that were distributed by PureFlix (before the Sony and Great American Media days). I directed one of those films. Bucket list filled. Oddly, that experience got me thinking about getting into distribution. Once again, there was no plan, just ambition. With many closed doors and a few that opened wide, that's where I landed. As I have often said, "I don't recommend my career path to anyone, but it worked for me."

I had no roadmap—just a hammer and the spark of curiosity. Every step forward exposed new gaps I didn't know existed. Cameras, editing, storytelling, contracts, finance—I learned it all the long, hard way. Most filmmakers do. They leap in with passion, unaware of what they don't know. Passion is important, nothing important happens without it. Moving before you're fully ready has risk, but you need to start somewhere. It's likely that you'll never be fully ready, but wisdom asks, when are you *ready enough?* Not being ready enough means that diving into something as significant as a feature film with passion alone is almost guaranteed to derail you, because the techniques and nuances of the business of filmmaking are impossible to capture with passion alone. This book helps you get ready enough to make the dream happen without a train wreck.

Years after that summer of learning how to build a house and also working in other construction crafts through my young life, I built my two-story dream home in Amarillo on twelve acres just west of town. My wife, Shellie, and I moved in a week before our son, Clayton, was born. There were mistakes, but none so significant that the house was not completed or collapsed in a pile of splinters. It still took a team to accomplish this; I didn't know everything, nor did I have the time, knowledge, or horsepower to do every process myself. However, my past construction experience made it possible when a large construction project would have otherwise been foolish to tackle.

I wasn't fully ready, but I was ready enough.

My story demonstrates the power of mentors and having a plan. Mr. Mohr provided me with a foundation and taught me how to read blueprints. With mentors, you learn techniques and nuances that you don't have to learn the hard way on your own, and the inevitable mistakes won't be severe enough to face plant you in the dirt. My story also demonstrates the importance of having a team. Never in life will you accomplish greatness as an island.

By the way, our son, Clayton, now operates Ragtown Media in Scottsdale, Arizona. He's taken the company to entirely new heights, and he got his foundation by toting lights, tripods, and batteries for his papa.

So, now that you've heard our stories, we're stepping back. From here until the Epilogue, this book speaks to you not from Kirk or Roger as individuals but from our combined experience and *as a team*. We wrote the rest in the third person to provide clarity, structure, and a roadmap shaped by both our scars and successes. Let's get to it.

— Roger Lindley & Kirk Roos

Introduction

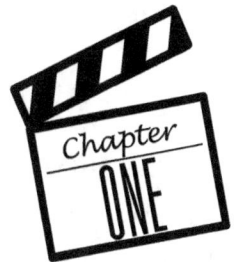

The Curious Evolution of Indie Film

"Seize the day, boys. Make your lives extraordinary."

—John Keating, *Dead Poets Society* (1989)

Indie and studio films share the same industry, but that's where the similarity ends. It seems obvious, yet we constantly see indie pitch decks propped up with studio comps. Comparing indie and studio films is like putting a cheese sandwich next to a five-course dinner at the Waldorf. Indie and studio financing, distribution, marketing, creative control, and business models are worlds apart. Sure, once in a while a studio acquires an indie, but that's still apples to peanuts.

Grasping that difference is foundational to why *every choice you make* as an indie filmmaker must distinctly follow an indie playbook.

But what does indie actually mean? We throw around the word 'independent' like a badge of honor. And it should be if done correctly. Is indie a budget level? An aesthetic? A festival screening? A film shot on weekends with maxed-out credit cards? You're not independent when you're hoping A24 or Sony Affirm will swoop in and pick up your film. That's not independence—that's a corporate buyout. It makes you a gambler with a half-baked plan, praying someone else will fix it. That dependency is fueled by misguided expectations, and nothing screams 'indie' less than begging for the attention of a suit while wearing skinny jeans.

True independence doesn't mean making your film *outside* the system; it means building a strategy that doesn't *depend* on it. And sustainable doesn't mean banking on a breakout film to magically launch your career. It means pushing past the wreckage of dreams sunk by filmmakers who never learned how the business works. It means raising capital, defining a strong marketing strategy, and mapping a viable pathway to distribution from the start. It means understanding the business as deeply as the craft, surrounding yourself with the right team, and treating every project like the foundation for the next.

The goal that we hope you'll focus on isn't just to make a film, it's to build a career, a reputation, and a body of work that continues to open doors well into your future. It means building toward a long-term career where you own the wins *and* the losses. It means doing the hard, sometimes dull, business work that makes your art sustainable.

So, are you building a business or simply hoping for a miracle?

One puts you in control. The other leaves you waiting at the gate, hoping someone lets you in.

Hollywood: The Beast

Independent film didn't appear out of thin air. Early adapters were rebels in the eyes of the Beast, the studio system, a vertically integrated monster. In the so-called "Golden Age of Hollywood," the Beast controlled everything; development, production, distribution, and exhibition. They owned the lots, the theaters, and the people. Actors were under long-term contracts. Writers and directors were essentially employees. Studios cranked out movies like candy canes at Christmas, efficient and profitable but creatively suffocating.

Then the mold cracked.

In the 60's and 70's, filmmakers like Cassavetes, Hopper, and Scorsese found ways to bypass the Beast. By the 90's, the indie boom had arrived. Filmmakers like Tarantino, Soderbergh, Linklater, and Kevin Smith proved you could make it without studio muscle. Sundance turned into the holy land for filmmaking. The Independent Spirit Awards were no longer a punchline.

The System is Broken

Yet, we still rely on that system with equal degrees of nausea and reverence. It's evolved from the absolutes of the Golden Age, but the Beast still breathes.

Today's indie world borrows heavily from the old playbook: Opaque accounting, institutional gatekeeping, and creative decisions are often shaped more by pre-sales formulas than storytelling. The legal labyrinth is still real; chain of title, rights agreements, deliverables, insurance, permits, residuals. And while you can make a film without a name actor or sales agent, the road is steeper without them.

And adding to the sucky part, right around 97% of all independently produced films fail to recoup the money spent to make them. Investors know it.

And distributors don't care if you make money. It's not their responsibility.

It's *yours*. Yes, you read that correctly.

That means you're playing chess on a board rigged for someone else's victory.

We're still trying to break the rules as rebels while dragging around the same old debris, the same gatekeeping bureaucracy, but mostly the exact outdated and misguided expectations that keep most filmmakers chasing squirrels of obscurity. And now, the big studios have their own "indie" divisions — Searchlight, Focus Features, Sony Affirm, and Sony Pictures Classics. It's as if they show up to the bake sale with a Costco cake and swipe their fingers in our frosting. While they benefit some higher-end indie films with studio-level release strategies, they're still the Beast, one we'll continue to feed until indie goes full direct-to-audience. There are pockets of that happening, but not on a scale that makes a real difference. One of the bottlenecks is with indie filmmakers themselves: They cause most of their own problems, and the Beast will keep its fangs in their throat until they figure out its game.

There is an important balance to consider here. Making a film takes passion, tenacity, skill, knowledge, and faith—and yes, breaking rules is part of the indie spirit. But hear this: You can't hope to walk around, over, through, or within the Beast until you know how to "play the game."

Hope Is Not a Business Plan

If you plan your film to check the acquisition boxes for a company like Sony Affirm or A24, that's a valid way to play the game. You're then building your project with a distributor's criteria and market demand in mind. But if you're hoping they pick you up just because you have made something you *hope* will sell, that's just wishful thinking.

Distributors are buyers looking for content that fits their market, but they won't do your homework for you if you haven't already done it yourself.

So, Why Do This at All?

You're here because something inside you won't shut up—some restless, beautiful calling whispers, "Make the film!" Maybe you've had the dream since you were ten. Maybe it hit you last year like a bolt of lightning. But now it's in your blood, and nothing else will do.

The gates are open. You have easy access to cameras, editing software, crowdfunding platforms, and direct access to your audience. The era of asking for permission is over.

That said, passion and access to tools alone won't get your film sold for a profit or build a sustainable career for you. You need to dial in discipline and a plan. You must move like a filmmaker building something that lasts, not rely on a roll of the dice.

Faith-Based Films

We'd be missing a big piece of the indie conversation if we didn't talk about the rise of Christian films, a movement in the indie world that came into focus at the turn of the millennium.

Mel Gibson's *The Passion of the Christ* (2004) broke into the mainstream, but it did so in a very unusual way. It was unapologetically faith-centered, spoken entirely in Aramaic, Latin, and Hebrew with subtitles, and packed with intense violence. By all normal market logic, it should have been niche. Instead, it became a global cultural event driven by controversy, curiosity, and event-style marketing that pulled in both devout believers and people who simply wanted to see what all the buzz was about.

Two years later, *Facing the Giants* (2006) was the indie film world's answer, an overtly faith-based story produced by Sherwood Baptist Church in Georgia. Made for just $100,000 with volunteers filling most of the cast and crew, it didn't break into the mainstream. But inside the Christian market, it performed far beyond expectations. Its theatrical run and strong DVD sales proved there was a loyal audience ready to support faith-themed films, even when production values were modest. That success helped cement the early viability of faith-based films as a market segment.

The studios noticed. 20th Century Fox launched Fox Faith in 2006. Sony followed in 2007 with Affirm Films. From that point forward, "faith-based" wasn't just a category in the church library—it was a business vertical with real revenue performance.

Faith-based isn't a genre—it's a market segment with two lanes. One is overtly faith-based, aimed at Christian audiences and built around explicit spiritual messaging. The other is faith-adjacent—films with moral or redemptive themes that appeal to broader audiences while still resonating with believers. Each generally plays by different rules.

Over the past two decades, the quality of faith-driven filmmaking has improved. *I Can Only Imagine, War Room,* and *Sound of Freedom* proved that faith-based content can demonstrate strong storytelling and solid production value. *The Chosen* raised the bar further, showing that a series rooted in Christian themes could compete for global attention.

Still, much of the market remains stuck in safe formulas like predictable dialogue, oversimplified morality, and a reluctance to wrestle with the messy, unresolved, and even dangerous topics that the Church at large typically won't touch. Those films often resonate deeply with church audiences but rarely connect outside of them. And that's fine if you're clear about the intended audience you're making the film for.

Some filmmakers set out hoping their movie will win millions to Christ. While God can use any story, the reality is that overtly faith-based films usually serve the already-convinced. For secular audiences, exposure typically comes when a Christian friend or family member invites them to watch—an approach that can open doors in some cases, but more often reinforces the sense that the film is "for someone else." Mainstream audiences rarely engage, and sometimes the tone can close doors instead of opening them. *God's Not Dead,* for example, was financially successful but framed an "us versus them" narrative that energized the base while likely alienating the very people the church is trying to reach. That doesn't look good on a résumé.

Another common practice in some Christian circles is that everyone on a film set—from the Production Assistant to the lead actor—should be a professing believer. While that may come from a desire for unity, it can unintentionally limit quality and the opportunity to be a witness. You're an employer, not a pastor overseeing church staff. Hollywood consistently produces technically excellent films because they hire the best people for the job. Faith-based filmmakers should aspire to excellence in quality and potent storytelling—and then lead with integrity, kindness, and professionalism that speak louder than any sermon. *That's* a unifying message.

If Christians truly want to raise the bar, the aim shouldn't be to just match Hollywood, it should be to surpass it. Faith is not a shortcut to excellence, and "anointing" is not a substitute for skill. God may *give* you the talent, but it's up to you to *develop* that talent. Calling may open the door, but craft, discipline, and tenacity keep it open. The message is too important to be buried under weak writing, uneven performances, or poor execution.

If you're called to make faith-driven films, treat that calling with the same professional rigor as any other filmmaker tries to achieve. Know your audience. Be honest about your goals. And build something that can stand on its own, whether or not the viewer shares your faith.

A Rising Tide Lifts All Boats

Your Success = Everyone's Success

Imagine an indie film world where success is normal and not a happy accident. Picture an ecosystem where investors make money regularly, crew members get paid fairly, project after project, and audiences trust that "independent film" means a great experience, not a gamble on some incoherent vanity project. Sounds a bit Utopian, but this vision starts with individual filmmakers like you building sustainable careers and racking up wins more often than losses.

When you win, the entire indie community wins. Filmmakers who build a track record of solid outcomes create a halo effect that benefits others. Sustainable careers lead to more consistent success stories, building trust with investors and partners. Think about it: if an investor loses their shirt on 9 out of 10 indie films, can you blame them for fleeing the sector? But if suddenly 6 or 7 out of 10 films return a profit, even a modest one, that investor will be much more excited to reinvest in new projects. They might tell their rich friends that indie film isn't a fool's errand. More wins = more money circulating = more films getting made. It's simple math and psychology.

As a filmmaker, you have a stake in the larger ecosystem. You're essentially advocating for the independent film industry whenever you treat your project professionally and hit your marks; schedule, budget, quality, audience engagement, and ultimately, returns. You become proof that this can be done right. That makes it easier for the next filmmaker to pitch to an investor, distributor, or high-profile actor's agent. Conversely, when someone torches an investor's money on a poorly planned production, it hurts all of us by reinforcing the stereotype that indie films are a black hole for cash.

Think of the indie film world as a long-term game of reputation and results. It's like how specific film festivals get a rep for programming quality work; people start to trust anything from Sundance or Cannes' indie selections, for instance. Similarly, suppose more indie filmmakers in your circle or region are known for smart business practices and decent returns. In that case, local financiers or arts grants committees will be more inclined to bet on new voices.

There's also a mentorship and knowledge-sharing aspect. If you find a formula that works, say you crack the code of profitable self-distribution, discover a niche audience that supports your work, then share the love. That doesn't mean giving away all your secrets or doing others' jobs for them, but being open about lessons learned. Maybe you speak on a panel or mentor a younger filmmaker (remember that "mentor" concept? Be the mentor you wish you had!). You're increasing the community's overall health by lifting others up and helping them avoid pitfalls. Fewer senseless failures mean more collective strength.

Also, when your career is sustainable, you'll likely reach a point where you become an investor or producer on others' projects. Many filmmakers do this; they reinvest their success into new filmmakers or interesting stories that aren't theirs. Why? Partly to give back, partly because they know a smart bet when they see one. When you're in that position, you'll appreciate those protégés who have their head on straight business-wise. You'll look for the same qualities of professionalism and long-term planning that we're urging you to develop now.

Lastly, consider the audience, the lifeblood of indie's entire ecosystem. When indie films consistently improve in quality and reliability, delivering a satisfying experience rather than just passion fluff, audiences will trust indie creators. They'll take more chances to see your weird little film because the last few films they watched were good. This growing audience's trust loops back into financial success, and the cycle continues.

So, the takeaway is that your career is bigger than just you. Every time you score a victory, no matter how small, you're pushing the indie film world forward. And every time you avoid a disaster by using solid business sense and preparation, you prevent a setback for yourself and others. It's a team sport, even when it doesn't feel like it. Embrace that responsibility; it can motivate you. And wouldn't it be nice if that culture were known for success and sustainability instead of caution and heartbreak? Be part of the change, one smart career move at a time.

Greenlight Yourself

That requires clarity, courage, knowledge, and preparation. You win by showing up *so ready* and *immutable* that the path forward can't deny you. You won't win the game by waiting your turn.

If filmmaking is encoded in your genes, you owe it to yourself to do it right. Stop waiting, but stop winging it. Step into the role of a creator who knows how to deliver.

But the low barrier to entry is buried under an avalanche of amateurish, weekend warrior mediocrity, destroying investor sentiment and tarnishing the indie spirit. (If you're guilty, don't sweat it. Admit that you don't know what you don't know. We're here to help, and you'll do better next time)

You really want to be indie?

Okay, then. Let's sharpen your blade.

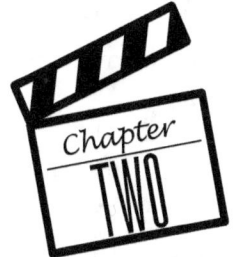

Welcome to the Indie Playground

"You want something, go get it. Period."

— Chris Gardner, *The Pursuit of Happyness* (2006)

The indie playground, where you climb high on the jungle gym of ambition, only to have reality shove you into the dirt. It's a place to run wild and free with your vision and can be a magical place, but it's an obstacle course that leaves you with skinned-up knees and a bruised ego more often than not.

You likely have a story you cannot let go of and you'll do what it takes to make it happen. That's the beauty of indie filmmaking: creative freedom, risk-taking, and complete control over your voice. But are you ready enough? Freedom has a price. You still must play nice with the Beast for things like distribution, contracts, and deliverables. And the Beast doesn't care how noble your vision is. It was built to serve itself, and if you don't know how to navigate the business, it will ignore you and move on.

This chapter reveals what the indie world demands from you, how the system is stacked against you, and what it takes to survive and stand up stronger.

Take Roger's Amazon documentary, *The Kurdish Factor: The Untold Story of the Gulf Wars* (2018) on Amazon. There are two takeaways here: story and distribution.

First, the story. Roger traveled to Iraq five times, filming in the semi-autonomous Kurdish region. Initially, the focus was on Dr. John Thomas, an Asian Indian general surgeon who had joined a medical mission led by Dr. Gazi Zibari, a renowned transplant surgeon and Iraqi Kurd who had fled Saddam Hussein's brutality in 1975. After the Gulf War, Dr. Zibari returned to help rebuild Iraqi Kurdistan's medical capacity. It was a compelling character setup, but Roger saw a larger story unfolding when he arrived. The Kurds are the largest ethnic group in the world without a country of their own, and in Iraq, many Kurds credited the U.S. for their liberation from Saddam's murderous savagery.

That gave Roger a solid backdrop but not a solid story spine. He kept shooting, hoping the story would take shape. It wasn't until real-world geopolitics delivered the third-act climax. In 2017, the Kurdish government declared independence from Iraq, and Baghdad swiftly responded with tanks. Their referendum collapsed, and the film finally worked not because of narrative mastery but because history handed Roger structure by sheer luck. But relying on luck is not a strategy.

Second, distribution. Lacking a clear understanding of the business at the time, Roger signed a deal with a shady European distributor. There was no oversight, no clear contract, and ultimately no money despite a release, just a hard lesson.

Story first, strategy always.

Humility: Ask for Help (a.k.a. Don't Do Your Own Root Canal)

Kirk has said for years, "Don't do your own root canal just because you're the one paying for it." And yet, indie filmmakers do this metaphorically all the time. They raise money, and suddenly, they think they must wear every hat: Writer, director, producer, distributor, publicist, sales agent, lawyer, and social media team. They're afraid to ask for help. Or worse, they believe they don't need it.

Many filmmakers "fake it until they make it," but that's just shorthand for pretending to know instead of learning to grow. That attitude looks confident on the surface, but it's performative, a façade of competence that avoids the vulnerability required for real growth.

Think more about someone like Teddy Roosevelt, who is often credited with saying, "When you're asked if you can do a job, tell 'em, 'Certainly I can!' Then get busy and find out how to do it." This business is way too complex to master alone. You might've learned how to light a scene in film school, but did anyone teach you how to negotiate an agency contract? Or how to structure waterfall payments in your distribution deal? Or how foreign rights can be sold in Europe without getting ripped off by a shady distributor?

Filmmaking is infrastructure with art on top. Pretending you have it all figured out might make you feel confident, but in reality, it makes you confidently reckless. True confidence is knowing your limits and surrounding yourself with people who make you better. Hollywood (or Hollyweird, as Kirk likes to call it) is full of people who smile and nod quietly, thinking, "They have no idea what they're doing." Be the one who says, "I don't know everything. But I'm here to learn." Teddy Roosevelt also said, "Do what you can, with what you have, where you are."

Do you know someone who grabs on to a few industry buzzwords or phrases and throws them around without knowing what they really mean? "Yeah, we're targeting ROI of ten million and four-walling this as a tent pole. I was talking to the gaffer at the wrap party and he thinks it might be franchisable. He's been on some big movies, so he would know." Do what? Can that someone's financial plan defend ten million in profit? What data do they have that justifies paying for theaters themselves? Tent pole? Is their little $250k no-name indie film about camping? That's someone trying to fake it till they make it, and it's arrogant. This industry mocks arrogance, but the humble, the learners, the listeners, and the collaborators build careers. And they make better movies. So yeah, you might be footing the bill, but please let someone else hold the drill.

Myth vs. Reality in Indie Film

Independent film gets romanticized as a freewheeling creative utopia where bold, purpose-driven stories thrive without studio interference. And yes, the indie playground can be a haven for daring storytelling and cultural impact. But let's pump the brakes.

A leading film industry analyst, Stephen Follows, studied 37,472 U.S. feature films from 1999 to 2018. Of those, 94.3% were independent. Only 3.4% of the independently produced films returned a profit, meaning 96.6% lost money.

Let that sink in.

Practically every indie investor goes home in the red. That's unsustainable for the industry, yet many filmmakers, driven by well-intended passion and blissful naivety, keep convincing investors to fund their films, while the failure rate remains unchanged. Why fight for "meaningful indie cinema" in an industry indifferent to the passion of its participants who might know the art but they don't know the business? That's not game-winning strategy.

The game isn't hopeless. But it is rigged, unless you learn how to play it smarter.

Bursting the Bubble (So You Can Build Better)

Your brilliant debut film will not automatically get into Sundance and spark a bidding war. Yes, it's possible—and we'll cheer if it happens—but planning on that is like planning to win the lottery. Only a tiny percentage of indie films ever secure any distribution at all, and even fewer make a profit. Most indie filmmakers struggle to get their movie seen by an audience larger than family, friends, and the crew that helped make it. This isn't said to scare you off but to dismantle harmful myths that could set you up for painful disappointment. We will replace those myths with a solid understanding of how the industry works so you can beat the odds.

Resourcefulness is key for an indie film shoot. You might find yourself filming in unconventional locations with a bare-bones crew. Embrace the creative challenge; it's part of the indie playground experience.

So, let's bust a few of those myths:

Myth: "If I make a great film, the world will find it."

The romantic notion is that a masterpiece will naturally rise above the noise. Not so. Even quality films can languish unseen in today's cluttered streaming world, buried in the abyss of platform foldering. Thousands of indie titles are out there chasing the same crumbs of viewer attention. Without a plan to stand out, your film can easily get lost, no matter how great. We'll explore avoiding obscurity in later chapters with smart marketing and distribution strategies.

Myth: "Film festivals will launch my career."

Film festivals can be fantastic—they can be a springboard and a networking goldmine. However, submitting a film to Sundance is not a business plan.

Festivals are highly competitive, and even if you get in and maybe win, it does not ensure that any distribution or revenue will follow. Festival buzz for your film helps with marketing awareness, but that's typically all you get. Many filmmakers have ridden the festival circuit to come home with empty pockets and no distribution deal. We had a film submitted to us that won Slamdance. Even with that *impressive* notoriety, it took a long time for the film to sell, and the deal wasn't all that great, which shows that winning a major festival does not automatically translate into big money.

In a later chapter, we'll discuss how festivals fit into a larger distribution plan and how to leverage them without hoping for miracles.

Myth: "I Can Produce Because I Have To – No Experience Needed"

A Big Problem facing indie filmmakers is that too many well-meaning dreamers step into the producer role for whatever reason. Maybe it's because no one else will. But producing isn't a fallback position; it's a skilled profession. If you wouldn't give yourself a root canal because of the pain and complexity involved, why would you try to handle your film's marketing and distribution without knowing what you're doing?

Like dentistry, filmmaking takes skill, planning, and a crystal-clear understanding of where things can go sideways. Yes, the best way to learn is by doing. But what if you didn't have to learn the hard way? What if you had someone on your team who's been through the fire and could help you navigate it without derailing the odds of your film succeeding?

There are three main reasons why inexperienced filmmakers try to tackle the producer's role:

Creative Control: Filmmakers want to protect their vision. By producing, they can oversee script, casting, and editing decisions, avoiding interference from external producers who might prioritize commercial interests to the perceived detriment of art.

Limited Resources: Independent filmmakers, especially early in their careers, may lack the funds to hire experienced producers. Taking on the role themselves allows them to move forward with their project, leveraging passion and resourcefulness to fill the gap.

Career Ambition: Producing offers a chance to build a broader skillsets and industry clout. Filmmakers see it as a way to gain credibility, network with financiers and distributors, and position themselves as multi-hyphenated talents in a highly competitive field.

The greatest myth is thinking passion alone will carry you through a job that demands negotiation skills, budget sense, crisis management, investor diplomacy, legal literacy, a stomach for nonstop pressure, and instincts built on experience. It's everything from managing crew dynamics to having serious and productive conversations with distributors and sales agents while still juggling the daily fires of production.

Most first-time filmmakers have no idea how complex this role is until it's too late. They take on the title without the training because no one tells them otherwise. And that's where things typically go sideways. Distribution falls apart. Investor expectations weren't managed. No marketing strategy. Deliverables weren't accounted for. And now you're in a deep hole, wondering why the film you bled for isn't going anywhere.

That's the default mode of indie filmmaking, unfortunately.

We'll cover more about producing in a later chapter, but we want to encourage you not to do your own root canal. You don't know what's coming to ruin your day, so surround yourself with people who do.

Most indie filmmakers don't fail because they lack talent. They failed because they never saw the storm coming.

Myth: "I don't need to worry about business – I'm an artist."

Oh, sweet summer child. Thinking, "I just want to create, so someone else will handle the boring stuff," is career-damaging. If you learn only one thing from this book, let it be this: **your film IS a business recognized by the IRS, the Securities and Exchange Commission, and various state agencies.** Treating it like one can make the difference between a film that goes nowhere and finds its audience (and maybe even makes money). The film is both a business and an art; the two must work together. We'll hammer this home throughout this book, but from day one, you need to think about budgets, marketing, and distribution, not just your cinematic vision. This is what separates the doers from the dreamers. It's setting up your film and yourself for financial and career success.

Myth: "I just need the money."

If you're walking around saying, "I just need the money," then you're not ready.

That may sound harsh, but we're saying it with love. We've been there. And we've made all the same mistakes you're probably making right now.

Saying "I just need the money" is like saying "I just need gas money" when the car hasn't even been designed. Saying that skips over all the most important stuff, and it screams "Amateur in the house!" to experienced producers and investors who know what you don't.

There's a persistent fantasy in the indie film world that goes something like this:

"We have a great script. Everyone loves it. If someone would just give us the money, we could make the movie and blow everyone away."

It's a lovely thought, but it's not the real world.

Because "just the money" is never *just the money.* It's legal structures. It's the capital stack. It's foreign pre-sales, state incentives, revenue projections, debt lending, waterfall charts, distribution pathways, deliverables, marketing strategies, and so on. It's months (or years) of spreadsheets, calls, contracts, and plan B's. If you don't have all that mapped out, then what you should be saying is:

"I need a plan."

Because without that, asking for money is like showing up at a bank for a loan with no collateral. That might work on your cousin, but it won't work on professionals. And that's okay! We're optimizing your collaboration skills, so when filmmakers come to us with wide eyes and big dreams saying, "We just need the money," it's a giant red flag. If you really just needed money, you'd be bank-loan ready. You'd have your LLC formed, your legal documents in place, your distribution strategy vetted, your tax credit paperwork queued up, and a sales agency on the line saying, "Let's go."

We're not trying to be gatekeepers. Quite the opposite. We want more filmmakers to succeed. But it starts with a truth that you don't "just need the money." You have to understand the business. If you don't, that's okay, just be honest about it. Find partners who do and stay humble. Learn. Share equity with people who can take you farther.

Ignorance isn't bliss in this business.

Old-School Structure and Why It's Falling Apart

15 to 20 years ago, there was a system, a formula, really, for financing independent films. It worked something like this:

> • 30% foreign pre-sales (if you had a name actor like Nick Cage)
>
> • 30% tax credit or rebate[1] (from Canada, Louisiana, Georgia, etc.)
>
> • 15-20% equity[2] (from investors, usually friends and family)
>
> • Remaining 20-25% from soft money[3], gap financing[4], or deferrals[5]

This worked when DVD was king, foreign buyers had appetites, and name actors moved product.

But streaming turned that game on its head. DVDs died. Foreign sales collapsed (unless you're Marvel). Buyers got picky. And most importantly, consumers learned they didn't always have to pay for individual movies.

Today, Minimum Guarantees[6] (MGs) are shrinking. Revenue share is

---

1   Film incentives are government-backed financial perks that lower production costs. Tax credits reduce tax liability and may be refundable or transferable. Rebates are post-production cash refunds based on in-state spending.

2   Equity capital is funding raised in exchange for ownership in the project. Investors are repaid from profits after debts and expenses are covered.

3   Soft money refers to non-recoupable funds like grants, product placement money, tax incentives, or rebates that reduce a film's budget without giving up equity or incurring debt.

4   Gap financing is a loan secured against unsold distribution rights, used to cover the shortfall between confirmed funding and the full budget.

5   A deferral payment is compensation postponed until the film earns revenue, often used to reduce upfront costs during production.

6   A Minimum Guarantee (MG) is an upfront payment from a distributor for distribution rights. It's an advance against future earnings—if the film under performs, the distributor absorbs the loss.

the new model. AVOD (advertising-based video on demand) is becoming the dominant force. And if you're not planning for this on the front end of your financing model, you're playing from the wrong rulebook.

The Capital Stack Matters

The capital stack is the breakdown of all the money coming in including debt, equity, soft money, tax credits, etc. Have you priced in interest? Recoupment waterfall[7]? Delivery costs? E&O insurance? Marketing? Do you have a pro forma[8] showing how the film could make money, and under what conditions, and are the numbers real? Have you considered:

- Whether your state incentive is transferable?

- Whether you can borrow against the incentives (i.e., tax credit loans)?

- If your cast is union, non-union, or a mixture of both?

- Whether your distribution and marketing plan is in place and realistic?

Most filmmakers don't have an LLC formed or understand they need one, much less a finance plan.

So if you're saying, "I just need the money," but you can't answer those four questions, then you're not ready for the money. If you don't know what to do, then you need to find someone can help you make a plan.

---

7   A recoupment waterfall is the order in which film revenues are distributed—typically repaying investors and lenders first after distribution fees and expenses, then profit participants.

8   A pro-forma is a financial projection estimating a film's costs, revenues, and returns to help investors evaluate potential profitability.

Collaborate, Don't Posture

Here's a better way to start the conversation:

"I have a strong script with great coverage[9], I've built a realistic budget, but I don't know what I don't know. I'm looking for an experienced producer who can help structure the financing and distribution side of this. I'm willing to learn, roll up my sleeves, and collaborate."

That's the kind of pitch we can work with.

Understand the New Math

The new equation for indie film financing requires creativity, humility, and a deep understanding of the new market. Some key realities:

- Pre-sales are nearly dead unless you have major stars.

- Tax credits only help if you know how to monetize them (via loans or structured investment).

- Equity needs a clear ROI[10] pathway, which means a real distribution plan, a back-end waterfall, and someone with a track record managing both.

- AVOD and FAST[11] channels are the future, but you still need to advertise to drive views.

- Filmmakers need to take responsibility for marketing their

---

9   Script coverage is a standardized industry report that provides a brief synopsis, character breakdowns, and an analysis of a screenplay's strengths and weaknesses. It is used by producers, agents, and executives to quickly assess a project's potential for development or production. Three separate reports are ideal.

10   ROI (Return on Investment) measures the profitability of an investment, calculated as the net gain divided by the original amount invested.

11   A FAST (Free Ad-Supported Streaming TV) channel delivers scheduled, linear content over the internet at no cost to viewers, generating revenue through ads. Examples include Roku Channel, Pluto TV, and Tubi.

films and not rely entirely on a distributor.

In the current era, marketing needs to be part of the budget. You don't call your film complete at picture lock, you finish it when your audience sees it. And if you don't budget for that, you're not greenlighting anything.

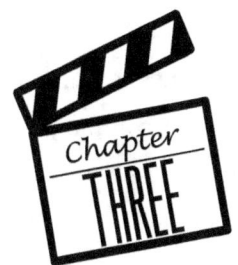

The Most Common Mistakes of Indie Filmmaking

"The greatest teacher, failure is."

— Yoda

Almost every independent filmmaker starts with good intentions and big dreams. Yet many promising projects end up on life support or dead on arrival. The most crash-and-burn failures trace back to common mistakes that plague first-timers (and sometimes even veterans who should know better). This chapter will reveal those mistakes in all their ugly glory. This is a mirror that shows the flaws—you might not love what you see, but it could save your film. We're going to be forthright about each mistake, why it happens, and how to avoid it. If you think, "Nah, I wouldn't do that," be careful—these pitfalls often come disguised as seemingly brilliant ideas. Learn from others' failures now, and you won't have to learn from your own.

Let's count down the most common missteps that derail the most indie filmmakers:

Mistake 12: Neglecting Entertainment Value

Many filmmakers set out to create work that raises awareness around important issues. That's a noble impulse, but one of the most common mistakes is prioritizing the message over the movie. If your film isn't entertaining, it won't matter how urgent or meaningful the subject is. People will tune out.

Take, for example, a documentary about children with Down syndrome. It may hold deep emotional power, but without a strong story structure to deliver that emotion with clarity and resonance, it's likely only to reach those already connected to the topic. To connect broadly, the message must be woven into storytelling that captivates, engages, and moves the audience.

The most effective advocacy films strike this balance. *Taare Zameen Par* (2007) explores the inner world of a dyslexic child through a rich, emotional narrative. *An Inconvenient Truth* (2006) turns climate data into a story with stakes and urgency through Al Gore's engaging presentation. Both films inform, but first, they connect.

Story is the gateway to resonant impact.

The mental health doc *Spyral* is a textbook case of advocacy films done right. When the producer brought it to us, the film was strong, and a pragmatic marketing plan was already in place.

They partnered with National Alliance on Mental Illness (700 chapters) and the NFL Alumni Association. They screened at Riverbend Church during SXSW buzz and premiered at Dances With Films, landing a *Variety* write-up.

Spyral had the trifecta: a timely message, a solid film, and a grassroots campaign that turned outreach into an audience.

Mistake 11: Losing Perspective – AKA Going Crazy in the Process

This one's more psychological but just as serious as the other mistakes.

Filmmaking can feel like life or death when it's your passion project. You eat, sleep, and breathe your film. But that kind of intensity, unchecked, can destroy relationships, burn out your crew, or wreck your health. As filmmaker Maureen Ryan said, "It's just a movie, and you're not curing cancer."

Translation: Keep perspective.

If every minor setback feels like an existential crisis, you'll drive yourself and everyone around you into the ground. Some indie directors push their crews to the brink, screaming about a prop being the wrong color or a line being flubbed three times. Why? Because "This film is everything!" But it's *not* everything; read the news. The wheels are falling off the world, and you're losing your mind over a boom mic in the shot. No one wants a boom mic photobombing their movie, but what's more important: snapping at the boom operator and killing morale, or preserving your team's trust and your reputation?

Toxic behavior has no place in life, especially not on set. Being an ass might get short-term results, but when that's your leadership style, it breeds fear, not respect. And that always costs you in the end. So, chill. Do you want to get yourself fired on Roger's set? Start screaming at his cast or crew, and he'll have you escorted out of their lives.

Leadership matters. Kirk often talks about what he learned in his MBA program: group dynamics. He uses the LA Lakers as an example. You have 12 guys on the team. Change even one of them—even the 12th man—and it's a different team. Maybe that guy was Kobe's favorite practice partner. Perhaps he was the emotional glue. Swap him out, and suddenly, the vibe shifts.

Your film crew is the same. One toxic person, one unchecked ego, one person not aligned with the mission, and the energy of the entire production tilts sideways. Leadership isn't just logistics. It's protecting the culture.

By staying centered and grounded, you make better decisions. You keep morale high. And you make a better film. Just as importantly, you give yourself the stamina to do it again. This film shouldn't be your entire life, but it should be the start of your career.

Mistake 10: "Fix It in Post" Syndrome

This mistake is a close cousin of rushing the script: the belief that most problems—story, performance, technical issues—can be fixed later in post.

Indie filmmakers often fall into this trap, usually from inexperience and wishful thinking. They don't get enough coverage or alternate takes, assuming they'll "cut around it." Or they skip clean dialogue takes because "we'll ADR it later," forgetting ADR costs money and time, and it's tough to match the performance.

Post-production won't hide your mistakes; it will *expose* them. The edit bay becomes a house of pain if you skimp on preparation and quality control during the shoot. Your options shrink, and your creativity suffocates.

Fix it now, not in post.

Sure, some things should be handled in post such as color, sound design, VFX, but those are intentional choices, not desperate repairs for sloppy development or prep.

This is where storyboards, shot lists, and honest prep work pay off. Some filmmakers skip them, claiming they "stifle creativity." That's a polite excuse. The real reason is they don't know how to prep; they're overwhelmed, lazy, or afraid that planning will expose what they haven't figured out yet. Sometimes, it's ego, thinking they can wing it like a genius auteur.

Prep unlocks creativity, especially when the clock is ticking and the budget is sucking air. Your job is to shoot only what the story demands. That means revisiting the script, clarifying your visual intent, and mapping the emotional flow of each scene before production.

Storyboards, location photos, and overhead diagrams protect your time, crew's sanity, and editing frustrations. When you know exactly what the audience needs to feel, you stop chasing bonus shots that don't matter.

Shoot only what matters. Leave the rest to your imagination, or save it for the next film.

Mistake 9: Failure to Plan (a.k.a. "We'll Figure It Out Later")

This one is broad but might be the deadliest: jumping into production without a solid plan. A shocking number of indie filmmakers charge ahead without a proper schedule, budget, or logistical strategy, usually out of enthusiasm, naivety, or both.

Roger learned this from his experience on *Taken by Grace*: All planning, including creative choices, should be completed before walking on set, so when the wheels fall off, you're improvising from a plan, dramatically reducing panic modes.

The *Blair Witch* Effect

Many indie horror filmmakers love to say, "Our film is the next *Blair Witch*." And hey, we get it, it's the holy grail of low-budget success stories. The stratospheric success of *Blair Witch Project* wasn't based on how scary the movie was, and it certainly was, but its success points to a solid *plan*. Sure, they had locations, actors, and a shoot schedule, which any film should have. But what made it work was the plan behind the *marketing*, in this case, the *myth making*.

So, when someone tells us they're making "the next *Blair Witch*," our first question is usually: Oh, cool—so did you run a fake missing person campaign? Did you create a website full of clues and phony evidence? Do you have a low-budget movie that feels like it could've been found in a forest on dusty old DV tape? *Blair Witch* didn't break the mold. It made one. The found footage concept wasn't new, but they made it *feel* new. They backed it up with a PR stunt that was so convincing that it turned a tiny indie film into a global conversation.

Yeah, the camera was shaky. Yeah, people complained. But that shakiness made it feel real. It told your brain that it was a spontaneous, unexpected event when in fact the movie was a brilliantly-coordinated mind job. And that's where the genius lives. The whole rollout was like something Andy Kaufman or Sacha Baron Cohen would do: pretend long enough, convincingly enough, and people stop asking if it's real.

So, before you call your movie "the next *Blair Witch*," ask yourself if you're just shooting in the woods or building a legend.

And don't stop there. Create a real budget. One that includes everything, not just the sexy stuff like cameras and Fisher dollies. A line producer is worth the money to create a budget and production schedule.

Budget. For. Everything

A common rookie mistake is raising just enough money to shoot the film. They scrape together enough for production, then run out of cash with an unfinished movie collecting digital dust on a hard drive.

There is no money for music, sound mix, color correction, deliverables, or a marketing and PR budget.

Then they beg and launch a desperate finishing fund campaign, hoping people still care. Meanwhile, their project loses steam and leverage. You have no power with a distributor if you're broke and unfinished.

Now flip the script: Imagine wrapping your film with $150,000 set aside for marketing and advertising. That's leverage. That's when you can negotiate theatrical.

Budget for the Entire Lifecycle

Development, production, post-production, distribution, and marketing. All of it. Don't schedule production until you've secured hard cash, signed commitments, or extremely credible pledges, to pay for everything you need to finish and release the film.

If that means scaling down your script, then scale it down. It's better to make a smaller film that's finished than a big one that dies half-born.

Planning also means hiring wisely. Another common trap is working with only friends or saying yes to whoever is available, cheap, or enthusiastic without vetting their skills or attitudes.

One toxic crew member can kill your set—taking morale, momentum, and focus with them. If someone is incompetent or has a garbage attitude, talk to them once. If it doesn't change, fire them. You're protecting the morale of the set and the quality of your film. And the rest of the crew will thank you.

Yes, even if they're working for free. *Especially* then. Low pay is a magnet for red flags.

Finally, once you have a detailed plan, respect the schedule. Spontaneity blows timelines, burns locations, and scares off actors who still have day jobs.

Great planning doesn't translate into rigid inflexibility, it means you have a baseline for pivoting when that plan runs into problems, because at some point it will. Your plan is a map for getting from point A to Z, but a map will show you alternate routes for navigating any roadblocks. Without the map, you'll either sit there staring at the obstacle in front of you, or you'll wander around looking for another way and maybe run out of gas.

Chaos is coming, and preparation is how you stay in control when it does.

Mistake 8: Skimping on the "Invisible" Things

New filmmakers often obsess over cameras and visuals. Absolutely, it's a visual medium, but they treat sound like an afterthought. Bummer, that.

Then there's the actor-turned-director who focuses entirely on witty dialogue, forgetting they must capture it properly. This is a noob mistake.

Kirk's been on a set where multiple actors were improvising simultaneously. None were mic'd individually, so none of the audio channels were recorded separately, which should have been mandatory. That's the stuff of nightmares for audio post, trying to manage wildly different volume levels. Don't get too clever with your dialogue if you can't capture it cleanly.

Another film was submitted to us that looked decent until the dialogue hit. The filmmaker recorded all the audio with the camera's built-in mic, and the actors sounded like they were yelling across the Grand Canyon. Hard pass in less than 15 seconds.

Bad sound will make your film unwatchable, no matter how beautiful it looks.

Muffled dialogue, jarring audio levels, distortion, and overbearing background noise are all fatal. Audiences will forgive a soft focus or imperfect lighting but won't forgive bad audio.

Invest in Sound

Hire a skilled sound recordist. Your DP's cousin with a boom mic does not count unless they know how to use it. Use quality microphones and record room tone. Then, monitor each take as it happens. Sound is invisible, but it's everything.

And while we're on invisible things, don't blow off continuity or data management either.

Continuity Matters

Hire a script supervisor or assign someone to track wardrobe, props, hand positions, and eye-lines. One continuity error won't kill your film. A couple are sloppy. A dozen is a straight-up amateur hour.

Data Matters

Back up your footage, label it clearly, and store it redundantly. Losing footage, or worse, overwriting files, is one of the fastest ways to sink your project. It happens more than you think and is usually the result of lazy or nonexistent planning.

These aren't glamorous roles. They don't win awards. But in the indie world, they're the difference between a professional film and weekend warrior mediocrity.

Mistake 7: The One-Person Show Will Wreck You (The Control Freak Syndrome)

Wearing multiple hats is normal in indie filmmaking. Refusing to delegate isn't. Whether it's ego, control issues, or budget anxiety, trying to do everything yourself leads to burnout and, usually, a worse film.

Remember the root canal analogy from Chapter Two? Same deal here. Just because you *can* do it all doesn't mean you *should*.

If you're directing and producing, bring on a true producer or at least a line producer or Unit Production Manager to handle logistics, so you're not solving location issues while directing actors. If you're editing your film, get a second set of eyes. Better yet, an assistant editor or someone who knows when to say, "This isn't working."

Feedback is Not a Favor

Host test screenings, ask other filmmakers, and use people who can give constructive and meaningful notes. The job of test screenings isn't to feed your ego; it's to catch the blind spots before your paying audience does.

The best directors collaborate. They trust their DP, their designer, and their sound team. They let experts be experts. They know their strengths, admit their weaknesses, and build a team that makes them better. This is the type of craftsperson to emulate. Yes, it might bruise your ego. Life isn't easy, nor is it fair. Take the note.

Roger sets defined boundaries for his keys by giving them the essential elements of the vision: color palette, style, mood, etc., but then he provides department heads a strong level of autonomy and then relies on them to do their job. They have done this before, after all. He still approves choices, but this strategy adds two essential layers to the production:

- When everyone owns their lane, the film levels up.

- The sum is exponentially greater than the parts.

Mistake 6: Picking the Wrong Team

Film production is a high-pressure, short-term marriage. Choose your collaborators wisely.

Don't hire a DP just because they own an FX6. Don't partner with someone calling themselves a "producer" who doesn't understand what that means. And don't bring in a 1st AD with a toxic attitude just because they have credits.

Vet people. Call references. Trust your gut. If someone's giving off bad vibes in pre-production, it'll be ten times worse when the pressure is on. Replace them early. Don't "wait and see."

Don't hire people you can't fire.

That means it's best that friends and family are off-limits unless qualified to work on a professional film set, but even then, it can be dangerous to do so. One bad shoot can wreck a friendship, and the risk to your relationship isn't worth it.

Know What Kind of Producer You Actually Need

Not all producers are the same. The producer in charge is defined by the Producers Guild of America (PGA), not by the owner of a one-man-band production company who produces corporate videos. Those are two completely different crafts with limited crossover in skillsets. Know the difference so you hire the right kind of help:

Title	What They Do
Producer	Oversees the entire project from development through distribution
Executive Producer (EP)	Secures financing or resources. Often limited creative input
Line Producer	Manages budget and day-to-day logistics during production
Co-producer	Shares responsibilities, often focused on specific areas like post or casting
Associate Producer	Assists with coordination, logistics, or deliverables
Development Producer	Helps develop the script, package the film, and attract talent
Creative Producer	Collaborates closely with the director to shape the story and tone. Many times the Producer serves this role.
Post-Production Producer	Oversees the edit, sound, color, and final delivery

The fun part is your eighteen-day shoot. The real work happens over roughly two years, before and after production. The entirety of those two years looks like this: Development, financing & packaging, pre-production, production, post-production, pre-release, release, and post-release.

- **Development**

Script, initial budget and rough schedule, comparable films, decks, marketing, and distribution strategies.

- **Financing & Packaging**

Adjust budget and schedule, formalize legal and finance structure, finalize key attachments, lock financing through equity, grants, pre-sales, soft money like film incentives and product placement.

- **Pre-production**

Hire full crew, finalize locations and permits, cast remaining roles, script breakdown (scheduling, shot lists, DOOD report[1]), lock the budget and production timeline, build sets, secure costumes and props, conduct rehearsals and tech prep.

- **Production (AKA Principal Photography)**

Shooting the film.

- **Post-production**

Project is edited, sound is mixed, visual effects are added, and the final cut is completed for delivery and distribution.

- **Pre-release**

Building your film's awareness through marketing, festival submissions, test screenings, and securing distribution deals.

- **Release**

The film is made available to the public through theaters, streaming platforms, or other channels, often supported by

---

1   A Day Out of Days (DOOD) report is a production schedule showing which days each actor or element is needed on set. It helps plan shooting efficiently and control costs.

marketing, publicity, and promotional events.

- **Post-release**

The phase after a film's public debut, focused on ongoing marketing, revenue tracking, awards campaigns, additional distribution windows, and long-term monetization.

And you need people who stick around. A DP who ghosts when you need pickup shots is useless. A producer who vanishes during deliverables is an existential threat.

- **Hire for the journey, not just the shoot.**

- **Hire to your weakness, not your ego.**

- **Smart teams fill gaps.**

If you're a writer, find a detail-oriented producer. If you're a director, bring on a seasoned 1st AD. If you're new, bring on a producer who's been there.

- **Great teams catch mistakes you'd never see alone.**

Filmmaking is not a solo act, even if you're the driving force. You are going to greenlight yourself, but that doesn't mean doing everything alone.

Mistake 5: Rushing in with an Unripe Script

We recently spoke with a group of Regent University students who asked, "What's the most important phase of filmmaking?" The obvious guesses came first: financing, production, and post. It's the script. But deeper still is the story. A script without a strong story is like a house without a good foundation; it'll fall apart at the worst possible moment.

Too many filmmakers go into production before the script is ready, mainly because they want to start shooting and can't stomach the thought of a tenth rewrite. When your best friend says the script is great, it feels good. But unless they're professional readers, their praise is meaningless. They love *you*, not your screenplay. Real script development requires honest feedback from pros who understand character arcs, inciting incidents, pacing, conflict, mid-journey turning points, market trends, etc. A new writer's first script is rarely good. That's not a slam; it's just the way it is.

Too often, filmmakers ignore development notes, rush to shoot, and blame distributors when the film flops. But no amount of stellar camerawork or award-winning performances can save a weak story. Do the hard work upfront. Everyone will have notes regardless of how good your script is, but develop it until professionals give minimal notes. Lock it down before you go into production. Rushing through this phase is the single most preventable mistake you can make.

Filmmakers are often guilty of a creative myopia. They are so deeply entangled in their own scripts that they either fail or, worse, refuse to acknowledge the glaring flaws in their work. When someone with experience points out a weak structure or overwrought dialogue, they get defensive. One of the most selfless and effective things you can do for your film is to listen when experience gives you solid advice, and then *really* listen when multiple people point out the same problem.

One of the most pervasive problems in independent film are filmmakers who won't take script notes, especially those who are funding their own film and want to hire us to produce. They get in their mind that once the film is complete, everyone will see the brilliance that, until then, has been pent up in their minds just waiting to take the *Academy Award*®. "Just wait and see. I don't care that you're an expert storyteller; I'll prove your notes wrong, because I know this story better than anyone." We do not work with people who harbor that attitude. It would be easy to take their money, produce, and even distribute their film, but guess who gets the blame when the film fails?

Kirk once consulted on a comedy script with solid actors and funny moments but major story issues. He pointed out the problems. The writer, who also funded the film, dismissed the notes because "the jokes are good." The film was shot anyway. The result was a feature with a few laughs and yawner recoupment.

Imagine every word in your script costs $100. Suddenly, you start writing with purpose: tight dialogue, punchy action, clean visuals, and a solid story arc. Think of every wasted word as a debt because if those words make it to set, that debt multiplies in real dollars. Invest wisely. Make every syllable count. Don't rely on what you "see in your head." Pay for professional script coverage more than once. Do a table read with actors. Once you're on set, bad writing gets very expensive, very fast.

Roger began with an unripe script when he directed *Taken by Grace* (2012), starring Angus Macfadyen and Haylie Duff. The script had a broken third act, but time constraints forced the film into production anyway. Everyone—from Roger, to producer Bradley Dorsey, to the distributor— knew the climax didn't work, but they shot the rest of the film and paused production before the final sequence.

There was a mandatory five-day break because Roger was obliged to complete another project in Amarillo, and Bradley also turned his attention to another project and was unavailable for collaboration. While gone, Roger and Angus traded emails, trying to rewrite a workable ending. When Roger returned to LA with a new version, Bradley flagged new problems. So, Roger rewrote again—this time overnight—and presented the revised climax the next morning, the day the climax scene would be shot.

It still didn't work.

Adding to the pressure was that Angus and Danielle Hoetmer, who played Angus's ex-wife, had never met, and there was no time for rehearsal.

At lunch, Bradley, the 1st AD, Angus, Danielle, and Roger met to discuss what to do. The deadline to shoot was fast approaching. Finally, Roger acknowledged three beats that Angus and Danielle had to nail.

With the 1st AD tapping his watch and no better option, they improvised the film's emotional climax in three high-stakes takes, each on a different camera setup. Watching through tears, Roger had no idea if the wildly diverse takes would cut well. Thankfully, the scene came together in the edit and the film worked beautifully, but the third act climax worked because of the exceptional acting talent of Angus and Danielle, not because of good script development. The stress, uncertainty, and risk came from rushing development and hoping to fix it later.

Lesson: In this case, the broken climax wasn't because of lazy writing; it was because multiple schedule conflicts forced an incomplete script into production. But the point is clear: do not count on magic in the moment to rescue your movie. Develop your script thoroughly.

Mistake 4: Getting Caught in Genre Trends

Indie filmmakers can sabotage themselves by chasing genre trends without strategic thinking. They say things like, "Horror is hot right now," or "Faith-based films are killing it," and then jump into development with no plan beyond wishful thinking.

Genre isn't just a creative choice. It's a positioning decision. A long-term brand decision. And it needs to be made with data, not desire.

Trends Do Not Equal Opportunities

Yes, horror is having good days. Back in 2023, horror accounted for over 10% of total box office revenue, double what it pulled a decade earlier. That sounds amazing until you realize half of the theatrical horror films still lose money.

So, what gives?

The ones that win, films like *Barbarian*, usually combine a killer concept that hooks quickly with a lean budget that respects the genre's ceiling.

You're not competing with *Get Out*. You're competing with every other low-budget filmmaker banking on horror's "low cost, high return" myth. If your budget is bloated, your hook is flat, or your release plan is sloppy, a hot genre won't save you.

Abigail (2024) had a $28 million budget but opened to a modest $10 million. That's a warning.

Five Questions Every Entrepreneurial Filmmaker Should Ask Before Choosing a Genre

1 Who is your audience, and how do they consume media?

Don't just assume horror = young people. Which platform are they on? Do they prefer streamers, YouTube trailers, or festival buzz? If your audience lives on TikTok but you're cutting two-minute trailers for Facebook, we don't need to finish this sentence, you'll figure it out yourself.

2 What's the average budget and revenue range in this genre?

Don't chase success stories; study the mids and pay attention to the failures. What does a typical genre film of your budget range make (indie produced, not studio)? And is your planned budget still viable when compared to those comps?

3 How will you de-risk this choice?

Are there proven pairings of genre + actor that help sell? Are certain territories easier to pre-sell with this genre? Are there grant opportunities or niche festivals built around it?

4 Are you launching a horror brand?

Is this your calling card, or are you just blindly following trends? Know where the genre fits into your career arc.

5 What are you building long-term?

A single film is rarely enough to sustain a career. Are you building a slate around this genre, or is this a one-off experiment? How does this project fit into your long-term strategy: brand-building, career positioning, or just checking a creative box? Know where this film will take you next.

Quick Self-Check

Be honest with yourself. Are you making any of the mistakes we've covered?

Is your script shaky, but you're pushing forward anyway? Is your budget still scribbled on a napkin? Is your distribution plan basically "we'll figure it out later"? Are you prone to snap at people under pressure?

We're not here to beat you up, we're here to *build* you up. If any of these mistakes punch you between in the eyes, now's the time to course-correct. Tighten your script. Build a real budget. Start researching distribution (we'll walk through that more deeply in a later chapter). And if you don't know how to do those things, or you're not confident doing them, hire someone who does. Yes, it'll cost you. But that's what professionals do.

The Hard Truth About the Crowd

The industry is crowded. No surprise there; it's easier than ever for someone with a DSLR and a dream to call themselves a filmmaker. Lower barriers mean more voices but also more amateurs. Many people jump in unprepared, burn their money, and blame the industry when things fall apart.

But it's not the industry's fault. Usually it's just a failure of learning.

Greenlighting yourself means learning. Failing. Getting back up. Learning more. Keep improving. Becoming a pro, which means *don't keep repeating the same mistakes.*

Feeling overwhelmed is normal. Even veterans feel it. But the difference between those who burn out and those who build a career is the filmmakers who learn from mistakes—hopefully from someone else's—ultimately succeed.

That's why you're reading this book.

Avoiding mistakes isn't just about saving your project. It's about building your reputation and brand, which attracts better collaborators, real investors, and long-term success.

You made it through the hard truths of Chapter Three. Now, let's shift gears from surviving mistakes to setting up wins.

Mistake 3: Ignoring or Overlooking Legal and Paperwork

Again, we'll dive deep into this subject in another chapter, so consider this a preview.

Some indie filmmakers operate on a handshake, especially those shooting with ultra-low budgets. They either don't know or don't bother with the stuff "we don't need for a no-budget film," like contracts, releases, insurance, and so on, but those are things that can destroy your film before it ever has a chance.

Here's the nightmare scenario: you finish the film, a distributor shows interest, and they ask for your paperwork; signed contracts, appearance releases, music licenses, and chain of title[2]. You freeze. You have none of

---

2   Chain of title is the legal documentation proving a film's ownership rights—from the original concept through all transfers—ensuring the producer has the authority to sell or license the project.

that. No paperwork equals no cabbage; you greenlit yourself into a mega-loss.

Distributors don't care how solid you are with your actors or how tight you are with your DP. They want signed documents: crew deal memos, music licenses, appearance releases, location agreements, proof you have all rights secured, and E&O insurance. If you can't deliver, you're not getting the deal, simple as that. Even worse, if you skip contracts, you open yourself up to legal chaos. An actor might claim you never had permission to use their performance. A location owner could object. A former "collaborator" might demand a piece of the film. And you have no paper trail to shut it down.

The mindset of "We're friends, we don't need contracts" or "No one's going to sue us, we're too small" is indie suicide.

Kirk has seen this multiple times, and it always ends badly.

He's personally lost major deals—*plural*—because someone claimed they had chain of title but didn't. In one situation, the writer and producer were close friends. They had recognizable names attached, and everything looked solid on paper, but when it came time to finalize contracts, the writer suddenly changed their mind and wouldn't sign. Deal gone, friendship gone.

It's happened to Kirk at least three other times. Two of those were on significant projects. One was more of a dead-end, but it still left a crater. People were being paid, locations were being scouted, and plans were being made around a planned schedule. Only to find out the writer changed their mind and decided not to be besties with the director anymore.

And then there was a film with an A-list actor. He was on board, ready to go. But the producers couldn't get the writer to sign off. They wasted his time, and that kind of mistake follows you in this business. Mistakes affect your income, too.

So, when we say that chain of title matters, we don't mean "we have a verbal agreement," "we're cool," or, more commonly, "we have a letter of intent." We mean locked down, signed, and legally clean. If you can't prove you own the rights, you're done. Don't let the door slam you in the ass on the way out.

Whether it was shot for free or not, every film needs to get its legal house in order. Ignoring this *will* be catastrophic.

Mistake 2: Money Mismanagement and Budget Blunders

HANDLE THE MONEY OR YOUR FILM DIES.

Money is the lifeblood of your project. Mismanaging it will kill your film fast. And not in a cool, wind-in-your-hair cinematic way. It dies in a sad, broke, "the film never got finished" way.

Let's walk through the most common money mistakes and how to avoid them.

Budgeting Like a Dreamer, Not a Producer

Rookie filmmakers often wildly underestimate costs, skip contingency plans, or overspend on the wrong things. For example, blowing a third of your budget on renting the latest high-end camera because you think it'll make your film "look like Hollywood." Meanwhile, you can't afford a good sound mixer, a decent production designer, or enough shoot days.

That's a trade-off you'll regret in the edit bay.

Your camera doesn't save the film; sound, execution, and story do. A great story will work even if the movie is shot on a good quality DSLR.

Budget Like a Pro

A real budget isn't based on your credit limit or what you hope to raise. It's based on actual costs. And it'll probably be higher than you want.

Start with what the script requires, then scale down intelligently where needed. Don't build a budget from blue-sky guesstimates.

And always budget with your market in mind. Your story might be personal, but your film is a product intended for the masses, whether for large audiences or a niche, so the budget should match. Research your audience, study comparable films, and understand buyer expectations before locking your budget. The limited appeal of a niche film makes it difficult to justify a large budget.

"Free" Has Value. Track It

Borrowed gear. Donated locations. Volunteer labor. Mom's catering. Favors in post.

These are gold, but they're not "free." They're in-kind contributions, and smart producers track them with assigned fair market value. It reflects the true cost of your production that helps:

- Strengthen your pitch to investors

- Boost your perceived production value

- Qualify for grants, incentives, and soft equity structures when appropriate rules and laws permit.

Plan for no freebies and assume you'll pay for everything. Then, when the favors roll in, you're ahead and not depending on goodwill that might vanish mid-shoot.

The Film Stock Trap

Another expensive mistake is insisting on shooting on 35mm or 16mm "for the aesthetics." Yeah, celluloid looks beautiful. But it's not a good business decision unless you're able to clearly defend how it serves your story and bottom line.

Film stock is expensive. Processing, scanning, storage, and every step bleeds money. Most audiences won't notice the difference. Or care. And digital filters can convincingly emulate the film look without nuking your budget.

The bottom line is knowing the difference between a critical creative and expensive vanity option.

Don't Go into Debt for a Dream

One of the worst moves you can make is maxing out your credit cards or taking personal loans to fund a film with little to no profit potential. We respect the passion. We admire the hustle. But passion doesn't pay back debt with interest any more than stacking your life savings on a single roulette spin.

Going into personal debt for a passion project can wreck your life. You want a career, not a cautionary tale for your grandkids.

Don't Overspend on an Unsellable Movie

Spending a million dollars on your first indie feature is a mistake unless you have name actors in lead roles, not day players (actors or crew members hired and paid on a daily basis, not the entire show), a proven team, a high-concept story, and a clear pathway to profitability. Otherwise, you're burning investor cash on a film the market has no interest in supporting.

Keep it lean. Low six figures. Bravo to you if that means fewer locations, fewer shoot days, and a tighter script. But it also means a much higher chance of breaking even or at least coming close.

The reality is that a million-dollar movie with no stars rarely recoups, and only fools play those odds.

Understand Pre-Sales (and Why They Matter)

Distributors do sometimes offer pre-sales commitments, which are agreements to purchase distribution rights to a film before it's completed. These commitments are made with the expectation that the film will be delivered according to agreed terms. Pre-sale commitments are based on your project's commercial potential, which includes:

- Bankable lead actors

- Genre

- Budget

- Director's track record

- Market trends and appeal

- And—once again—story along with the quality of script.

Pre-sales are often used to secure production financing, as they can be collateralized with lenders. You can then take that contract to a lender and borrow against the distributor's reputation for paying filmmakers an advance. This doesn't come easy, but when it works, it's a great way to help finance your film and reduce equity exposure to your investors.

Remember that pre-sales are unlikely if you lack stars, a marketable concept, or strong execution. Plan accordingly.

Track Every Dollar

Every dollar you spend is a dollar that must be repaid to someone with interest. If capital is deployed by a distributor, lender, or equity investor, interest is charged to the film's LLC. That's that.

Use a spreadsheet. Track every expense. Build in a contingency. Adjust as needed. And if numbers make your head hurt, hire a line producer or production manager who knows film bookkeeping.

> ***Pro tip:*** Line producers help manage money, but a seasoned producer who's taken films from development through distribution is often the most valuable hire you'll make. They won't raise money for you, but they'll help you not burn it.

Keep your budget as low as possible without compromising your vision.

Spend on what matters:

- Story

- Performance

- Sound

- Crew morale

- Completion and distribution

- Everything else is noise.

If your first film breaks even, that's a huge win. It's not as fun as turning a profit, but it means your investors got their money back, and you now have credibility.

Respect the money. Use it wisely. And don't forget this is a business. Treat it like one.

Mistake 1: Neglecting the Business Side (Treating Your Film Only as Art)

We touched on this in Chapter One and will continue hammering it because it's that important.

Too many filmmakers pour every ounce of energy into the art such as the locations, the performances, the look, while completely ignoring that they're also creating a product for the marketplace.

If you make your film with someone else's money, you are not just an artist, you're a businessperson with the responsibility to recoup your investor(s) capital. That means you must produce an artistically and *commercially* viable film. It's the ultimate crossroads between creativity and commerce.

And yet, one of the most common and costly mistakes is treating distribution and marketing as someone else's job.

Just like a great screenwriter starts with a logline, a synopsis, or even the final scene already in mind, you need to know where your film is going *before entering pre-production.*

Distribution works the same way. If you know how and where you want your film to land, whether that's a theatrical run, niche streaming, a classroom, or a faith-based platform, distribution will shape everything:

- How you cast

- What genre you choose

- What tone you strike

- How you finance it

- How you pitch it

Know your destination, then build toward it.

Making a film without a plan for reaching your audience is like setting out on a road trip without gas money. You won't go far.

And yet, this happens way too often. Indie filmmakers spend every dime on production and pray that a distributor will swoop in and save them.

That's not in a distributor's job description.

Many filmmakers assume the film will "get into festivals and get bought" or that some magical distributor will handle everything you should have already planned for.

Delusional thinking and misguided expectations seem hopelessly embedded into the gene code of the indie world. It is a belief that you can make the movie, walk away, and somehow, it'll find an audience (and fill your bank account).

That fantasy is dead.

The dream of selling your indie in a big, splashy festival deal is rare. Just look at Sundance in recent years: more films than ever, fewer sales, and a sea of heartbreak for projects with no audience strategy.

We're not saying you shouldn't concentrate on great art; quite the opposite. But we *are* saying make the art *strategically*. If no one sees your film, if it generates no revenue, you fail to finish the job. You can easily rise above the status quo and conquer the indie world *if* you'll embrace the wisdom of this book. The industry needs filmmakers like you who not only know how to do it right, they won't settle for less.

Start Thinking Like an Entrepreneur

Identify your audience early. Who is this for? Where do they watch content?

Build your distribution strategy before you shoot.

Budget for marketing; between 10% and 100% *or more* of your total spend, depending on the release strategy.

It's hard to do all this. But watching your finished film collect dust is even harder because you ignored the business side.

Make the art and make it memorable. But you're also launching a business.

USUALLY a Mistake: Starring In Your Film

While this isn't a one-size-fits-all mistake and therefore not included in the list above, it's usually a bad idea to star in your film unless you have a demonstrable track record of moving the sales needle. While it's common for filmmakers to write, produce, raise the financing, and cast themselves in the lead role, it's a gamble that usually doesn't end well.

But hey, if your goal is to build your acting reel or check a dream off your bucket list, that's legit. No shade. Just be honest about what this is; a personal project, not an investment vehicle. Suppose you're raising money from friends, family, or outside investors, and you're also the star. In that case, you must be transparent about what they're funding because the odds of returning that money dropped significantly. We're not saying it's impossible; you can have some modest success doing so, but with so many odds stacked against you already, why add another layer?

Why It's a Problem: Market Reality

We can't tell you how many times we've been in a conversation where someone says, "Hey, we could get this semi-famous actor from the '70s to play the cop at the diner." We try to talk them out of it, because it doesn't move the audience needle. But once a filmmaker gets their money, they hit the gas and chase that name anyway. Half the time, it's not even about the movie; it's about hanging out with the guy from that show they loved. It's fanboy fantasy disguised as strategy.

The problem is that if the actor isn't one of your top three leads, it doesn't matter. Some distributors will actively avoid the film if they see that casting. Some actors are known in the sales world for showing up in every tiny indie, and while there's nothing wrong with that (God bless those actors who love to work), it becomes a red flag from a business standpoint. Distributors say, "Please don't bring us another movie with him; we already have seven, and we can't move any of them."

The trap is filmmakers believe what they want to believe. They'll say things like, "Yeah, but that movie from the '70s has a cult following!" There is no argument there, and that's why people line up at Comic-Con to get his autograph. But putting him in your indie film in a two-scene role is an amateur tactic. It simply *does not* add backend value, and you pay more money for that role than you should have.

So, when you cast the cop at the diner, cast a great actor who deserves a shot, maybe someone you've always believed in. Then, focus on getting real value with the three lead roles. Especially if you're casting yourself in one of them, the other two better bring name recognition and credibility beyond your own. You've greenlit yourself, awesome. But now you must be honest: are you greenlighting your writing, directing, producing, or acting career? It's hard—maybe impossible—to greenlight all four simultaneously. Be clear about which number you're betting your chips on.

We once had an excellent documentary submitted to us narrated by James Earl Jones. Darth Vader himself! The filmmakers believed his international notoriety would significantly move the needle, but it did nothing for sales. The story centered on musicians in South Africa, which worked great for what it was. It was beautifully shot and well produced, but it didn't have strong market relevance outside of South Africa. If the documentary had been *about* James Earl Jones, the film would have had significant market relevance worldwide. Do you see the distinction?

When It Can Work, and What to Do Instead

Films can succeed with a no-name lead, but it's much harder. If you go that route, be prepared to compensate with:

- A killer concept

- Brilliant execution

- Significant marketing spend

- And a ton of luck and timing

Otherwise, the smarter move is casting a bankable actor in the lead. Take a supporting role if you want to be on screen. You'll get more credibility by delivering a great film that sells than by insisting on top billing.

Ego vs. Strategy

Again, if your real goal is personal growth, creative expression, or building your reel, then own that. Just be transparent with your team and your backers. Let them know the return they're betting on is you, not profit. That kind of support comes from people who believe in you.

But if you're trying to build a career and attract repeat investors, you must get out of your own way.

Put your film first, not your face.

"Ego is expensive. And few will pay for yours."

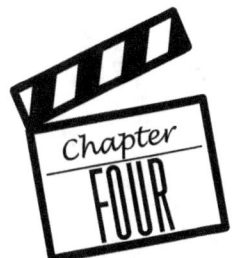

The Two Most Important Questions

Chapter FOUR

"No plan survives contact with the enemy."

— Helmuth von Moltke the Elder, quoted in *Valkyrie* (2008).

Not everyone cracking this book is a producer or wants to be one. Some of you are writers, directors, and actors. But if you're trying to get a film made, regardless of your role, this chapter demands your attention.

You may have your script and a ragtag crew ready to roll. You're fired up to make your indie masterpiece. Before you spend a dime, there are two questions you must answer. Ignore them or phone in answers and your film's already in trouble.

These two questions are a cold-blooded, investor-facing, distributor-driven, no-nonsense gut check that separates the professionals from the Jr. Starter Kits. They're what sales agents, platforms, and festival programmers want to know, even if they never ask you directly. The questions are:

————————— ● —————————

1. Why would anyone pay to see this movie?

2. How does it fit in the market?

————————— ● —————————

They sound simple, but they're dangerously deceiving at first glance. These two questions force you to toggle between your creative instincts, business sense, and a cold dose of reality to drill down to the bottom line: Who cares?

It's hard to evaluate your own work objectively, because you're emotionally attached to it. But it's critical to step back from any bias about your film's market value, audience potential, or financial viability. You need to defend your position with real data and strategic thinking, not "I know in my heart this will be a hit." It's normal to feel that way, but gut instinct alone won't make a successful film. Passion is essential, but passion needs proof. And if the data points elsewhere, you adjust. Maybe even walk away. That's the level of discipline required to answer the two most important questions.

The answers become the bedrock of your concept, screenplay, pitch, investor deck, budget, marketing plan, and distribution strategy.

We're approaching these questions from the money side. Art matters, but great directing won't keep you out of the 97% fail club. Let's break down the questions:

1. Why Will Anyone Pay to See This Movie?

People pay for entertainment, a thrill ride, an escape that makes them go, "Oh yeah, that's worth my ten bucks," and your film must deliver.

What were the last three movies you spent money to watch? Were they indie films? Based on industry trends, there is roughly a 3:1 preference for studio films over indies on streaming platforms. Studio films, backed by major Hollywood companies, dominate due to larger production and marketing budgets and robust execution, while indie films typically gain presence through niche platforms. The point is that indie films are at a distinct market disadvantage because of the marketing power of the studios. So, you plan accordingly.

Sure, your artistic heart's screaming, "My film is a beautiful story!" or "The visuals are dope!" Cool, but that doesn't get the credit cards a-swipin'. Business-wise, mushy messaging must be sharpened into a hook that grabs an audience by the throat.

Here's how you crack it:

Who's your audience? Aim your story at the hearts that'll beat for it. Horror freaks? Doc nerds? What's their happy place? What gets them off the couch? (Or on it, depending on where they watch.)

Why watch your movie instead of countless other movie titles? What's the juice, the twist that melts brains, a truth that stings, laughs that kill? Be specific.

Boil it down to a logline that screams, "Watch me, NOW!" Write a thrill ride that'll scramble your brain 'til Tuesday. "The Secret They Don't Want You to Know" documentary. Think *Food, Inc.* (2008) or *The Corporation* (2003).

Say it's a faith-based film. Craft a hook that'll be the most soul-stirring, faith-fueling journey they'll ever take, not "and glory ensues." Considering the competition for eyeballs, you *must* deliver. Promise a spiritual knockout that'll have 'em weeping on their knees, but hand you a snooze-fest with bad lighting, and they'll ditch you. In a world drowning in free church live streams and preachy feel-good fluff, your "why" should be a sledgehammer of divine inspiration. *I Can Only Imagine* (2018) and *The Passion of the*

Christ (2004) are just two great examples.

2. How Does This Movie Fit in the Market?

This is about knowing where your film lands in the infinity of movie titles. It's not enough to make a film; you must know what's already out there, who's watching it, and how to elbow your way into the chaos. From a business lens, this is your money map.

Researching comparable films is essential. It gives you insights into the market, what genres are trending, what audiences are responding to, and what kinds of films are picked up by which distributors. But—and this is where many filmmakers blow it—you must compare apples to apples. Don't pull a $20 million studio release with global stars out of the sky as a comp for your $500k no-name indie. That's like comparing a Ferrari to a bicycle and trying to convince someone it'll win the same race.

While we're on the subject of comps, let's chase a rabbit for a moment to address a trend that is increasingly creating stumbling blocks for filmmakers:

Using AI to Create Comps

AI is an amazing tool. Its importance is akin to the transformative impact that the discovery of fire made upon humanity. In the film industry, it can brainstorm scripts, help edit footage, analyze stripboards, generate sales estimates, and much more. And we love it—as a *tool*. But that's all it is. AI isn't a distributor; it doesn't buy your movie.

Yet, more filmmakers are submitting investor decks with AI-generated estimates pulled from various sources. These decks look clean and impressive, but when you analyze more, they fall apart.

Here's why:

Data Is Often Based on The Wrong Comparables

We recently had a filmmaker with a $300,000 micro budget film who ran their numbers through an AI tool. Their comp was *Napoleon Dynamite*. The AI plugged in box office data from that movie and spat out a potential return of $78 million. Even their "conservative" projection was $10 million.

But where's the logic? *Napoleon Dynamite* was produced as an indie, but it had a studio P&A push behind it, massive festival buzz, and years of hindsight. Your movie might have similar quirks, but that doesn't make it equally bankable. One of the biggest disconnects in indie film is that everything changes when a studio picks up your movie. With a smokin' P&A (prints & advertising) budget and a promo machine behind it, you're not in the same playground anymore. You're not even playing in the same league. And even if you do get a studio deal, don't expect to make any money from it. The studios have a knack for expensing away all the revenue so you don't see a dime. Regardless of the accounting, most indie films will never be released through a studio distribution deal, so your projections need to reflect that reality.

The Cost Side is Ignored

Most AI reports don't account for real-world costs:

- Marketing and P&A
- Sales agent fees
- Distribution fees
- Legal, deliverables, insurance
- Recoupable expenses

We keep seeing spreadsheets full of projected revenue with zero line items for expense deductions. That's blind faith in technology without even a basic understanding of the film business.

OK, back to the 2nd question.

There is No Contract. No Commitment. No Risk Mitigation

Estimates are acceptable if they're based on realistic comps that reasonably match production budget, casting, genre, and release strategy. If you show an investor a chart that says "$10M potential" without that basis, you'd better also show them estimates from a sales agent or distributor who'll confirm the projections. If you don't have that, you are misrepresenting risk. What if your film makes $0? Did you show that projection also? You need to show the full picture.

Filmmakers say, "But AI gave us these numbers." We ask, "Is AI distributing your movie? Because unless a real distributor is backing those projections, they're just numbers that you hope are true." Investors will see straight through the façade.

Perceived revenue does not equal actual profit.

Everyone loves talking about how *The Blair Witch* grossed over $248 million on a $60,000 budget. But after all the fees, buyouts, backend deals, and distribution costs, the producer's revenue cut wasn't nearly as life-changing as people assume. While no public information is available for detailing what the producers personally earned, a reasonable estimate would be anywhere from mid to high six figures to 4 million. Not bad, but in the shadow of a $248 million box office, it's a rounding error.

The same is true for *Paranormal Activity, Whiplash, Clerks,* and any other indie film that hit big from a studio distribution deal. The headlines don't show what was lost to distribution structures, intermediaries, or back-end point dilution.

Here's what you're sizing up when researching comps:

- Genre performance (especially in your budget range)

- Cast value and sales traction

- Festival strategy, if any

- Streaming vs theatrical outcomes (streaming revenue is hard to come by, but you can pay for that research)

- Marketing hooks that landed

- Who distributed it, and where it found its audience

Use this research to help shape your pitch deck, distribution plan, and investor conversations. It proves you understand the business you're walking into.

Also, as you may have figured out by now, never use theatrical box office gross as a proxy for investor return. Gross theatrical numbers are not what investors take home. That number gets chopped up between exhibitors, distributors, and various fees long before a dime returns to investors. We'll break that down in full in the Distribution Decoded chapter, where we walk you through the revenue waterfall and explain where the money goes.

Use AI. But Use It Honestly and Practically

- Label projections as speculative.

- Get real-world validation from agents or buyers.

- Bring on an attorney to review your deck and business plan before it goes to investors.

Your film is a business. If you're not a sales agent, then don't fake being one just because a machine gives you a classy number.

Fair warning: if you use unrealistic comps to raise money, you're setting yourself up for legal trouble when things go pear-shaped, and they probably will. Misrepresenting the market potential of your film to investors, even unintentionally, can potentially put you on the wrong side of a fraud accusation. So, keep your comps realistic and relevant. Match them by budget level, release strategy, genre, and cast profile. Find other indies in the same general financial and distribution tier and ensure they're recent, like in the past five years. Audience tastes change quickly. A film that blew up in 2014 might flop today.

Why These Questions Are Your Lifeline

These two thought provokers are your film's business backbone. They tell you who's buying, why they'll care, and how to shove it in their faces. If you ignore these questions, you're almost sure to become part of the 97% statistic, broke and whining.

Get this right, and you have a better shot of dodging obscurity. We respect the effort, but the game doesn't care.

Creative GPS: Knowing your audience shapes your cast, shots, and story. Where's it going to play? Theaters are a long shot; streaming's a jungle, and festivals are a crapshoot, so pick your poison. Or put them all in one awesome cocktail. Plan your distribution strategy before you shoot. Knowing where your audience watches movies helps you understand how yours would ideally be released.

Who's in your lane? A million indie horror films are clogging the pipes; how's yours not just another turd? That weight rests heavily on the marketing hook and the uniqueness of your story.

What's your edge? The unique hook that screams "me, not them."

Making a low-budget sci-fi? You're one of a thousand. Your edge better be a mind-bending twist or effects that punch above your weight, not "it's got a twist." Sure, you can make it for $35,000 and maybe sell it for $45,000, and you might make a small profit. But that assumes no one got paid, including you. So. Did you make the film for your demo reel? Fine. But know going in that your film is likely not the next *Blair Witch*. And if it is, it's probably because you came up with a brilliant marketing and PR plan and hit the zeitgeist.

Are you making a cultural deep-dive doc? If there is a hungry niche out there, find 'em and feed 'em. Market fit isn't artsy navel-gazing; it's knowing your target so you don't get buried in the content glut.

Money talks: Market fit sets real goals. Investors fund returns. If it's someone who doesn't know the business, you must protect their money and accurately inform them of the actual risk; a film is a highly speculative venture, and investors could lose all their money.

Distro roadmap: Hot genre? Theater shot niche gem? Streaming or fest circuit? Develop an understanding of what you're dealing with.

Marketing ammo: Your pitch and market slot are the soul and spine of your trailer and social media, so plan them early.

How to Not Screw This Up

Dig like a detective: Stalk similar films; box office, buzz, flops. Social media is your microscope. What's trending? What bombed? Not casual glances, you need deep dives.

Read the industry rags like *Deadline, Hollywood Reporter, Variety,* etc., to get a feel of what's selling. Go to festivals, conferences, and markets. Join film business chat groups. That'll help inform you about how you fit in.

Talk to your marks: Chat up potential viewers. What hooks them? What bores them?

Sharpen your hook: One sentence—why your film is a must-see.

Slot it smart: If research says a horror boom is here, lean in, but rise above. Does your film have a social issue ripe for trending? Hit it, but do it better than the last guy and position like a pro.

Keep circling back: Script changes and market shifts; recheck the two most important questions often.

Stay sharp.

This isn't weekend homework, it's your film's foundation. Answers evolve, and that's fine as long as you're not fooling yourself about what's real.

That's a lot to consider, and it can easily overwhelm you, especially if you've never done it before. Another reason to hire an experienced producer on your first film, a producer who knows how to do all the above.

Be Inventive and Progressive

Most filmmakers try to build a skyscraper before learning to build a dog house. We've mentioned this before, but one way to hone your skills, including knowing and building your audience, is to make a short film. It's one of the most innovative ways to hone your craft, develop your voice, and create the audience you'll eventually need for your feature. And short films are great for your resume, something you can show investors, for example, when you finally level up.

Much like :30 commercial spots, short films force clarity. They teach you how to think in frames, build tension quickly, manage resources, and direct under pressure, all with stakes low enough that mistakes won't damage your career. You'll learn to work with actors, plan your shots, schedule production, deal with on-set surprises, and avoid fixing things in post to solve the story and production problems. Every lesson you learn on a short film will scale directly into the feature world.

Even more importantly, shorts help you build an audience. Not just family and friends, but actual followers; people who resonate with your work and want more. Use social media intentionally: post behind-the-scenes content, storyboards, concept art, editing clips, and even your failures. Invite people into the process. Platforms like TikTok and YouTube are testing grounds for tone, voice, and reach. And YouTube is no longer a dirty word in distribution. Some distributors now use branded YouTube channels as their primary AVOD strategy. It's the largest streaming platform in the world and the second-largest search engine. When you launch your feature, your short film fans become your first advocates for your feature. Remember: your short still needs a stellar story and the best production value you can deliver. You can't take shortcuts just because it's not a feature.

If you do it right, a short film can work as a launchpad for your career. One great short film, well executed and strategically promoted, can do more for your career than a rushed, forgettable feature ever could. So, no worries if you're not ready to shoot your magnum opus. Make a short, but don't compromise: It *must* stand out. And make sure it speaks to the audience you're trying to build.

The Bottom Line

Indie filmmaking is a cutthroat playground with scarce cash and terrible odds. These two questions aren't optional: they're vital to your success. Detailing why someone pays and where your film fits forces you to marry your artistic soul to a business brain, and—sorry, not sorry—the business side is *at least* 50% of this conversation. We cannot stress enough how important it is for you to embrace this reality. You're not just crafting a film; you're crafting a shot at being seen, maybe even paid, by people who don't owe you anything.

So, before you burn your savings and your crew's goodwill, stare these questions down. Answer 'em with guts and grit. We respect that you're in this fight, but the indie graveyard is full of dreamers who didn't do their homework. Make your film the exception, not the rule.

Setting Up Your Film Like a Business

"The night is darkest just before the dawn.
And I promise you, the dawn is coming."

— Harvey Dent, *The Dark Knight* (2008)

L et's say you open a donut shop. You spend a year perfecting your secret recipe with fluffy dough and next-level glaze, and you even have a signature maple bacon crunch thing that freaks people out. Now imagine that after all that work, you say: "Okay, I'm done. Now I need someone to figure out how to sell them and pay the costs to advertise my store." Sounds crazy, right?

But that's exactly how most indie filmmakers treat their movies.

They write a script, maybe even shoot it, and then act like the rest is someone else's job. They expect someone to swoop in for distribution and promotion. But you need to "own the shop" if you "make the donuts." It's on you to figure out who's buying, how to reach them, what the packaging looks like, and how to get your product on shelves. In film terms, that's your audience, branding, release strategy, and deal structure. If you're not thinking about those things from day one, you hope your donut sells itself while it sits in a box behind the counter, and you watch the cars drive by, oblivious to your existence.

Filmmaking is a creative business, but it's still a business. That means budgeting, branding, marketing, and planning for how your movie gets seen. Don't hand off that responsibility because you "don't like business stuff." Own it. Learn it. Or find a partner who lives for it. But don't assume your artistic brilliance will carry you across the finish line.

Make your movie, but run your shop.

Why Most Indie Films Aren't "Real" Businesses

Traditionally, too many indie filmmakers shrug off business concerns. Many operate from a hobbyist mindset, whether they realize it or not, which is the key reason why some films fail financially.

Making back a fractional percentage of an investment is not a success story in any other business. Indie filmmakers shrug and say, "Well, that's how it goes." Too many filmmakers spend investors' money on films that never return a profit and then call it a day. If a startup company followed that model—raise money, spend it all with no plan for revenue, then close shop—its founders would likely be sued! But in film, this status quo is oddly accepted.

Treating your film like a business starts by creating a business plan. It should be a serious formal document if you're approaching serious investors, but at minimum, it needs to be a clear roadmap for how you'll develop, finance, produce, market, and distribute your film in a way that gives it the best shot at recouping costs and, ideally, turning a profit. It means thinking beyond "I want to make this film" to "Who's going to pay to watch this film, how do I reach them, and how do the economics work?" This level of planning begins with a well-crafted pitch deck, but ultimately lives in a full business plan that investors can evaluate, even if it's a wealthy relative.

Your key calling cards are a film pitch deck and supporting business materials that serve the role of an investment prospectus. You use them to spark investor interest, land a producer, attract a cast, and help prove you know what you're doing. It's not just pretty pictures and vibes; it's a sales document designed to show that your film is creatively compelling and financially viable.

Ultimately, investors want to know two things:

———————— • ————————

1- You know what you're doing.

2- You have a clear pathway to profitability.

———————— • ————————

The Importance of This Chapter

The emphasis of this book is the business of filmmaking, and we make every attempt to align your brain to not only the importance of treating your film like a business but giving you the tools to help make it happen. There are multiple components involved with starting a new business, and in this chapter, we will apply common components for creating a viable business environment for your film. Those include:

1- How to Create a Pitch Deck

2- How to Create a Business Plan

3- Building Your Financial Strategy

4- Seed Capital - The Smart Money

How to Create a Pitch Deck

A well-crafted pitch deck is a summary of your business plan that's tight, efficient, and commands attention. It's like a restaurant menu that shows the finished dish, the price, and why you'll love it, but it's not the recipe. The goal is to spark appetites. If investors are interested, they'll ask for the full business plan to see who runs the kitchen, how it's managed, and whether the manager can actually deliver.

Your pitch deck will be the first visual introduction of your movie concept to investors, so first impressions are critical. Putting on our investor hat for a moment, we can tell by a few key slides whether the film is a viable investment (Most of the decks that hit our desks are not). Visual appeal should grab our attention, and great design goes a long way (your mother was wrong; people DO judge a book by its cover. Sorry, Mom), but the logline is the doorkeeper of your entire deck. If the logline is meh, we're out. In the marketing chapter, we go in-depth into why a strong logline is fundamental to project viability.

If the logline hooks us, we'll flip over to the synopsis. We're looking for three paragraphs of two or three short sentences each. Each paragraph represents an act: The first paragraph is Act One, and so on. While the logline should capture our attention, the synopsis should hold us hostage.

Then, we'll scout the deck for attachments, namely who is directing, who is producing, and who has the lead role. If no actor attachments, who is on the wish list?

What's your marketing strategy? If your plan says, "We have an LOI from distributor X who will handle all that," you've just revealed you don't know what you're doing. An actionable marketing strategy should be developed before production begins, *regardless* of your distribution strategy. The good news is that we'll walk you through how to build one in the next chapter.

What's your release strategy, and how realistic is it? If you say, "We'll release in theaters, then go to Netflix," you've just signaled that you don't understand how distribution works. Netflix doesn't buy indie films off the street, and they won't return your call when you try. To help you avoid that trap, we'll walk through real-world release strategies in Chapter Seven.

We highlight these common issues because most pitch decks share many of the same flaws. Our goal is to get you thinking critically about your planning. It's not necessarily fun or easy, but it's essential if you want to run your film like a business and, more importantly, a successful one.

The ideal deck is 10–15 horizontal (landscape) slides: clean design, visually sharp, with tight, sizzling hot copy. Less is *way* more. Your deck should summarize the business plan, not explain every detail.

Think of it like a billboard; you're sparking high-level interest and prompting a clear next step. A good deck respects the investor's time. High-net-worth individuals (HNWIs) are busy. If your deck passes the smell test, they'll ask what's next, and that's when you offer the whole business plan.

Important: You must have their demonstrable permission before sending over any investment instrument (like a subscription agreement). Otherwise, you may violate SEC rules[1].

A great deck tells a great story. Below is an overview of the essential elements your pitch deck should include, with the culmination of every slide showing that you know what you're doing and have a clear path to profitability. We'll break down some of the tougher context in later chapters.

Note: There are plenty of online resources for designing a visually engaging deck. Our focus here is on the quality of your text, what you say, and

---

1   Under U.S. Securities and Exchange Commission (SEC) rules, you may not offer a security to someone who hasn't requested it or given prior permission, unless a specific exemption applies. Unsolicited pitches can violate federal law. If you reside outside the U.S., check your country's securities regulations.

how clearly you say it.

What to include in your deck

Title (cover) Slide – Film title, logline, and visual hook.

Story Summary – A short, gripping synopsis.

Genre & Tone – Comparison films (tone, audience, budget range, release strategy. NO studio films unless you have confirmation that yours will be, also.)

Vision Slide – Director/producer's intent, emotional impact, and why they should be the one who tells the story.

Audience & Market – Who it's for, why they'll care. Remember the two most important questions.

Team – Key creatives with notable bios and credits.

Casting Strategy – Talent that is confirmed or on a wish list that makes sense for the film's story and its budget.

Visual Style – Look book references or concept art.

Distribution Strategy – How the film will make money (TVOD, SVOD, festivals, etc.)

Budget – Top sheet numbers, how money will be used (use and allocation of proceeds).

Timeline – Pre-production through release.

Incentives & Risk Mitigation – Tax credits, gap financing, sales estimates.

Investor ROI[2] and IRR[3] – How investors get paid and what the upside looks like.

Call to Action – What you're asking for (amount, terms, next steps).

Contact Info – Clear, professional contact details.

Bonus Material:

- Press coverage if you've already generated buzz.

- Awards or past successes of your team on previous films.

- Awards for the script.

- Mood video / sizzle reel / proof of concept reel (link or QR code).

How to Create a Business Plan

Once your deck is solid, use it as the blueprint for your business plan. Just like you wouldn't write a screenplay without first locking the treatment, you shouldn't write a business plan until your deck is tight. The condensed messaging needed in a deck forces you to distill the essence of the film: Concept, strategy, market, comps, and team. The business plan is where you unpack all of that in full detail.

---

2   **ROI (Return on Investment):** A basic measure of profitability, calculated by dividing net profit by the initial investment. It shows how much gain or loss an investor earns relative to what they put in.

3   **IRR (Internal Rate of Return):** A metric used to estimate the annualized rate of return on an investment, factoring in the timing of cash flows. It helps investors compare profitability across different projects.

Can you get away without a business plan? Sure, if your investor doesn't care about getting their money back. They exist, but they're rare. Maybe it's a wealthy relative who is more interested in your growth as their return on investment and not the money or someone looking for a tax write-off. Investors who do expect a financial return can sometimes be convinced to part with cash without a plan, but those investors only make that mistake once.

The business plan is a comprehensive document that provides investors with the detailed information they need to evaluate if you know what you're doing and you have a clear pathway to profitability including the viability, risks, and return potential of your film. They'll rely on this for a significant portion of their due diligence[4]. A business plan is typically a fact-based, text-driven document designed to inform, not sell. It may include charts, tables, or graphs (e.g., budget breakdowns, ROI models, and timelines), but its tone should remain objective and professional. The goal is to present clear, credible, and *dependable* information an investor can use to assess risk vs. reward potential. It's a serious document, often 40+ pages, that includes everything from financial assumptions to legal disclaimers. Ours are almost at the level of private placement memorandums[5] (PPMs) but without the subscription agreement[6] and not prepared by an attorney. That

---

4   **Due diligence:** The process by which an investor reviews all available information about a project—financials, legal documents, team experience, risks, and potential returns—to assess its viability before deciding to invest.

5   **Private Placement Memorandum (PPM):** A legal disclosure document provided to prospective investors in a private offering. It outlines key details such as the business plan, use of funds, risk factors, capital structure, and legal disclaimers, helping protect the issuer from liability and ensuring compliance with securities laws.

6   **Subscription Agreement:** A legal contract between a company and an investor that details the terms under which the investor agrees to purchase shares or ownership interest in the project. It includes details such as the investment amount, ownership percentage, rights, representations, and legal disclaimers. It is typically signed after the investor has reviewed the business plan and completed due diligence.

means your plan should include everything an investor needs to evaluate the opportunity before requesting legal paperwork.

A strong business plan includes:

> **Executive Summary** – A 1–2 page snapshot of the opportunity: logline, synopsis, team, budget, and the ask.

> **Team Bios** – Relevant industry experience with prior credits and measurable success. No fluff, no filler.

> **Market and Industry Analysis** – A clear overview of the current landscape. Include comps with budget and box office, define your film's niche, and outline your strategic position. Provide a high-level look at the state of the industry and its growth potential—critical context for investor confidence.

> **Revenue Streams** – Outline how the film can generate returns across multiple channels (TVOD, AVOD, SVOD, international sales, merchandise, etc.).

> **Development Status** – What's completed, what's in progress, and what remains. Show momentum and a clear path forward.

> **Production Plan** – Where and when you're filming, union status, key crew, and a realistic schedule.

> **Distribution Strategy** – Your release plan and why it makes sense. Be specific and grounded.

> **Marketing Strategy** – How you'll reach your audience: festival approach, platform strategy, grassroots tactics, and digital marketing.

> **Budget & Use of Funds** – Top sheet and a breakdown of how capital will be allocated, including development, production, and marketing.

Capital Stack – Detailed structure of the financing: equity, soft money (grants, tax incentives, product placement), deferments, minimum guarantees, and how it all fits together.

Risk Factors – A full and honest list of the risks. This isn't optional—it protects you and shows that you take the investment seriously.

Investor Return – Detailed financial waterfall, recoupment structure, internal rate of return (IRR), profit participation, and expected timelines.

Exit Strategy – How investors will receive their cash. Include festival paths, sales agent plans, distribution timelines, and potential acquisition targets.

Legal Disclaimers – Includes standard SEC language, forward-looking statements, and disclosures to ensure compliance and limit liability. This language is widely available online. Examples are also included at profoundstudios.media/documents

The business plan is not something you slap together in a weekend. It's the investor-grade proof that you know what you're doing—requiring research, strategy, and clear thinking. It maps the entire project from A to Z and shows what happens if you hit a detour.

You can write it yourself—and you should. But once it's done, have an experienced attorney review it. If you're raising serious capital, this isn't optional. A single error could expose you to liability. A solid entertainment or securities lawyer will make sure your plan is sound, SEC-compliant, and credible.

Let your deck guide the structure, but expand each section with facts, data, and clarity. If your pitch deck is the billboard, the business plan is the operating manual.

If you want a professional head start, we offer a customizable business plan template—available for a fee at profoundstudios.media/documents.

Market and Industry Analysis

One of the first rules in business is to know your customers. Filmmaking is no different. If you can't answer who will watch your film and why they'd pay for it, you're flying blind.

And no, your film is not "for everyone." That's lazy thinking and wishful at best.

In indie filmmaking, the niche is your edge. As producer-director Jon Reiss put it, "In independent film, the niche is king and queen[7]." Without a massive marketing budget, you must be laser-focused. Know exactly who cares about your story and how to reach them.

Are you targeting horror fans? Autism advocates? MMA junkies? Climate warriors? If you try to reach everyone, you'll reach no one. Reiss again: "If you don't know who your film is for, you run the risk that it will be for no-one at all."

Forget mass appeal. That belongs to the studios with tens of millions in ad spend. You don't need everyone; you only need the right someone. It's better to be a must-watch for a passionate few than background noise for the masses.

Once you identify your core audience, study their behavior. What platforms do they use? What content do they already consume? What keywords, hashtags, or online communities gather them in one place? Start a dossier. These are your early adopters.

But audience targeting is only half the equation. Investors also want to know what kind of market are you selling into?

---

7   *The Film Collaboratives* blog, August, 2014

This is where industry analysis comes in. Look at current trends in the indie film landscape. Is your genre growing or saturated? Are niche markets like faith-friendly, horror or true crime expanding or pulling back? What does audience demand look like on platforms like Tubi or Amazon for your type of story?

Provide a macro view: box office recovery post-COVID, growth of streaming, expansion of AVOD platforms, or international demand for English-language content. This shows you understand not just your film but the broader market forces shaping its potential.

Why does this matter? During due diligence, investors evaluate not just your film but also the industry sector in which it operates. If you can show that your genre or audience niche has growth potential and that your movie is positioned to ride that wave, you've made their decision easier. It's part of demonstrating a pathway to profitability.

Pair this with strong comps: real-world films similar in genre, budget, and release strategy that found success. Back it up with numbers. That's what gives you credibility. That's what makes your plan investable. But don't just show the achievements; note a few failures as well. A hero filmmaker will research and disclose the ratio of wins to losses in the category their film will live in. Most investors appreciate that level of detail. And if the ratio reveals that most films in the category lose, how do you mitigate that risk with your film? Prove it's a story that stands out? Budget? Trendsetting? Multiple dynamics weave together to create a clear risk profile. If you can't show a credible risk mitigation strategy, you might consider abandoning the project.

Plan Multiple Revenue Streams

You identify every possible revenue stream in any other business, and your film should be no different. The days are gone when a distributor buys your film and puts you in the black before the ink dries on the agreement.

Create a comprehensive list of potential income streams for this project, even in small amounts, and develop a plan to pursue each one.

Think domestic distribution (theatrical, VOD, SVOD, AVOD), international sales (territory by territory), TV licensing (cable, airlines, educational broadcast), community screenings (paid showings at organizations), educational licenses (especially for documentaries), merchandise (shirts, soundtracks, tie-in books), and even festival screening fees (some fests—particularly international—do pay).

Not every film will tap every stream, but the more hooks in the water, the better your odds of recouping. And this strategy should shape your production. If targeting schools, build a study guide. And remember, exploitation starts in development, not distribution.

Budget Realistically, and Keep It Lean

Treating your film like a business means your budget is your startup cost, and smaller budgets are easier to recoup. A $50K feature could break even with a modest distribution deal, though success hinges on execution and market fit. With a $500K budget, you'll need recognizable talent, probably no higher than the B list (Don't expect current A-listers unless they're doing a favor, taking backend only, or joining for passion), savvy marketing, or festival buzz to compete. Sundance's Creative Distribution Initiative found that only one of 18 films budgeted between $200K and $900K broke even between 2018 and 2020, dubbing this range the "budget donut hole" where recoupment is toughest. Films under $150K, while not directly studied, face a lower risk by needing less revenue to turn a profit. Mid-budget indies ($300K–$1M) rarely succeed without standout elements like stars or a killer hook. That's why "budget to the comps" matters. If similar films sell for low six figures, spending multiples of that is reckless. Write lean: use locations you can access, simplify logistics, and weave constraints into the story. Every dollar spent should be at least a dollar you can realistically earn back.

Allocate Budget to Marketing & Distribution, Not Just Production

A classic rookie mistake is spending 100% of your budget on production and assuming, "If we build it, they will come." They won't unless you give them a reason. That reason will include a marketing and distribution strategy that excites audiences and buyers. A business-minded filmmaker sets aside a real marketing budget from day one, at least enough to build trailers, professional key art, festival strategies, and targeted digital campaigns. For a micro-budget feature, allocate at least $25,000 to $50,000 to cover the basics like key art, trailers, and deliverables. If that sounds too much, you're not thinking about the business. Industry wisdom suggests reserving 10% of your budget for basic marketing, with the goal of your film going directly to streaming platforms. Bump that to 50% or even 100% or more if you're planning a theatrical run of any size. That may sound extreme, but it's smart. Many successful movies have had marketing budgets of 5x or 10x their actual production budget. There's a reason.

Telling investors you're allocating $90K for production and $50K for marketing is part of showing that you have a reasonable pathway to profitability.

Protect your marketing bucket with no compromise. No other expenses come from that account, no matter what.

Marketing money lets you cut a solid trailer, design professional key art, submit to festivals, travel for networking, and build early buzz. It means hiring a publicist in the run-up to release when it matters most, running targeted social campaigns for streaming, and covering P&A if you go theatrical. Most importantly, it gives you leverage with distributors.

Make a Distribution Strategy Early

We'll cover this in-depth in Chapter Seven, but your business plan should include your intended route to market from the start. Are you aiming for a top-tier festival premiere and hoping for a sale? Good luck; that's a rocky field to plow. Self-distribution from day one is more cost-effective, but DIY is a heavy lift.

Plan A could look like this: Plan a strategy for getting into SXSW and other festivals for buzz momentum. In the meantime, secure a mid-tier North American distributor, use a sales agent for foreign rights, and retain the option to self-release if the offers are weak. It's wise to have plans B and C detailed and ready to go because plan C could easily become your landing zone. Plan B: Skip the festival circuit and go immediately to a domestic distributor and foreign sales agent.

Plan C: If no one bites, upload to iTunes/Amazon via an aggregator and push a grassroots campaign yourself.

The point isn't to lock in a single path. It's to have a plan—and a back-up—and a backup of the backup so you're not guessing when it's go time. You build confidence when articulating a real strategy to investors, cast, or crew. It shows you're not just making a movie but bringing a product to market.

Also, know the economics (we'll discuss in the next chapter): What platforms pay, what distributors deduct, and what percentages reach you. That way, you can run recoupment scenarios. Here's a basic one:

You spend $50K to make a micro-budget film. You release it on TVOD and get 5,000 people to rent it at $4. That's $20k gross. Amazon or another platform takes half, leaving you $10k. You license to a niche streamer for $10k and sell foreign rights in two small territories for another $5k. Now you're at $25k, halfway to break even. Add another $10K from long-tail revenue, and you've recovered $35k—a $15k loss but not catastrophic.

Now, imagine your budget was $100k instead. Same returns, but you're $65k in the hole.

This is the logic behind recoupment modeling. If the market for your film can return $x, then your budget should reflect that.

Company Structure and Legal Protections

An LLC is essential for raising money, qualifying for state incentives, and securing distribution. No distributor, investor, or tax credit office will work with you without it. Don't try to shortcut this by using an existing LLC and simply adding the film to it. Doing so can expose your other business to potential legal liability, financial entanglement, and tax complications. If something goes wrong during production—lawsuit, accident, unpaid debt—your original business could be on the hook. A film should always be held in its dedicated entity to protect your other ventures and to keep accounting, ownership, and rights clean and auditable. Investors expect a standalone structure. So do sales agents, state incentive offices, and insurers.

An LLC is the typical structure for most independent film projects because it's flexible, easy to set up, and provides a clear legal and financial container for the film. It protects your personal assets, simplifies tax reporting, and allows you to define ownership and profit participation in the Operating Agreement. As a pass-through entity, all profits and losses flow directly to the members and are reported on their individual tax returns— often a benefit to investors if the film generates early losses they can deduct.

If you're outside the U.S., look into equivalent business structures in your country—such as a private limited company (Ltd) in the UK, GmbH in Germany, or Pty Ltd in Australia. Local laws vary, so check your country's regulations and consult a professional to choose the right setup for your film. The principle is the same: create a dedicated legal entity that protects you and presents your film as a serious business.

To structure ownership, you'll need a Securities and Exchange Commission (SEC)- compliant Operating Agreement drafted by an attorney. This document outlines who manages the company, how decisions are made, and how profits are split. Investors buy into the company through a Subscription Agreement, which defines their "Units" (the amount they invest and what they get in return). Setting up the LLC usually costs a couple of hundred bucks, depending on your state. However, the real cost kicks in with drafting the legal documents—the Operating Agreement and Subscription Agreement. Think hundreds to thousands in legal fees, depending on complexity. It's not cheap, but it is mandatory if you want real investors.

Some insurance policies can be written for individuals, but most carriers prefer to insure an LLC. The same goes for tax incentives: most require that the production company applying is a properly registered entity in the state where the film will be shot. Every state has commercial services for registering and managing LLC entities, including providing registered agent services[8].

And if you're crowdfunding, running the money through a business account keeps things clean and shows backers you're legit.

The bottom line is that an LLC moves you from creating art to show business. We'll get in the legal weeds in a later chapter, but for now, know this: if you're serious about your film, setting up a proper business structure isn't optional. It's the price of entry.

Crowdfunding and Audience Building

A solid crowdfunding campaign can raise $20k and build an early fan base, but don't fall into the trap of thinking it's easy money. Crowdfunding

---

8   **Registered Agent:** A person or business designated to receive legal and official documents on behalf of a company, including service of process, government correspondence, and compliance notices. Most states require businesses to maintain a registered agent with a physical address in the state of formation.

is not for the weak-kneed. You're not pitching one investor but hundreds, and they all expect something back. Your campaign will likely struggle if you don't have a ready-made audience that already cares about your work. Crowdfunding success hinges on having a pre-existing, engaged audience. Without it, you're essentially cold-pitching hundreds of strangers, which is time-consuming and often ineffective. As Seed&Spark's Bri Castellini puts it, "Crowdfunding done right is audience building first and fundraising second." Platforms like Indiegogo emphasize that your campaign lacks the necessary support to succeed without a crowd. Therefore, building and nurturing your audience well before launching your campaign is crucial. If they bite, they're your first customers and emotionally and financially invested. So treat them right, deliver what you promised, and keep them informed. When it's time to launch, they'll help spread the word.

Crowdfunding is a full-blown marketing campaign: sharp hook, clear rewards, and solid execution. Yes, it's "free" money, meaning you don't re-pay it, but you're still accountable. Blow it, and you'll burn trust fast.

Traditional Business Model for Indie Film

The old-school "make it, screen it, sell it at a festival" model is all but obsolete.

Innovative indies are exploring new models: breaking features into webisodes, partnering with brands or NGOs[9], booking roadshow tours, or building recurring support through platforms like Patreon. These aren't magic bullets; they're strategic pivots grounded in adaptability and audience connection.

Branded content is also on the rise. In this model, a company funds all or part of a film in exchange for featuring its product, service, or values

---

9   An **NGO** (Non-Governmental Organization) is a nonprofit group that operates independently of any government, typically to address social, environmental, humanitarian, or development issues. NGOs can be local, national, or international and are often funded by donations, grants, or partnerships.

organically. This isn't traditional product placement; it's about alignment. The story must genuinely resonate with the brand's identity. For qualified filmmakers who understand how to weave messaging into the narrative without compromising quality, branded content can be a powerful funding avenue that also comes with built-in marketing support.

Have a Plan, But Stay Flexible

If your distribution plan flops, pivot. Execute your plan C self-release strategy. On the flip side, if a legit offer comes in and you planned to go DIY, evaluate it like a business deal. What are they offering? What are you giving up? Is it worth it?

The bottom line: don't wait for someone to do it for you. That's what real producers do—they greenlight themselves and stay in control, even when it's not fun. Especially then. A smart plan isn't rigid. It exists so you know how and when to change course.

Building Your Financial Strategy

Capital stacks were built on equity, debt, pre-sales, and tax incentives for years in the independent film world. It worked—at least on paper. If you had a major actor attached (say, Margot Robbie, Ryan Gosling, or Timothée Chalamet), you could often generate millions in projected foreign sales before the film went into production.

Let's say your movie had a $5 million budget. You could project $3 million in global pre-sales, secure gap financing, and borrow against those future sales. Add another $1.5 million from a tax rebate in a place like

Georgia or New Mexico (which you might also borrow against), and suddenly, you're only looking for $500,000–$1 million in equity.

But the market has shifted.

Pre-sales are no longer as reliable, especially if you don't have a bankable name actor. Tax credits can be slow, complicated, and vary wildly by state.

Meanwhile, most indie producers still run into the same chicken-and-egg dilemma:

"We need money to get the actor, but we need the actor to get the money."

Get the egg first, the money.

Secure at least 30% equity in your budget in escrow before you approach talent or financing partners. That's what gives your project credibility.

And remember, one size does not fit all. A $300,000 micro budget film probably won't generate meaningful tax credits or attract an MG (Minimum Guarantee)[10] because it likely won't have the cast to support a presale.

So, whatever your budget, build a capital stack that makes real-world sense:

- Don't list speculative foreign sales, get actual estimates from a real sales agent.

- Don't assume a tax rebate until you've talked to the film office and a lender.

- Don't expect someone else to figure it out; do the math

---

10   **Minimum Guarantee (MG)**: A pre-sale or distribution advance paid by a distributor or sales agent in exchange for rights to the film. The MG is typically paid upfront or in milestones and is recouped by the distributor from revenue before any profits are shared with the producer or investors. It reduces risk for the filmmaker by securing early capital but often comes with rights restrictions and revenue participation terms.

yourself, then verify it.

Hire an accountant. Talk to an entertainment attorney. Get a financial advisor or an experienced line producer who's done this before. And don't expect them to work for free.

Treat Your Film Like a Business All the Way to the Finish Line

Once production wraps, many filmmakers breathe a sigh of relief and go on vacation. This is a big mistake. After production, the real grind begins. Real businesses track performance, study what worked, and use the data to improve. You should, too.

Track expenses against budget and income against projections. Did DVDs sell better than expected? Did your email list convert into rentals? Use that info to guide your next move, not just creatively but strategically as well.

What delivered ROI? Which channels fell flat? What festival brought valuable contacts? Document it. Every film is research for the next one.

This mindset shift may feel awkward and overwhelming. But business planning protects your art by ensuring you can finish, release, and recoup. And it doesn't kill creativity. If anything, it fuels smarter decisions: A drama built around one location might get made while your WWII epic sits in a drawer.

Investors, distributors, and even festivals are sizing you by how well you speak their language. When discussing comps, target markets, and revenue strategy, you separate yourself from the 97 out of 100 dreamers who show up with passion only.

Successful Filmmakers Show Up with Passion *and* a Business Plan

Treating your film like a business takes the sting out of rejection. Didn't land that festival? Adjust the plan. The distributor ghosted you? Pivot. And when you track your wins (like audience growth or strong niche sales), you'll realize you're building momentum, not chasing validation.

Seed Capital

The Smart Money Step

By now, you may be thinking, "This is a lot," and you're not wrong. Setting your film up within a sound business structure can feel overwhelming. That's normal. Many filmmakers reach this point and panic. Some skip it altogether, raise money from friends and family, and start shooting without a foundation. But the wiser path is raising seed capital first.

We alluded to this in the last section, but seed capital is the money you raise to build the business. Not to shoot the film. To create the plan that gets you to the shoot. In other words, you're raising development money.

This early capital allows you to:

- Form your LLC and pay the filing fees.

- Hire an entertainment attorney to draft your Operating Agreement and Subscription Agreement.

- Have that same attorney vet your business plan and deck before investors ever see them.

- Hire creatives to design professional key art (even a mockup) and help build a high-quality deck.

- Hire a line producer and accountant to help with budgeting and financial advice.

- Make a legitimate offer to a lead actor, including holding funds in escrow.

- Pay for consulting, strategy sessions, or look books that improve investor confidence.

Development costs vary based on your total production budget, but here's a rough ballpark:

Category	Low-End Estimate	High-End Estimate
Legal (LLC, agreements, vetting)	$5,000	$15,000
Creative (key art, deck design)	$2,500	$10,000
Casting Offer (escrow, deposits)	$5,000	$25,000 +
Misc. Development Expenses (line producer, accountant, script polish, etc.)	$2,500	$10,000
Total Seed Capital Range	**$15K**	**$60k +**

Yes, that's real money—but it's what separates the weekend warrior dreamers from the self-greenlit doers. You'll use your seed round to fund legitimacy—which is what gets real investors to take you seriously.

Now a quick word on actor attachments—and why LOIs (Letters of Intent) no longer have value.

It used to be that filmmakers could get an actor to sign a letter of intent (LOI) and wave it around to raise money. But that strategy was always shaky, especially now. Distributors don't value LOIs, and agents know exactly what they are: an attempt to leverage their client's name to secure financing. Bottom line: the LOI game is dead.

When you approach an agent, they'll ask a few immediate questions:

- Who's directing?

- What are the dates?

- What's the offer?

- And most importantly: Is the money in place?

If you don't have funds in escrow, or at least a clear plan to secure them, agents today won't engage. Requesting an LOI without cash is a red flag. It marks you as inexperienced, no matter how good your intentions are.

Even seed money makes the project real. If you can say to an actor, "We're shooting on this date, here's your shooting schedule, and airline tickets are standing by," that's a completely different level of conversation than, "Can I get an LOI? We're hoping to shoot next spring if everything falls into place." And real money can help persuade agents and actors to overlook their caution of working with a first-time director.

See the difference?

When an actor or their agent sees real money and a real schedule, they'll typically respond in one of three ways:

- "I'm available. Let's go."

- "I'm booked then, but I'm free on this date—can you adjust?"

- "I'm not interested, because of X."

All three responses are useful. They move the process forward. But none of them happen unless your offer is real. Having seed money to make a legitimate offer to a lead actor is smart, even if you don't have all the money raised yet. Because once you have a signed offer from a recognizable actor and can tell investors, "They're contractually attached and ready to shoot on this date," you not only look professional, you have greenlighted yourself into a far more likely scenario of getting serious investors to write real checks. You can escrow actor offers, but you'll need cash for all the rest.

That, paired with a clean, professional business plan that shows you know what you're doing and have a clear path to profitability makes it far easier for an investor to write the check. Especially in an industry this risky.

Marketing Unpacked

"I love it when a plan comes together."

— Col. John "Hannibal" Smith, *The A-Team* (2010)

I n this chapter, we'll break down the marketing stack—logline, tagline, title, key art, and trailer—and show you how to build each element effectively and timely: The earlier, the better. Then we'll present options for rolling out your campaign through ad placement and social media awareness before, during, and after release. It's one of the longest chapters of the book, but it's also one of the most important, because marketing is where films either vanish or rise above the ocean of noise. On several occasions, we've mentioned budgeting for marketing. Let's have a closer look.

Budgeting for Marketing
To Build Leverage

A significant source of frustration for indie filmmakers develops after a movie is finished. Filmmakers enter the distribution phase feeling blindsided, suddenly claiming they were "taken advantage of" by sales agents or distributors. And maybe, in some cases, they were. But what leverage did they have when they walked into that deal?

They might expect a minimum guarantee, what the industry calls an "MG." They get excited when a distributor offers them $50K, $100K, or more upfront for their film. But if their movie costs $1 million and the MG is $50,000, what exactly are they celebrating? That small advance often comes with the cost of control. You gave the distributor the upper hand because they fronted the money.

Imagine a different scenario: what if you had a $200,000 marketing budget in the bank and ready to work? Suddenly, the conversation with that same distributor changes. Instead of begging for an MG, you could say, "We're handling our limited theatrical rollout, and we have P&A funds."

That shifts the power dynamic. Now, you can ask for a higher revenue share. Or, if you do want an MG, you can say, "We're bringing $200K to the table. Can you match us?" That's magic sauce.

That's how savvy filmmakers move in the modern era. The landscape has changed; more distributors now expect filmmakers to actively participate in the marketing of their films. Gone are the days when you handed off your movie and expected someone else to "take care of the business side."

We've said it before in earlier chapters: greenlighting yourself means taking full responsibility, not just for the creative execution, but for the market execution. Your marketing budget is a power move.

Marketing vs Advertising

Pro tip: To avoid confusion and not sound like a noob when talking shop, remember this:

———————— • ————————

Marketing is the strategy. Advertising is the tactic.

———————— • ————————

Marketing is the big-picture game plan: Identifying your audience, positioning your film, and crafting your message. Marketing defines *what* you say, *who* you say it to, and *why* it matters.

Advertising is how you *deliver* that message: Paid placements, social ads, trailers, promoted posts, etc. It's *how* you say it and *where* you place it.

Marketing budget includes the costs for marketing and advertising.

Marketing and Story Concept

Too many indie filmmakers start thinking about marketing during or after post-production as something they'll "figure out later" once the movie is done. That mindset is a trap of doom. The closer you get to picture lock without a marketing plan, the more challenging it becomes to create one that works. Especially if you made a film with a weak concept and no clear audience, no marketing guru, distributor, or festival whisperer can save it from the 97% club. Maybe—*maybe*—your film catches fire down the road. But most likely, it joins the digital graveyard of thousands of well-meaning projects that have never stood a chance.

That's tough to hear. But hearing it now is easier than wasting years learning it the hard way.

At this point, your best move is to muddle through and squeeze what you can out of what you have. The strategies later in the chapter may help you recover some ground. But like they say in the oil business:

"You can't sell dry wells to farmers for fence post holes."

If you fell victim to the "we'll worry about marketing later" mindset, that's most filmmakers, not just you, so no shade. We've seen many talented filmmakers make the same mistake, *including us.* So, we offer you a shift in how you think about marketing:

———————— • ————————

Marketing and story concept are not separate.
Your concept should be your marketing hook.

———————— • ————————

Did you catch the *significance* of that? Let it detonate in your brain and rearrange your molecules. If it lands, your entire career just shifted and can now be defined as *before you read this and after.*

At first glance, the statement might seem rather droll. But this is about baking resonance into the DNA of your idea from *day one* so that the concept *is* the hook. It's significant because *most* filmmakers don't think about marketing and story concept in the same sentence.

This is far beyond hoping someone watches your film just because you think it's a good story. Maybe it is. But does the essence of the concept sear itself into your audience's soul? Does it stir something primal that's beyond language? Does it echo in their minds, burning brain cells for days?

The most magnetic concepts do that. And great marketing doesn't invent that resonance out of thin air, it exploits it. If it takes you ten minutes to explain the concept of your film, you do not have a marketable concept, and a film based on it should not be produced. You should be able to explain your movie in one fast, potent logline, or even better, in a tagline.

We'll discuss both in a moment. We know some of you will ignore this warning and shoot the film anyway. Too bad you have to learn the hard way.

There are examples when developing marketing after producing the film makes sense. You can get away with a shorter runway if your movie has a built-in audience, say, fans of a famous band, actor, beloved author, or viral subject.

The documentary *Brothers in Blues: Jimmie and Stevie Ray Vaughan* is one of those cases. The film had a built-in audience of millions of Vaughan brothers fans and a strong concept; the untold stories of two legendary musicians told by the people in the room when it happened. Eric Clapton, Billy Gibbons from *ZZ Top*, Jackson Browne, legendary producer Nile Rodgers, and early band members told an hour and a half of rare stories. Pure gold. We co-distributed the film with Freestyle, who launched the marketing campaign just one week before release, and the audience showed up. *But the majority of indie films don't have the luxury of a built-in audience.* They need a strategy and time to nurture a paying audience, and they need to start early. That's when a strong concept is mandatory because no famous names will move the needle without a killer concept. The marketing stack will reveal itself like a magic trick if your concept is sharp.

The Marketing Stack

Think of this as stacking one marketing tool on top of another to build a plan that syncs with everything in the life of your film, from development to cult following fifty years from now (we can fantasize, yeah?). The marketing stack keeps you laser-focused on seamlessly integrating marketing and story:

> **1. The Logline** – One or two sentences that make someone say, "you have my attention."
>
> **2. The Tagline** – One emotionally-charged phrase that captures the spirit of the concept.
>
> **3. The Title** – The first (and maybe only) thing they'll remember.
>
> **4. The Key Art** (poster) – The emotional snapshot that sets the tone.
>
> **5. The Trailer** – The deal closer. The "Take my money, NOW" tool.

Let's unpack these.

The Logline

A logline is a one or two-sentence summary of your film's premise that clearly reveals the protagonist, their goal, the central conflict, and the stakes. It's the pitch distilled to its essence; it's what you'll say if someone asks, "What's your movie about?" If their eyes gloss over while you're still trying to explain the story ten minutes later, you don't have a logline, and your story's validity is questionable, to say it politely. The power of a strong logline is that it can sell the film's concept without anyone reading the script. Someone should hear it and say, "Wow, I wanna see THAT movie!" The logline is your strategic success magnet for pitching, packaging, and

positioning your film to investors, distributors, festivals, and other potential stakeholders.

Basic storytelling starts with a spine, the protagonist's journey, and
how they change themselves or the world to achieve their goal. That's the
heartbeat of any great story, whether it's told around a campfire or in a $200
million Oscar Best Picture. It's not just what happens; it's *why it matters*.
Your protagonist wants something. Something real. Something urgent.
But obstacles stand in the way, both internal and external, and watching
them overcome those challenges makes the story worth telling. The higher
the stakes, the stronger the story. The logline captures all this in a couple
of lines, each word pulling its weight like it owes rent. It's the gene code
of your film. Every scriptwriting book, course, or weekend screenwriting
clinic explains these concepts, and if you're writing your film's script, you
have no excuse for not knowing those concepts instinctively. But for some
reason, translating a compelling idea to paper sometimes seems to be one
of the most difficult tasks known to humanity. Especially given the sheer
volume of mediocrity that tests the patience of excellence but still gets
funded.

Common Logline formulas

There's no one-size-fits-all "best" logline formula, but the strongest ones
usually follow a core structure that combines character, conflict, stakes, and
a clean and compelling hook. Here are a few of the most effective formulas
used across the industry:

The Classic "Who + What + Why + Stakes" Formula

**When [INCITING INCIDENT] happens,
a [PROTAGONIST] must [GOAL], or else
[CONSEQUENCES].**

Great for high-concept, mainstream films.

Immediately communicates the setup, urgency, and dramatic stakes.

Example, *The Matrix:*

When a disillusioned hacker discovers the world is a simulation, he must embrace his destiny to lead a rebellion, or humanity will remain enslaved forever.

The "Somebody Wants Something But Obstacles Stand in The Way" Formula

A [PROTAGONIST] wants [GOAL], but [OBSTACLE], so [ACTION TAKEN].

Simple and effective, especially for character-driven stories.

Emphasizes internal and external conflict.

Example, *Finding Nemo:*

A timid clownfish wants to rescue his son, but his fear of the open ocean holds him back, so he embarks on a dangerous journey that pushes him beyond his limits.

Genre-Tailored Formula (for Thrillers, Sci-fi, etc.)

In a [SETTING/GENRE], a [PROTAGONIST] must [DO SOMETHING], before [TICKING CLOCK/ANTAGONIST] causes [HIGH STAKES].

Useful when your setting or concept is part of the hook.

Builds urgency and tension right into the logline.

Example, *A Quiet Place:*

In a post-apocalyptic world overrun by sound-hunting

creatures, a family must live in silence—or face certain death.

"Irony Hook" Formula (Used in Hollywood Pitches)

It's about a [PROTAGONIST] who [SITUATION], until [IRONIC TWIST].

Powerful when your concept has a big irony or reversal.

Often used in high-concept comedies or dramas.

Example, *Liar Liar:*

It's about a lawyer who lies for a living—until his son's birthday wish forces him to tell the truth for 24 hours.

More Tips

- Use active voice.

- Highlight unique genre elements, especially for sci-fi, horror, or fantasy.

- Keep it under 35 words.

- Don't include character names unless they have power (e.g. Beyoncé or Jeff Bezos).

The Tagline

While the *logline* is generally used to sell your film to potential stakeholders—investors, producers, distributors—the *tagline* helps sell the finished film to a paying audience. It's a marketing tool, not a pitch. Whether it's thrilling, heartbreaking, hilarious, or haunting, the tagline captures the soul of your film in just a few words.

A tagline sells the *feeling*. It's not about plot or structure. Where the logline *tells the story*, the tagline *teases the experience*. It's what lives on the poster, the trailer, the lips of anyone trying to hype your movie in one line or maybe just a few words. A great tagline is short, sharp, and emotionally loaded. It hints at tone, genre, or theme without explaining anything. It makes people lean in. You're not writing a summary; you're casting a spell.

Compared to the logline examples above, here are their counterpart taglines:

The Matrix (1999)

> Tagline: "Reality is a thing of the past."
>
> • Mysterious and cerebral. It hints at the film's central theme, questioning what's real, without giving away the plot.
>
> • Bonus tagline used in some campaigns: "What Is The Matrix?" — A brilliant move that created intrigue and viral curiosity before viral marketing was a thing.

Finding Nemo (2003)

> Tagline: "There are 3.7 trillion fish in the ocean. They're looking for one."
>
> • Funny, clever, and epic. It scales the stakes emotionally and geographically while making you laugh.
>
> • Also used: "Fish are friends, not food." – More of a character-driven line, but became widely associated with the film.

A Quiet Place (2018)

> Tagline: "If they hear you, they hunt you."
>
> • Tense and terrifying. In one line, you understand the premise, the stakes, and the core rule of the movie's world.

Liar Liar (1997)

Tagline: "Trust me."

- Perfectly ironic. Two words that capture both the premise and the humor of a lawyer who literally can't lie. Short, punchy, and dripping with sarcasm.

How to Write an Effective Tagline

Unlike loglines, taglines are not formulaic and, therefore, trickier to nail, but here are a few tools for dialing in on a keeper:

1. Start with the Emotional Core

What should the audience *feel* by watching your movie? Dread? Wonder? Hope? Suspense? Grief?

The best taglines are *emotional*, not explanatory. Think less about what it's about and more about what it feels like.

> *The Shawshank Redemption*: "Fear can hold you prisoner. Hope can set you free."

(Emotion: adventure, hope, determination)

> *Alien:* "In space no one can hear you scream."

(Emotion: terror, isolation, vulnerability)

2. Keep It Short. *Really* Short.

Aim for 3–8 words. The best taglines are punchy and repeatable. If someone can't remember it 10 seconds later, it's not working.

> *Ghostbusters:* "Who you gonna call?"

> *Apollo 13:* "Houston, we have a problem."

> *Poltergeist:* "They're here..."

3. Think Like a Copywriter, Not a Screenwriter

Pretend you're writing a billboard for a movie you want people to see as they're driving by at 70 miles an hour. You're not explaining plot points. You're planting a hook in someone's subconscious.

4. Use Wordplay (When It Serves the Tone)

Double meanings, irony, and contrast can be powerful, if it fits your genre and audience.

> *The Social Network:* "You don't get to 500 million friends without making a few enemies."
>
> *Superman:* "You'll believe a man can fly."
>
> *The Truman Show:* "On the air. Unaware."

5. Test, Don't Guess

Write 15–20 options. Say them out loud. Put them on mock posters. See what grabs attention and what doesn't. Ask non-filmmakers for their gut reaction. If they say, "Ooooh," or "I'd watch that," you're tracking.

6. Match the Genre and Tone

> **Romantic Comedy:** "Can two opposites attract when everything's falling apart?"
>
> **Thriller:** "He knows your secrets. He's just waiting."
>
> **Drama:** "Some wounds never heal. Some heal you."

7. Avoid These Common Mistakes

- Too long
- Too vague
- Too generic
- Sounds like every other movie
- Explains the plot
- Reads like a rejected logline

The tagline isn't there to explain your film. It's there to haunt your audience. It's the line they remember when they can't quite remember the title. It's the whisper that sells the emotion. Get it right, and you've already won half the battle.

The Title

Here, sports fans, are where a lot of filmmakers get *very* defensive.

They cling to their movie titles with white knuckles, even when every distributor, sales agent, and marketer tells them, "This title doesn't work."

Some indie film titles are so cryptic that you'd think they were passwords to the director's therapy sessions. They get poetic, mysterious, or way too clever. But a good title is about clarity. Your audience should know the tone, genre, and even the movie's theme they're about to pay for in three words or less.

We've had to change the titles of several films we've worked with. At times, filmmakers got very upset. At other times, they'd say, "Well if it helps with sales, I guess that's okay..." That reluctance and insecurity comes from not realizing their title has a purpose for the poster, the campaign, and the audience that within two seconds decide whether to click the thumbnail or not. It's the first impression your movie makes. You don't wait to brush your teeth until after the job interview, do you?

There are famous examples. *Pretty Woman* was initially called *3,000,* which referred to the amount of money the lead was paid for a week as a sex worker. Sure, it was accurate, but not memorable or marketable. *Edge of Tomorrow* had a box office flop title but later found new life when they started marketing it as *Live Die Repeat*, a tagline that became a better title than the title itself. And *Snakes on a Plane* is the holy grail of clarity. You knew exactly what it was.

Test it. Say it out loud. Picture it on a poster. Ask someone who hasn't read your script, "What kind of movie do you think this is?" You're on the right track if they say something that matches your vision. If you're making a rom-com and they respond with a question, "Is it a documentary?"— Start over.

Filmmakers often love their title like their first born child. So we offer strong advice:

───────── ● ─────────

Nothing is sacred but the concept itself.

───────── ● ─────────

And it better be an amazing concept.

Your title. Your temp score. Your script. Your dialogue. None of it is sacred. If it doesn't serve the concept's spine, it doesn't stay. It's *that hardcore simple.*

Titles communicate clearly and powerfully. If you want to keep your title, it's up to you to prove it works to people who've been down this road a thousand times before. If it doesn't hook, communicate, or resonate, then let it go.

Your title is the tip of the spear for capturing the audience's attention. It's the first thing people see. It's what they say out loud when they tell a friend:

"Did you see *Lord of the Rings?*"

"What did you think of *Sound of Freedom?*"

If your title doesn't trigger curiosity, clarity, or connection, nothing else in your marketing stack will get a chance.

Your title is everywhere. It includes the script, pitch deck, website, marketing materials, IMDb page, streaming platforms, festival listings, and press releases. It has to carry the weight of your whole film in just a few words. So:

- **Be memorable** – Can people recall it the next day without checking their notes?

- **Be searchable** – Is it searchable without pulling up nineteen other movies, a screamo band, and an Etsy store?

- **Reflect genre and tone** – Don't give a romantic drama an thriller-sounding title (unless you really know what you're doing).

- **Create curiosity** – It should raise a subtle question: What's that about?

- **Connect emotionally** – A strong title sparks feeling. Dread. Hope. Nostalgia. Tension.

Compare *The Notebook* to *Love Story, 1940*. Which one lands? Exactly.

Common Title Mistakes

Let's call out a few indie sins:

- **Pretentious nonsense:** *"The Ephemeral Whispers of Yesterday's Echo."* Stop.

- **Generic sludge:** *"Choices." "Home." "Truth."* These say nothing.

- **Spoilers:** Don't give away your twist in the title.

- **Unpronounceable words:** If someone doesn't know how to say your title out loud at a party, it's dead weight.

How to Find the Right Title

1. Start with your theme. What's the core truth of your story? What's the emotional anchor?

2. Check availability. IMDb, Google, and domain searches will save you pain later.

3. Write 20–30 options. Don't stop at the first cool-sounding one. Push deeper.

4. Say them out loud. Seriously. Hear how they roll off the tongue.

5. Test it. Ask non-filmmakers. Do they get it? Do they want it?

6. Think long-term. Can this title live on a poster? A T-shirt? A franchise?

If you're stuck between two good ones, choose the one that plays better in your audience's mind. Emotion trumps cleverness.

A weak title is like opening a Michelin-star restaurant and naming it "Food Place." You might serve incredible meals, but no one will be inspired enough to come in to find out. Give them a reason to care from the beginning.

Cutting the Trailer

The Art and Science of Success and
the Missteps That Kill Audience Interest

The movie trailer is one of the most misunderstood and botched pieces of marketing in indie films. A pitch deck is important, but it doesn't have the same pucker power as an amazing trailer.

A trailer is a strategic piece of psychological warfare designed to hook the viewer in less than five seconds, and most indie filmmakers suck at it because they don't understand the dynamics of great trailer editing, not because they have no talent. Some people specialize in them. Whether it's a distributor, a sales agent, or your lead producer, someone with real marketplace experience should have eyes on your trailer's genesis. Write a treatment for it. This is a marketing asset; give it the love it needs.

The Trailer's Job

Your movie trailer has only one assignment, and that's to convince someone that they cannot live another minute without watching the movie it's advertising. Too many filmmakers try to over-explain their movies with the trailer. A trailer isn't a story outline; it doesn't explain the plot; *it sells the film.*

Keep it under 90 seconds, no more. Less is better. Think of any 30-second trailer you've seen that prompted you to buy a ticket. Can your trailer do that? In fifteen seconds? Can you blow minds in ten seconds? If so, you're a kingmaker. That's the level of compression and clarity we're aiming for.

What to Include in Your Trailer

The hook. Show the core concept or question that makes your film intriguing. Think about the "one" thing people will be talking about. Your trailer should pose or ask the One Big Question, which ties directly to your concept and core marketing hook, which we talked about earlier.

The genre tone. Viewers should know within five seconds whether this is faith, thriller, drama, comedy, etc. This is not the place for nuance.

Visual impact. Even if your film is subtle or character-driven, use the most visually arresting moments you have. Motion, composition, lighting, whatever grabs the most attention but sells the hook.

Pacing that builds. Think rhythm. Momentum. Start slow if you must, but your trailer needs to grab fast and crescendo like a symphony. We'll talk more about pacing in a moment.

A taste of the characters. Not all of them or their whole arc. Just enough to show stakes, tension, relationships, and conflict.

Awards or recognitions. If your film or team has won something worth mentioning, flash it on-screen. Festival laurels = social proof.

Call to action. End with something clear: "Coming to streaming," "World Premiere at [Festival]," or even "Watch the full film at [URL]." Tell the viewer what's next.

What *NOT* to Include in Your Trailer

The whole plot. This should go without saying, but we'll say it anyway. Leave mystery. Trailers should tease, not explain. If I can predict act three from your trailer, you blew it.

Random filler scenes. Not everything needs to "look cinematic." Cut it if it does not sell the hook, tone, or stakes.

Technical weaknesses. Don't include bad audio or sloppy shots. Even if they work in the film, they'll ruin your film's perceived quality by including them in the trailer.

Exposition-heavy dialogue. Avoid long-winded lines that require context to make sense. Stick to impactful, tight lines and visual storytelling.

All the best reveals. Keep something in the chamber. You're not trying to win a Shorty Award for showing every twist in 90 seconds. Make them want more, not feel like they've already seen it.

Generic music. Music sets the mood. Use it wisely. Don't use cheap stock music that sounds like a YouTube tutorial. Invest in proper trailer music, custom if possible.

Why Most Indie Trailers Fail

Mostly because they're cut like a mini-movie, not a marketing tool.

Filmmakers tend to get precious. They try to be subtle, or they edit their trailers themselves without any distance from the material. The result is a three-minute edit that says, "I love my film," but not, "You should love it, too."

If you don't know how to do that, hire someone who does. Or, at the very least, get someone who wasn't on the film to edit the trailer. You need objectivity. You need someone to cut the fat and focus on what will sell.

Pacing

The foundation of a great trailer is the pacing of the edits and the content that supports the pacing. Think of it like this:

———————— ● ————————

Build - Pause - Drop the Hammer - Build - PILE DRIVE.

———————— ● ————————

Build: Initiate with an introduction that quickly sets the scene, genre, and tone. This phase often employs longer shots and a steady tempo, allowing viewers to acclimate to the story's world. Remember, you have only five seconds to hook an audience or buyer's attention. And for the love of cinema, do NOT slap your company logo at the front... Unless you're Netflix. No one cares about your production company; they only care about the content. If including your logo matters to you, place it between story beats or at the end, *after* you've established a compelling tone.

Pause: Introduce a deliberate moment of silence or minimal sound, creating a stop down, a moment for viewers to take a deep breath. This intentional break captures attention, heightens anticipation, and sets the stage for what's to come.

Drop the Hammer: After the pause, hit the audience with something they can't ignore; a jaw-dropping visual, a killer line of dialogue, a strategic comedy punchline, or a shocking reveal. This moment should jolt them awake, reignite momentum, and raise the stakes. Think impact. Think ignition.

Build: After the hammer drops, shift into overdrive. Tension climbs, pacing quickens, excitement builds, and every shot should feel like a heartbeat. This phase stacks intensity fast—faster cuts, bigger stakes, deeper emotion. The story charges forward.

Pile Drive: Culminate with the trailer's most exhilarating segment; a rapid-fire montage of high-stakes scenes, intense action, or emotional peaks. This climax aims to leave the audience exhilarated and eager for more.

By thoughtfully combining these beats, you create a trailer that showcases the essence of your film and captivates and maintains the audience's engagement throughout.

Trailer editing is part art, part science. Under pressure, you're creating a dopamine bomb. You're building tension, establishing genre, introducing a world, dropping a few wow moments, and wrapping it in a rhythm that makes viewers forget they're watching a trailer.

"Cut" Your Trailer During Development—Seriously

You'll do it on paper, of course, but the exercise is worth its weight in gold. It forces you to ask: What moments sell this story? That discipline leads to sharper, more intentional writing. Scripts written with trailer moments in mind tend to be tighter, more visual, and more emotionally resonant by default.

Most amateurs don't think about trailers until post. Smart filmmakers build it in from the start.

They write key trailer moments into the script.

They know they'll need a jaw-dropping moment in the first five seconds. They plan for striking visuals, punchy dialogue, and a mic-drop cut to black.

Build-Pause-Hammer-Build-PILE DRIVE

Write with that pressure. Shoot with that awareness. Cut with that clarity.

Nail it, and people will hunt your film down.

All-Time Great Movie Trailers

Alien (1979) – Best. Teaser. Ever.

Built pure suspense with minimal footage, launching a cultural legend.

Psycho (1960)

Hitchcock's marketing genius: voice-over misdirection, calm delivery, built shock even before the film's iconic shower scene.

Dr. Strangelove (1964)

Graphic title cards, fast edits, dry satire—it introduced trailers as an art form.

Jaws (1975)

A slow-burn build-up to tension and terror.

Citizen Kane (1940)

Orson Welles created a four-minute pseudo-doc trailer—a bold self-promo, not just footage.

Modern Standouts

It (2017)

Designer sound, eerie pacing, record 197 million views in 24 hours.

Logan (2016)

Empire's top trailer of the year; mournful tone, powerful narrative setup.

Guardians of the Galaxy (2014)

Smart use of the song, *Hooked on a Feeling* by *Blue Swede* delivered 22.8 M views, and even changed the final film cut.

Why These Trailers Work

They understood resonance: Using mood, pacing and imagery to echo the film's core.

They hit primal triggers: Dread, humor, nostalgia, or pure awe.

They are marketing masterpieces: Crafted by specialist editors, not just studio compilers.

They changed expectations: Showing trailers could be art. Look them up on YouTube. You'll see.

The Key to Key Art

Let's talk about key art, aka your poster. That single image that's supposed to grab attention in half a second. Posters and trailers share the job of selling the film. But unlike trailers, posters are silent and still. They don't have the benefit of motion, music, or voiceover. They get one silent, motionless frame to capture tone, genre, and intrigue.

A good poster is often your film's first impression, which gets someone to watch the trailer or click "play." Whether it lives in a theater lobby, on a streamer, or as a social media banner, it's your visual handshake with the audience.

So, don't phone it in.

What a Good Poster Must Do

Stop the scroll. Whether online, at a festival, or on a VOD platform, your poster has about 1.3 seconds to grab someone's attention. You're done if it looks amateur, generic, confusing, or uninteresting. If it gets them to stop scrolling, you have a chance.

Establish the genre and tone instantly. Your design should clearly say, "This is what you're getting." If I can't tell what kind of film it is at a glance, your poster has failed.

Create intrigue. You don't need to show every character, location, and plot twist; you only need to make people curious. Your image should raise just one question in potential viewers' minds: "Is this film worth my time and money?"

Work as a thumbnail. Most people will see your poster as a 200-pixel image on a streaming platform or pitch email. Your font needs to be legible, and your image needs to translate when it's the size of a postage stamp.

What to Avoid

Photoshopped actor head-collages. Don't do the "floating heads" poster unless you have A-listers. No one cares about unknown actors; they care about the story and the concept. Unknown head shots screams amateur and kills credibility. This ties in with the mistake of starring in your own movie and inserting your company logo at the head of a trailer.

Low-resolution stills from your film. Just because a shot looks cool in the edit doesn't mean it belongs on a poster. Screenshots from the film rarely translate well. Design something from scratch and with intent.

Overly complicated design. Too many elements confuse the viewer. Simplicity sells. Think of one bold image, one compelling typeface, and one emotional hook.

Fonts that say 'student project.' Your poster shouldn't look like it was built in Microsoft Paint. You're not making a high school flyer. If you're not a graphic designer, hire someone who is.

Trying to be clever instead of clear. Symbolic art can be influential, but it still needs to communicate. A blurry flower next to a pair of broken glasses isn't "deep." It's confusing.

> *Pro Tip:* Design key art early. Like trailers, smart filmmakers start thinking about their key art during development.

If you're serious about marketing, you'll plant iconic visual moments in your script, moments that deserve to be on the poster.

Think:

- The silhouette of a character in a defining moment.

- A location that holds story power.

- A single, symbolic image that captures your theme.

Start visualizing that image long before the shoot. Make it part of your pitch deck, even as a mockup. We often create effective mockup key art, and visually generative AI can be a great tool used in conjunction with Photoshop and Illustrator. Your poster should feel inevitable, and you should build anticipation around it.

More Key Art Thoughts

Don't DIY the final version unless you're a designer with key art chops. Invest in it. Take it seriously. Because if you can't make someone care with a single image, the odds of them sitting through your feature are microscopic.

Your poster is ammunition first, art second. Load it carefully. Fire it with intent.

Kirk once sourced poster designs for the film *A Better You* from thirty people with the intention of selecting just one. In the end, the top contender was a so-so idea, but it helped to motivate the final poster that was eventually used.

We'll discuss AI later in the book, but for development purposes, we routinely use Midjourney and other generative AI along with Photoshop and Illustrator to create mockup posters. We'll never use these posters publicly, but they work great for informing stakeholders what the final could eventually look like. The strategy is worlds away from plagiarizing Google Images like for mood reels or look books, and it has a customized and professional-level appeal. It takes some time and a LOT of patience to get the right look, but the effort is worth it.

Once we get an AI image we like, Photoshop and Illustrator dial it in.

Rolling Out Your Marketing Strategy

Now that your marketing stack is complete—sharp logline, punchy tagline, vetted title, lethal trailer, and slick poster, it's time to roll it out. Done right, your campaign has three distinct phases:

Pre-release, release, and post-release.

Pre-Release: Build the Foundation

Goal: Generate curiosity, establish legitimacy, and prime your audience.

This is the invisible groundwork phase. You're building presence before most people know your film exists. Think of it as loading the cannon.

Build Your Audience Early: Social Media Isn't Optional

Building an audience is a critical part of pre-release, and it doesn't require a massive following, just a real one. Start as soon as you have regular content to post. You're ready to begin if you can commit to one solid update per week.

This isn't about shouting into the void. It's about starting conversations, planting curiosity, and warming up the algorithm.

Strategy Tips for Building Followers

Pick 1–2 platforms where your target audience hangs out. Instagram for visual storytelling. Facebook for older demographics and community groups. TikTok for youth. YouTube for trailers. X for film industry chatter. Don't try to conquer them all; pick where your film lives best.

Create a posting rhythm you can sustain. Weekly BTS stills, trailer sneak peeks, character spotlights, director diary clips, or countdown posts. Consistency is greater than quantity.

Engage, don't just post. Ask questions, poll your audience, share progress, reply to comments, show gratitude, and let people feel like they're part of something. The "This is our journey" vibe is greater than the "Buy my stuff" chest thumping.

Leverage hashtags and niche tags. Depending on your genre/audience, use film-centric tags like #indiefilm, #setlife, #filmmaker, #womeninfilm, #horrorfans, #drama, or # faithfilm.

Turn your team into ambassadors. Everyone on the cast and crew should be sharing the journey. Make it easy by giving them templated graphics, captions, or video clips.

Post content that provides value. This could be inspiration, humor, insight, or emotion. A BTS post that reveals your shooting challenges and how you overcame them is more compelling than a generic "Day 12 shoot!" caption.

Test, track, adjust. What gets engagement? Lean into that. If nobody clicks on your character bios, try video Q&As. If behind-the-scenes photos spike engagement, make that a series.

Refine your hook early. If it doesn't resonate now, it won't later. Adjust your marketing stack accordingly so that all elements work together.

Finalize your logline, tagline, title, and key visuals. These form the language of your campaign.

Mock up poster concepts and trailer moments before production. You're writing for marketing, not just story.

Cut a teaser or proof-of-concept scene, even if it's rough. It helps pitch and build hype.

Build your press kit (synopsis, cast/crew bios, director's statement, early stills).

Establish your digital presence. Website, email list, social handles, all consistent with your branding.

Start posting early to build an audience. Behind-the-scenes content, visual tone drops, crew shout outs, short videos.

Submit to film festivals strategically. Aim for credibility. Use festivals to build press quotes and collect laurels, not to land a mythical distribution deal.

Press outreach. Niche outlets, local press, film blogs, and podcasts often welcome compelling indie stories if you lead with a clear angle.

Release: Hit Every Channel with Precision

Goal: Drive attention, convert interest into action, and create the illusion of ubiquity.

This is your launch window. The audience needs to feel like your film is everywhere.

> *Pro tip:* Anticipation peaks on release day—then it's a race against fading interest. That's when excitement peaks, curiosity spikes, and your audience is most ready to act. Pre-sales help, but the biggest rush happens when people realize they can finally watch your film. Don't blow that moment with sloppy communication. Where and how to see your move

should be crystal clear in every post, email, and trailer outtro. No guesswork. No broken links. No "DM for details." We've said it before, make it stupid simple for people to watch your movie.

Push press with newsworthy headlines. Frame your story, don't just drop links.

- "Local Filmmaker Debuts at [Festival]."
- "New Thriller Tackles [Topical Issue]."

Maximize any festivals you get into.

- Capture reactions, shoot photos, snag quotes, record your Q&A.
- Use it all to build credibility online.

Social posting goes into overdrive.

- Daily countdowns, trailer clips, influencer reposts, cast & crew behind-the-scenes, and memes (yes, memes work).
- Every post should drive people to one goal—watch the film.

Run micro-ads if the budget allows. With laser targeting, $50–$100 on Facebook/Instagram can deliver real ROI if your creative is sharp.

Look big, act loud, be everywhere. Build momentum instead of just releasing a movie.

Post-Release: Keep the Fire Burning

Goal: Extend the shelf life, create sustained interest, and build long-term brand value.

Most indie filmmakers go dark after launch. Big mistake. You're only dead when you stop talking.

Repurpose content

- Break the trailer into :15s and :30s.

- Share deleted scenes, on-set stories, cast reactions.

- Post "how we made this" videos—audiences love behind-the-curtain.

Keep press alive

- Pitch to blogs or trades as the "little film that   could."

- "How [Your Title] Built Buzz Without a Big Studio."

- "Why This Film About [X] Struck a Nerve With [Audience]."

Engage the audience

- Share fan reactions, host Q&As on Instagram Live, encourage grassroots screenings.

- Build a community around the message or aesthetic of your film.

Target niche audiences

- Is your film educational? Push it to schools.

- Faith-based? Reach churches.

- Deals with trauma? Seek mental health orgs.

- International? Translate it and target foreign markets or diaspora groups.

Keep posting strategically

- Weekly or biweekly content drips are enough to stay in the algorithm.

- Think of your film like a campaign, not a one-time drop.

Marketing timelines

Every film demands a unique marketing strategy. Below, we created a hypothetical timeline to help you visualize how marketing flow works, but your job is to think beyond the template. This isn't about following a formula but learning to think strategically. The more you understand what to plan, the better you'll know how to prepare. That's where real momentum and magic begin.

Pre-Release Window

6 Months Out (Month -6)

→ **Launch Socials & Website**

- Secure film handle & domain.

- Build a basic one-pager website with email capture.

- Post "film is in post" announcement.

→ **Create content and calendar**

- Map 6 months of weekly posts.

- Prep categories: Ideas include behind the scenes drops (20-30 seconds), story themes, director notes, meet the cast & crew interviews, photos, etc. On set, capture on-the-spot action of crew saying what's happening now. Cast in makeup making comments and sit-down interviews with main cast discussing what the film means to them. Ask the cast to record candid moments on their phone during and after production.

---

5 Months Out (Month -5)

→ **Begin Weekly Posting**

- One meaningful post per week.

- "What this film is." Building an audience begins with them understanding what they're being asked to follow.

- Include captions with emotional or behind-the-scenes insights

→ **Soft audience engagement**

- Ask early questions: "Which mood board do you prefer?"

- Begin hashtag use: #indiefilm, genre-specific tags

---

4 Months Out (Month -4)

→ **Poster Test Round**

- Post 2–3 early versions for feedback.

- Poll audience on tone, fonts, vibe.

→ **BTS Video Drops**

- Show the crew quirky moments, fun insights, scenes being filmed, and other voyeurism that engages audiences with what it's like to be on a film set. Cool stuff!

---

3 Months Out (Month -3)

→ **Trailer Tease**

- Release a :15–:30 teaser (not the full trailer).

- Include tagline. Call-to-action: "Follow our journey to the release date."

→ Cast/Crew Highlights Begin

• Weekly spotlight: "Meet our DP" or "Lead Actor Fun Fact."

---

2 Months Out (Month -2)

→ Poster Final Reveal

• High-res final poster drop, "Our audience has spoken!"

• Pre-order or RSVP CTA (if applicable).

→ Email List Push

• "Join for exclusive sneak peeks."

• Offer a small reward, such as an exclusive sneak peek of the movie's first five minutes with subscribers before public release. Or an exclusive Behind-the-Scenes clip: Share a fun or emotional moment from production that's not available anywhere else.

---

1 Month Out (Month -1)

→ Final Trailer Drop

• Official trailer (60–90 seconds).

• Include final release date + CTA.

→ Festival Strategy (if any)

• Submit to final wave of regional/niche festivals.

• Begin planning premiere or virtual event.

---

3 Weeks Out

→ **Final Countdown Begins**

- Daily or every-other-day posts.

- Clip snippets, cast reactions, emotional quotes.

→ **Reach out to press/blogs**

- Local press, film blogs, genre-specific outlets.

- Focus on story angle not just "film is releasing."

Release week

Day -4 (Monday)

→ **Final Trailer Blast**

- Drop the official trailer on all platforms.

- Include release date/time, direct CTA (watch link or RSVP).

- Email to list: "It's here."

Day -3 (Tuesday)

→ **Press Push + Influencer Mentions**

- Send press releases to blogs, podcasts, and local outlets.

- Encourage micro-influencers to share reactions or trailers.

Day -2 (Wednesday)

→ Behind-the-Scenes Highlight

- Share BTS video or stills with cast commentary.

- Social post: "We filmed this scene in one take because..."

Day -1 (Thursday)

→ Cast/Crew Reactions or Live Chat

- Go live on Instagram/YouTube for a short Q&A.

- Cast video shout outs "Here's why we loved making this."

Day 0 (Friday)

→ Release Day

- Blast the watch link everywhere: social, email, bio, website.

- Post quotes, trailer moments, emotional stills.

- Encourage fans: "Watch + comment + tag a friend."

Day +1 (Saturday)

→ Audience Reactions + Reviews

- Repost early viewer reactions and testimonials.

- "You watched. What did you feel?" Prompt in stories.

Day +2 (Sunday)

→ Post-release Push + Gratitude Post

• Thank your fans, team, and supporters.

• "If this film moved you, share it with someone."

• Reminder post with CTA to watch or review.

Social Media

Social's your front line, but yelling "watch me!" on repeat will cause people to ignore you. Strategize:

- **Pick Your Turf:** Facebook is for older folks, X for film nerds, and Instagram/TikTok for the young and visual. If it fits, try a faith skit on TikTok. YouTube is trailer central—searchable gold.

- **Engage, Don't Shill:** Polls ("Which poster vibe wins?"), questions ("Favorite faith film? Ours nods to those"), set trivia. Be a person, not a bot. Reply with thanks and ask for Shares.

- **Plan Out Weekly Drops:** Monday cast chats, Wednesday BTS pics, Friday diary snippets. Hashtags matter (#indiefilm, #faithfilm).

- **Email VIPs:** Social's crowded; email's direct. Website sign up ("First trailer peek!") builds a tight crew. 100 fans beat 1,000 randos. Keep it short, rare, juicy.

Public Relations: Your Force Multiplier

Advertising is what you pay for. Public relations is what you *pray* for. Earned media, such as coverage by editors, influencers, podcasters, or journalists, carries more weight than anything you pay for yourself. A 2013 Nielsen global study found that 92% of consumers trust recommendations from people they know, surpassing all forms of paid advertising. Additionally, word-of-mouth, which Nielsen categorizes under *earned media*, consistently inspires the highest levels of consumer action compared to paid ad formats.

PR offers what advertising cannot; credibility, third-party validation, and reach that feels organic. It's why a single review, radio endorsement, or podcast appearance can outperform weeks of social ads.

In some cases, a well-targeted *paid* PR campaign will deliver better results than paid advertising. For instance, leveraging media partnerships or targeted outreach can spark coverage that spreads organically across outlets—something ads alone can't match in either trust or momentum.

PR is about telling why your story matters and sharing your film in a way that resonates. That means giving journalists, bloggers, and podcasters a narrative they can't resist.

- **Topical hooks:** Does your film connect to current events, cultural debates, or anniversaries?

- **Human angle:** Is there a personal story behind the film that makes it newsworthy?

- **Local hero factor:** Hometown papers love "local-kid-makes-good" stories.

- **Underdog story:** Independent filmmakers scrapping to finish a feature is inherently compelling.

How to Run a PR Campaign

1- Create a Press Kit

Pro tip: You don't need to reinvent the wheel. If you've already built a pitch deck for investors, much of that material can be repurposed into a press kit. Swap financials for a clean synopsis, add production stills, and you have a solid foundation. This saves time, keeps branding consistent, and avoids doubling your workload.

- **Cover Page:** Title, tagline, poster image, contact info.

  - **Film Overview:** Short synopsis (50–75 words) and long synopsis (150–250 words). Genre, runtime, rating.

  - **Director's Statement:** 2–3 paragraphs on vision, purpose, and relevance.

  - **Cast Bios:** Headshots + 3–5 sentence bios with notable credits.

  - **Crew Bios:** Key team only (director, producer, DP, editor, composer).

  - **Production Stills:** 3–6 high-res, story-driven images, plus optional BTS.

  - **Festival & Awards:** Laurels, selections, nominations.

  - **Press Quotes:** Short pull quotes from critics or influencers (leave blank if none yet).

  - **Release Info:** Premiere date, streaming/theatrical details, CTA link.

  - **Contact Page:** Publicist/filmmaker email, phone, socials, website.

Export as a PDF under 10 MB, then create a cloud folder (Dropbox/Google Drive) for high-res assets like posters, stills, and trailers. Journalists love easy, one-click access.

2- Build a Media List

  - **Start local:** TV, radio, newspapers, and regional magazines.

  - **Expand niche:** blogs, genre sites, and advocacy outlets tied to your subject.

• **Include podcasts, YouTube shows, and newsletters**—often more valuable than mainstream press.

3 Craft Your Pitch

Keep it short. Lead with the angle, not "please review my film."

• **Personalize it:** "Your readers follow veterans' issues—our film explores PTSD through a Marine's eyes."

Always attach your press kit link and trailer.

4 Plan a PR Calendar

• **Pre-release:** Announce festival selections, teaser drops, or local screenings.

• **Release:** Push interviews, reviews, and topical think-pieces.

• **Post-release:** Highlight awards, grassroots reactions, and fan impact.

5 Follow Up (Without Stalking)

If no reply in a week, send a polite nudge.

Respect a "no." Burned bridges kill future coverage.

Paid PR—When It Makes Sense

PR is earned media, but you can pay to boost it:

• **Press Release Distribution Services** (PR Newswire, GlobeNewswire): $200–$500 to blanket your announcement across hundreds of outlets. Don't expect reviews, but you'll gain visibility and searchable credibility.

• **Sponsored Articles/Native Ads:** Paid editorial that looks like coverage. Works if it's a site your audience actually reads.

Always disclose.

- **Publicists:** Hiring a pro publicist for a festival run or release can cost $3K–$10K+ per month. At Sundance, SXSW, or TIFF, it's worth it. For smaller indies, you can DIY the basics.

How to Find The Right PR Firm

If you hire outside help, vet them carefully. Plenty of overpriced hype machines out there. Here's how to separate the real from the fake:

- **Check track record:** Have they worked on films at your level, not just studio projects?

- **Ask for media clips:** Can they show actual coverage they secured?

- **Call past clients:** Honest feedback will save you thousands.

- **Avoid vanity PR:** If their only plan is "send out a press release," run. Real PR is relationship-based.

- **Look for specialization:** Firms with indie film, faith film, or genre experience outperform generalists.

- **Demand transparency:** Know exactly what you're paying for—retainer, hours, or deliverables.

PR + Ads = Amplified Reach

The smart play is combining PR with paid promotion:

A blog review drops? Screenshot the headline and run a $50–$100 ad targeting your audience.

If local TV covers your premiere, boost the clip to your zip code so everyone sees it.

If you landed a podcast interview, push it with micro-ads to fans of similar shows.

Done right, PR creates a halo effect—your film looks bigger, feels validated, and gains trust. Pair that with ads, and you're not just telling the world your film matters. Others are saying it for you, and you're making sure the right people hear it loud.

More Notes

Guerrilla Grit

If you're cash-strapped, get crafty. The *Paranormal Activity* team let audiences "demand" local screenings through a viral campaign—a stroke of genius.

- **Contests:** Faith film? Instagram prayer challenge—winner gets a stream.

- **Influencers:** Micro-faith bloggers might plug you for a sneak peek.

- **Crew Power:** Ten teammates sharing reaches hundreds—give 'em easy posts.

- **Community:** Church screening? Local faith groups will spread it.

- **Crowd Backers:** Funded it? Task 'em—share trailers, review it. They're in.

Buzz to Action

Marketing's endgame? Action—screenings, streams, chatter. CTAs rule: "Premiere Oct. 10—tickets [link]!" Again, make it stupid-easy to watch; links everywhere.

Word-of-Mouth is King

Hit emotions—faith films need uplift. Show it in promos; ask fans to share: "Loved it? Tell someone!" A viewer tweet—"This indie faith flick shook me"—is platinum. Quote graphics are free hype.

Keep It Real, Keep It Going

No spam, no lies. Mislead on a film and get roasted. Be you: "I'm [Name], we poured our souls in, hope you'll see it." Marketing is not a sprint. Post-release, keep the fire alive with reviews and BTS bits. An indie can bloom late and stay on the trail.

The Takeaway

Marketing is hustle, smarts, and heart. Know your crowd, hit 'em where they live, and embed that hook from day one. You're the megaphone, and if you don't shout, who will? It's all about giving your film a pulse. The next chapter unpacks distribution and how to deliver after you've primed the pump.

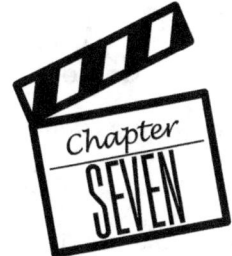

Distribution Decoded

"You're gonna need a bigger boat."

— Martin Brody, *Jaws* (1975)

You've hustled through scripting, shooting, and post-production with gritty determination – but now comes the final gatekeeper of indie filmmaking: *distribution.* In this chapter, we'll decode how money flows back to you (or doesn't), lay out the distribution game plans that are available to you, and shine a light on all those sneaky pitfalls that ambush filmmakers on the road to release. By the end, you'll see why distribution is often where dreams turn into nightmares and how to avoid your film becoming another sad statistic. Armed with this knowledge, you'll be able to tackle your film with more confidence.

Think Like a Distributor

The New Landscape of Distribution Platforms & Content

If you're hoping Lionsgate will give you a million-dollar MG (Minimum Guarantee) like it's 2005… those days are gone.

MGs still exist. Companies such as Lionsgate, A24, and Sony Pictures Classics will still pay MGs on select titles. But think about it from their point of view. If you were a distributor, would you throw down a massive advance on a film from a first-time director that hasn't been tested with audiences and that can't be guaranteed to blaze a trail through the mud? Not unless you were absolutely sure that film had a market and a monetization path. That's not easy.

MGs are leverage tools. They are investments that distributors use to gain exclusive rights and long-term profits. So, if you get an MG for your movie, the message is something like this:

"You made your film for $2 million. We're offering you $200,000."

That's the distributor's way of being honest by saying, "This is what your film is worth to us in today's market." You can't be mad about it, even if the offer isn't generous.

Sure, they might give you 65% of back-end profits. Maybe 75% if your film really stands out. The contract might even say you're getting 100% of 'net profits.' But net is after they deduct 35% for distribution fees, marketing costs, delivery costs, and "extraordinary expenses." The balance is 'net profits,' and you get 100% of it. It might be 100% of $0, but that's the deal you signed.

Welcome to "Hollyweird Reality"

If it were your business, would you hand out $4 million MGs to every filmmaker who showed up with a two-million-dollar passion project? You'd be out of business in a month and forced to flee the country.

Filmmakers think like artists, distributors think like entrepreneurs. They don't care one shiny penny about your dreams. They *invest* in content with strategy, metrics, and market alignment in mind. If your movie doesn't have a clear pathway to an audience, it's not getting an MG.

Netflix will not pay $4 million for your movie just because you made it for $2 million. That's not how streaming works. Distributors don't care about your investment, they're only concerned about theirs. Platforms reward value, not effort, and value is based on data, trends, viewership potential, and their own algorithmic calculus.

Most platforms today will not reward indie filmmakers with outsized checks. They offer short-term licenses, modest flat fees, or revenue share deals. The longer they license your film, the better it might look on paper, but don't expect a financial windfall.

The streaming platforms play a volume game. They are feeding massive audiences with endless content. Quantity, not quality, is the model unless you're A24, and even then, you need Sundance hardware just to start the conversation.

So, how do you survive as an indie filmmaker in this landscape? You stop fantasizing about bidding wars. You don't write "our plan is to attend major festivals and spark a bidding war" in your business plan. That's wishful thinking, and experienced investors will see right through it.

Get real estimated numbers from real distributors. Be transparent. Be honest. And temper your expectations.

A typical scenario is you make a movie for $2 million. A few platforms pick it up. You get some modest revenue share agreements, maybe 70/30 splits, maybe better, maybe worse. The point is: you are playing the long game.

To get there, choose a partner with relationships such as a producers' rep, a seasoned agent, or a producer who's been in the trenches. Someone who knows what the platforms want and who can steer the ship from start to finish.

The long game needs to be played correctly. Investors want their money back sooner rather than later, and most indie films run out of steam during the first year of release with a diminishing trickle of revenue after that. Investors are not standing in line to invest in a movie with a recoupment plan stretched over a 10-year licensing term. They want to be paid off early, and then the long tail revenue is gravy. The consensus is that if your film doesn't recoup in the first two or three years of release, it probably never will. So, develop a realistic three-year ROI plan with a trickle of revenue after that.

And for the love of cinema, don't promise your investors a double or triple return on an MG. Be realistic and honest. That's how you build trust. And that's how you build a career.

Now that we have you thinking more like a distributor, keep that frame of mind as we unpack distribution on a more granular level. There is a lot to consider with distribution, and there's much more to know about the subject than what we present here. But this is far more information than most filmmakers understand, which puts you in a rare club.

The Revenue Waterfall

How the Money Flows

Welcome to the pecking order of who gets happy first.

Theaters, platforms, distributors, and sales agents all take their cut before the stream reaches you. By the time it trickles down, it can become a drip for you and your investors.

Let's break it down:

Theatrical

In a traditional release, the first hand in the pot is the exhibitor (movie theaters). Studios might start with a 50/50 split. For indies, theaters typically take 65%—and in places like NYC, it can hit 75%[1]

So, in the worst case, if your film grosses $1 million theatrically, you're likely looking at just $300–350K back BEFORE marketing costs, distribution fees, or deliverables. That happened with the indie film *Columbus,* which grossed $1 million but only netted $305K after theater splits. They were fortunate. Here are others:

> *It Follows* (2014)
>
> > Budget: $2 million
> >
> > Grossed: $23.3 million worldwide

On paper, that's a 10x return.

But after exhibitor cuts (~$11M), distributor fees, and prints/ads (another ~$5–6M), the likely net back to producers was around $5–6 million.

It's still profitable but nowhere near the fantasy headline numbers.

---

1 Sundance.org, "Distribution Case Study: *Columbus.*"

The Peanut Butter Falcon (2019)

Budget: $6.2 million

Grossed: $23 million worldwide

Sounds amazing, but once you remove:

- Theater cuts (~$12M)

- Distribution fees & expenses (~$5–6M)

- Marketing spend (estimated ~$3–4M)

Despite the feel-good headlines, you're likely looking at a modest profit.

Honey Boy (2019)

Budget: $3.5 million

Grossed: $3.4 million at the global box office

Final result? Underwater.

Even with great press and awards buzz, it didn't recoup its budget theatrically. Most of the real value came later in streaming, awards exposure, and prestige for the filmmakers.

Skinamarink (2023)

Budget: $15,000

Grossed: $2 million+

Even after splits and distributor fees, this film likely netted a profit of close to $500–700K. Micro-budget + viral marketing + strong concept = true indie win. But this is the exception, not the rule.

Digital

Digital is cleaner; no theaters, fewer intermediaries, but it's far from squeaky clean.

TVOD platforms like iTunes take 30%, leaving 70% for the rights holder. Amazon's direct platform is a 50/50 split. Platforms are notorious for not reporting their earnings, so you may never know how much the film generated in gross revenue. If you go through an aggregator or distributor, they'll take their cut, too.

The Pattern

Everyone gets paid before you. And if you have investors, they're waiting in line too, right above you, meaning you get paid dead last.

Revenue will first cover distributor fees and expenses. Only then will anything flow to your production company or investors. Even then, that gets split again between producers, equity holders, and "net points." Net points often mean nothing because "net" rarely exists.

Why It Matters

This is why profit participation sounds better on paper than in real life. And why "my film made money" doesn't mean you made money. According to a Harvard/DASH report, the number of indie films released theatrically surged to 863 in 2019, up 53% from 2012. Most of those didn't return a dime to their creators.

So yes, the money is out there, but it's sliced up long before it gets to you.

These graphs, although generalized, demonstrate revenue waterfalls visually:

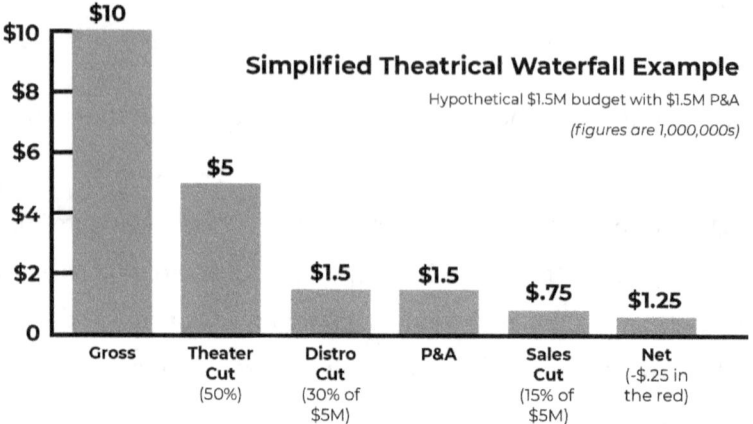

For indie films with both theatrical and digital releases, the general average revenue breakdown across both channels generally looks like this:

Digital vs Theatrical

- Digital has lower overhead.

- Theatrical costs (prints, marketing, travel, etc.) often eat up revenue before it reaches producers.

- For many indie films, theatrical is used more for prestige, reviews, and positioning, not profit.

Exceptions:

- If a film has a strong theatrical hook (faith-based, documentary with a following, or festival heat), a theatrical share might climb much higher.

- But in most indie cases, digital drives the majority of recoupment.

Because digital platforms typically do not disclose actual gross revenues, any figures presented represent what the platforms themselves account as gross revenue. Using the same hypothetical film referenced in the graph above and assuming the exact gross revenue figure of $10M solely for illustrative purposes, here is how revenue is generally divided:

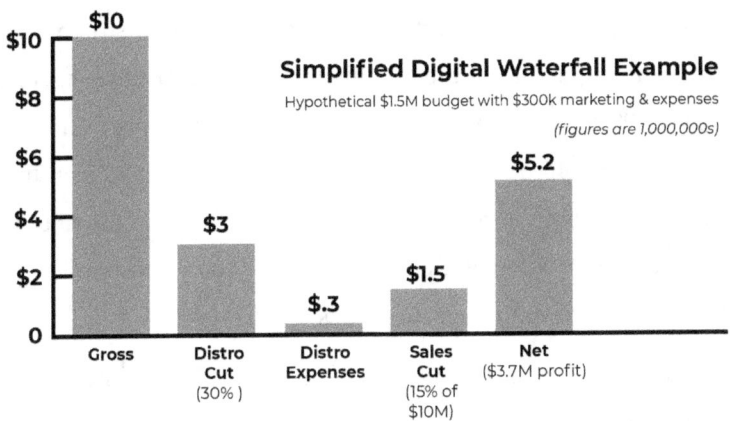

Understand the waterfall. Structure your deals wisely. But don't count on "net" anything.

The more you plan for the business side of distribution, the better your chances of staying afloat once the waterfall starts flowing.

Quarterly Reports & Getting Paid: The Waiting Game No One Warns You About

Let's talk money—specifically, when (and if) you see it.

Theaters typically settle box office revenue within 30–60 days after your theatrical run ends, depending on the exhibitor and how your release is structured. You won't get a flood of cash on Monday after the opening weekend.

Streamers are another beast entirely. If you licensed your film to a platform via a distributor or aggregator, payments typically come through that intermediary, not directly from the platform. These are often lump-sum deals paid upfront in the case of a presale or MG, or installments based on delivery and term triggers, but if it's revenue-share (AVOD, TVOD), you're in the same quarterly game as everyone else.

Distributors usually report quarterly, especially for the first two years of your film's run. After that, it often shifts to bi-annual. However, some distributors wait 90 days after a quarter closes to send the report, and payment can take another 45-60 days. So, revenue from your film's April–June activity might not hit your account until December. To make distribution even more charming, if your film earns less than $500 in a quarter, they might hold the payment until your total adds up. Yes, legally.

Quarterly reporting is based on the calendar, not your film's release date. So if you release in mid-June, you're only in the books for a couple of weeks of Q2:

- Q1: January, February, March

- Q2: April, May, June

- Q3: July, August, September

- Q4: October, November, December

Track every report. Distributors make mistakes or sometimes hope you're not watching.

Understanding Licensing

As we explained earlier, "foreign" is not a territory, nor is "Europe" or "Asia." These are lazy umbrella terms that sound industry-savvy but mean nothing without specifics.

Generally, each country is considered a territory; sometimes, even regions within a country are split. French-speaking Québec, for example, can be licensed separately from English-speaking Canada.

When someone says they're "handling foreign," your first response should be, "Which territories? And what rights in those territories?"

Rights: What Exactly Are You Selling?

There's more than one kind of right to license. Here is a list:

1. Digital / Streaming Rights

Rights such as SVOD (subscription video on demand), TVOD (transactional video on demand), and AVOD (advertising video on demand) for distributing content via online platforms, including subscription, transactional, and ad-supported models.

2. Broadcast & Cable TV Rights

Rights to distribute content via traditional television channels, including premium, free, and cable networks.

3. Physical Media Rights

Rights to distribute content in tangible home video formats.

4. Theatrical Rights

Rights to exhibit content in commercial cinema settings.

5. Non-theatrical Rights

Rights to license the exhibition of a film outside of traditional cinemas, including venues like schools, libraries, museums, military bases, airlines, cruise ships, and religious institutions.

6. Public Performance Rights

Rights to screen content in non-commercial or institutional settings, often requiring Public Performance Rights (PPR).

7. Specialty Rights

Rights for niche distribution channels outside traditional cinema or institutional settings.

8. Ancillary & Derivative Rights

Rights to create new works or products derived from the original IP.

9. Emerging Platforms

Rights for distributing or adapting content on new or evolving technologies.

10. Hybrid Distribution Rights

Rights that bridge traditional and digital distribution models.

A comprehensive breakdown of these rights is available in the Appendix at the end of the book.

What Does "North America" Mean?

In distribution terms, it usually includes:

- The United States, plus U.S. territories like Puerto Rico and Guam

- Canada (English and French-speaking markets)

- Usually the Caribbean (depends on the deal)

But even here, you can split things up. Digital only in Puerto Rico, all rights in the U.S., and theatrical only in French-speaking Canada.

These are carve outs, and they can be powerful. But you must know what you're doing. Bad licensing terms can kill your momentum or, worse, hand someone control over your release in a region they don't even serve well. Territory carve outs refer to specific geographic areas or markets that are excluded or separately negotiated in licensing agreements for media rights, such as theatrical, broadcast, digital/streaming, or other distribution rights. These carve outs allow rights holders to independently license or retain control over specific territories, often due to market-specific strategies, existing deals, or legal/regulatory considerations. In the entertainment industry, territory carve outs are common in international distribution agreements, where rights are divided by country or region to maximize revenue, accommodate local partners, or address cultural and regulatory differences.

Let's Talk "Foreign" – Country by Country

Every country is a separate deal. Some get bundled together. Some don't.

Territories are the foundation of international sales, and understanding how they're split can help you structure smarter deals. Here are common groupings:

Common Film Territories and How They're Grouped

North America

- United States

- Canada

(Usually sold together as a single territory along with the Caribbean.)

Latin America (LATAM)

- Mexico, Brazil, Argentina, Chile, etc.

(Sometimes sold as one bloc, sometimes broken out into

major markets.)

United Kingdom & Ireland

- UK and Ireland are typically bundled together.

Western Europe

- France

- Germany

- Spain

- Italy

- Benelux (Belgium, Netherlands, Luxembourg)

- Scandinavia (Sweden, Norway, Denmark, Finland)

- Switzerland, Austria

(Each can be sold individually or as regional packages depending on the deal size and film profile.)

Eastern Europe

- Poland

- Czech Republic

- Slovakia

- Hungary

- Romania

- Bulgaria

- Former Yugoslav territories (e.g. Serbia, Croatia, Slovenia, Bosnia & Herzegovina, Montenegro, North Macedonia)

- Baltic states (Estonia, Latvia, Lithuania)

(Often sold as a regional package, though Poland and select larger markets may be sold separately.)

These are often bundled or handled through pan-Eastern European distributors.

Asia

- China: Highly regulated; theatrical rights require a quota system and a local partner.

- Japan: One of the most profitable international markets; strong for animation, drama, and prestige films.

- South Korea: Thriving cinema culture with strong local distributors.

- Southeast Asia: Often sold as a bundle (Thailand, Vietnam, Malaysia, Indonesia, Philippines).

- India: Huge population, but challenging for Western indies without localization.

- Taiwan & Hong Kong: Sometimes bundled, sometimes separate; strong niche markets.

Other Major Territories

- Australia & New Zealand (ANZ): Usually sold together.

- Middle East: Often sold as a single bloc through a regional buyer.

- Africa: Can be difficult to monetize; North Africa is sometimes included with MENA (Middle East/North Africa).

- Russia & CIS: In flux due to political and economic challenges; often handled separately.

Sometimes the smartest move is to break it up and sell territory-by-territory to distributors specializing in each market.

Don't give away the farm to get a deal. Stay sharp. Stay specific. Control is how you win.

Ratings Are Not Universal

Another mistake indie filmmakers make is assuming all countries treat content like the U.S.

MPA (formerly MPAA) ratings (PG-13, R, etc.) are voluntary in the United States. Most streamers don't require them, but most theaters prefer them. TV broadcast ratings (TV-MA, TV-14, etc.) are expected but, again, still voluntary.

But in many other countries, you may be legally required to pay for and obtain an age rating before your film can be shown publicly, even on streaming platforms.

Here are a few examples:

- United Kingdom: Must be rated by the BBFC (British Board of Film Classification).

- Australia: Classification by the Australian Classification Board is mandatory, even for VOD.

- Germany: The FSK handles age ratings.

- France, South Korea, and others: Similar regulatory bodies often require paid submissions for approval.

- Some regions demand third-party rating services, especially for children's content.

These ratings take time and money, often months and hundreds to thousands of dollars. If you or your distributor didn't budget for that, your "foreign launch" might be delayed indefinitely.

Key Licensing Questions to Ask (Every. Single. Time.)

1. Which territories are included, and can we carve any out?

2. What specific rights are you licensing? (Theatrical, TV, SVOD, AVOD, etc.)

3. Is this exclusive or non-exclusive?

4. What's the duration of the license?

5. Are sub-licensing rights included? If so, to whom?

6. Who handles ratings and localization costs?

7. Can I retain festival or educational rights?

8. Is there a minimum release commitment in each territory? (If not, they may sit on it forever.)

Licensing is where the money appears or vanishes. Treat each territory as a little empire with its rules, challenges, and opportunities.

Know what you're selling. Know where. Know to whom. And know when to say "no."

And next time someone says, "We're taking your film worldwide," don't grin like a toddler with a new toy. Lean in and ask:

"Which countries? Which rights? And how are you handling ratings in each one?"

That's what a professional sounds like.

Release Strategies

So, why do filmmakers still chase theatrical deals, knowing the math rarely works out?

For decades, it was the holy grail: premiere at a big festival, land a distributor, collect a fat check ("minimum guarantee" or MG), and watch your film hit theaters while someone else handles the marketing and bookings. It's how you get on red carpets and Oscar radars. But the new reality is a lot messier.

In a typical theatrical deal, the distributor may have an exclusive window (often 90 days) where your film plays only in theaters. They front the prints and advertising spend, book your release, and recoup every penny before you see a dime. On top of that, they take a 20–30% distribution fee. Remember the revenue waterfall? Distributors sit on top.

The Ol' Loss Leader

A limited theatrical release, even if unprofitable, can yield strategic benefits: critical reviews, media buzz, awards eligibility, and brand credibility. Filmmakers often use it as a "loss leader" to boost visibility for SVOD, TVOD, and international sales. A24 (*Moonlight*) and Bleeker Street (*Captain Fantastic*) turned niche films into cultural moments with festival buzz or star power.

For lesser-known indies, theatrical deals are tough without genre appeal, a marketing hook, or proven demand. If you secure one, scrutinize the terms:

- **Release plan:** Cities, screens, and marketing budget?

- **Recoupable expenses:** Can you cap them?

- **Contract term:** Aim for 5–7 years, not 10+.

- **Bankruptcy clause:** Ensure rights revert if the distributor fails.

Distributors can go bankrupt, leaving films in limbo. Most indies peak in year one and fade unless they are evergreen (e.g., timeless docs, cult horror). Short contracts allow pivots if the distributor underperforms.

Bottom Line: Theatrical runs enhance profile but are risky and slow to recoup. Plan strategically, avoid long distribution terms, and don't romanticize the big screen.

Day-and-Date Releases: Breaking the Window

Day-and-date releases launch a film in theaters and on VOD simultaneously, a model popular for indie films and documentaries. It gained traction during the pandemic (e.g., Warner Bros.' 2021 slate) and suits smaller films aiming to maximize buzz and revenue.

In this model, your film screens in select theaters (e.g., art houses, boutique cinemas, or small chains) while available on platforms like iTunes or Amazon for rent/buy. This front-loads earnings, capturing digital revenue without delaying a traditional 90-day theatrical window. For example, *Snowpiercer* (2014) hit VOD three weeks after theaters, targeting sci-fi fans eager to watch at home.

> **Benefits:** Revenue starts accumulating immediately from multiple channels, leveraging marketing buzz. Indie distributors like Magnolia or IFC Films use this to boost smaller films.
>
> **Challenges:** Major theater chains often resist, fearing lost ticket sales, and some festivals or awards (e.g., Oscars) prefer exclusive theatrical runs. A one-week theatrical run in key cities can qualify for awards without delaying VOD.
>
> **Strategy:** Focus on niche audiences, use limited theatrical runs for reviews and prestige, and price VOD rentals at standard rates ($3.99–$6.99) rather than premium ($20). Coordinate

marketing to drive theater and VOD engagement.

Hybrid Distribution: Carving Up Rights

Hybrid distribution mixes strategies to optimize a film's reach and revenue, splitting rights by format, region, or timeframe. It's ideal for indie filmmakers seeking flexibility.

> **Example:** We used a hybrid distribution strategy for *Faith of Angels* (2024): Angel Studios and Living Scriptures shared a one-year SVOD co-exclusive window post-theatrical. Great American Media took AVOD and linear broadcast, and TVOD went multi-platform. The director handled physical media (DVD/Blu-ray), saving intermediary fees.

> **Another case:** *Running Wild* (2013) split rights. Screen Media managed a 22-city theatrical run and sold to Netflix/Amazon, while filmmaker Suzanne Mitchell retained DVD sales and website streaming rights for direct profits.

> **Benefits:** Control over profitable segments and diversified revenue streams. Aggregators (e.g., FilmRise) simplify VOD placement, allowing theatrical or self-distribution alongside.

> **Challenges:** Complex coordination, potential contract conflicts, and reduced appeal to distributors wanting all rights. Major studios (e.g., Lionsgate) often demand exclusivity, risking "Hollywood accounting" issues.

> **Strategy:** Use sales agents for foreign markets, retain niche rights (e.g., educational), and ensure clear contracts. Hybrid distribution requires proactive management but tailors each release to your film's strengths, maximizing success in a

fragmented market.

Self-Distribution: DIY or Die (Doing It All Yourself)

Self-distribution means you act as the distributor, handling theater bookings, marketing, digital platform placement, and press without a traditional distributor. Once a last resort, it's now a viable option for indie filmmakers, especially when distribution offers are lacking or predatory, or you want control to reach your niche audience.

Why Self-Distribute? You keep most profits (no 20–30% distributor cut) but bear the labor and upfront costs. DIY does not mean solo work; smart filmmakers build teams, hiring theatrical bookers, publicists, or aggregators to extend reach while retaining rights.

> **Example:** *Columbus* (2017) self-distributed after Sundance, rejecting traditional offers. With Sundance's Creative Distribution Fellowship, the team booked theaters (e.g., Landmark Theaters), used Quiver for TVOD, and negotiated an SVOD deal with Hulu. They came within $130K of recouping their budget, saving ~$400K compared to a distributor deal.

Aggregators. These services (e.g., Bitmax, Quiver) deliver your film to platforms like iTunes or Amazon for a fee or revenue share (15–20%). They handle encoding and quality control, as platforms often don't work directly with first-timers. Beware: some aggregators (e.g., Distribber in 2019) have gone bankrupt, leaving filmmakers unpaid. Research reputable options and read the terms carefully.

> **Strategy:** Combine self-distribution with partnerships (e.g., nonprofits for screenings) or direct-to-fan sales via Vimeo On Demand (90% revenue share). Focus on digital platforms, community events, or niche physical media. Self-distribution

demands effort but offers control and higher profits for savvy filmmakers.

Self-distribution is grueling, often demanding 60-hour weeks for 6–12 months on top of years of filmmaking. It requires swapping your "artist" hat for a business/marketing one. Many filmmakers burn out, underestimating the effort to market a film. Uploading to Amazon Prime with a few tweets won't cut it; you need a robust campaign strategy and a small team. Once again, treat it like a startup launch, with a dedicated distribution budget for deliverables and ads (as noted in Chapter Two).

> **Examples:** Ken Burns' *Lewis and Clark* (1997) used grassroots screenings and PBS partnerships for direct audience reach. *High Road* (2011) leveraged VOD platforms and social media buzz. *After-Meth* (2006) targeted recovery communities with event screenings. Shane Carruth's *Upstream Color* (2013) succeeded via self-managed VOD and Q&A theatrical events, proving strategic DIY can pay off. Kirk even sold 1,000 copies of a *How to Make Lefse* video through niche marketing to Scandinavian-American audiences.

Self-distribution offers control and higher profits. You manage marketing, artwork, and platforms, pivoting quickly if needed. Revenue flows directly to you after platform fees, bypassing distributor cuts or murky accounting. It's empowering; your indie spirit shines, as seen in *Upstream Color* (2013), which built a grassroots following via VOD and Q&A screenings.

However, without preparation, it risks becoming an expensive flop. Success hinges on a strategic campaign and realistic goals. Assess your film's marketability early: Does it resonate in test screenings? Lack of distributor interest may signal weak appeal. A sellable film, marketed smartly, can thrive DIY, but poor planning means shouting into the void.

Hustle strategically to avoid pitfalls and maximize impact.

Service Deals: Renting the System

This is where the power move is played. The service deal is a criminally underused tool in the indie filmmaker's arsenal.

Not the "sign your soul away" traditional distribution deal, not a complete DIY nightmare where you're running your release off a laptop, a service deal sits in the middle; it lets you hire a professional distributor to execute your release strategy while maintaining ownership, control, and revenue participation.

Instead of handing your film off and hoping for the best, you raise your marketing, advertising, and release budget and pay the distributor to do what they do best: book theaters, place ads, run PR, cut trailers, handle deliverables, and open the doors to platforms and press.

This model puts you in the driver's seat. You retain control of the film, determine where and how it's released, and negotiate a lower distribution fee. Service deal fees often land around 15-20%, a nice drop from the 25–40% typical in traditional deals. That means more of the revenue flows back to you and your investors.

Service deals only work if you raise P&A and/or marketing money. You're not just paying for services; you're stepping into a co-distributor or even the lead role of distributor, where you're doing the planning, and they're doing the legwork. That means overseeing strategy, marketing, timelines, and deliverables.

You need a dedicated marketing and distribution budget, not a few thousand dollars left over from your production budget.

For a streaming-only release, your marketing/distribution budget should be at *least* 10% of your production budget. So, if your movie costs

$500K to make, you need to raise another $50K to bring it to market properly. That's the minimum.

And if you want a theatrical release, even a limited one, a minimum of 50% of your production budget is a good rule of thumb. For a wider release, double or triple your production budget. You heard that right: *a theatrical release done right easily costs as much or more than your entire production.*

Theaters don't promote your film; you do. Ads, posters, DCP files, publicists, social media, travel, screenings, reviews, trailers, local ads, and in-theater ad spending add up fast. And if you're not prepared to bankroll it, your film will quietly vanish.

A note about theatrical screening: Most theater chains, such as AMC, Cinemark, and Odeon, will require a qualified lab to deliver DCP (Digital Cinema Package) files. Your deliverables budget should include around $1,500 for QC (quality control) and ~$60 per theater for DCP delivery. Many theater chains work with Digital Cinema United, which has labs in Culver City, California, Prague, Johannesburg, and London.

A service deal is only power play if you're willing to raise money and run your release like a startup launch. You'll work with pros, use real industry infrastructure, keep more of your rights, and manage the flow of revenue more transparently.

Here's what you get:

- A theatrical and/or digital rollout through legit platforms.

- Retention of ownership and control.

- Real-time access to revenue tracking.

- Better positioning to negotiate downstream deals.

- The ability to pivot and scale based on your film's

performance.

But again, this only works if you plan for it. Raise the funds early. Educate your investors. They're not just paying for the film's production but investing in the film business. A great product with no launch plan is still a flop.

So yes, service deals are one of the smartest plays in the game. But they only work if you're strategic enough to plan for distribution *before* production because you have to pitch this to investors as part of your initial plan, not as a last-minute fire drill.

Service Deal Snapshot

Category	Service Deal Approach
What It Is	You hire a distributor to execute your release plan but retain ownership and control.
What You Pay For	Marketing, PR, trailers, posters, ads, festival positioning, platform placement, theatrical booking, deliverables.
What You Get	Access to a distributor's relationships, infrastructure, and credibility. However, they should use that access wisely and respectfully; distributors tend to ghost problematic rookies.
Distribution Fees	15-20 % (negotiable), lower than traditional deals.
Revenue Control	You retain more of the revenue waterfall; funds flow faster and more transparently.
Minimum Budget Rule	For streaming, raise at least 10% of your production budget for marketing/distribution.
Theatrical Budget Rule	Plan to raise at least double your production budget. Best for filmmakers who want control, investor accountability, and professional release without giving up rights.
Red Flags	Waiting until after production to raise marketing funds = distribution death spiral.

Service deals are a smart play for many indie films, but only if you plan, raise the money, and treat your movie like a business.

Timing is Everything: Submission Windows and Release Timelines

Distribution is as much about when as about how. One of beginner film-makers' most significant mistakes is not understanding the timelines involved both in pitching to distributors and in the logistics of releasing a film. Let's decode the timing aspect so you can set realistic expectations and not be taken by surprise when things move slower than a snail on Quaaludes.

Submitting to Distributors or Sales Agents

If you're seeking a deal, you ideally start this process early. Often, the perceived window for getting a distributor's attention is around your festival premiere or after you finish your film. But reaching out after picture lock is fine. Sales agents and distributors will call grace on unfinished color grade or sound mix. Ideally, you'd be making relationships with distributors even before that. It has taken us years to know "who's who." That changes annually because, like any other company, distributors have turnover in staffing. Distributors go belly up or merge with other companies. Maintaining relationships (LinkedIn, for example) is essential. And if you wait a year after completion, many companies will assume the film is "old" or that others have passed it on.

It's harsh, but a film has a shelf life in the eyes of the industry. The hottest moment is when your movie is freshest and most exciting, maybe even during packaging but well before it's finished.

So, before you lock picture and have a solid screener, that's the time to quietly start reaching out, even if you're also doing festivals. Producer's reps can help here; they'll shop the film to buyers and foreign sales agents for a commission, as we covered earlier. If you can't afford to attract a rep, you, the producer or director, might need to hustle and send out queries. Like job hunting, don't put all your hopes on one email. Cast a wide net, follow up, and use any connections you can.

Now, if you attract interest, due diligence is key. Not all distributors are created equally. Some might show enthusiasm but drag their feet signing anything. Some offer what appears to be a good deal, but then the distributor schedules your release for two years out, if it happens at all. You need to vet them. And if multiple parties are interested, you can nudge them by politely letting each know that others are in the mix that can prompt faster action – nobody wants to lose a deal to a competitor.

Navigating the Streaming Ecosystem
Platforms, Platforms Everywhere

For indie filmmakers, the streaming ecosystem is both a goldmine of opportunity and a bewildering maze. On the one hand, you have more outlets than ever for your film. On the other hand, the competition is wild, gatekeepers are real, and the economics can be opaque.

Let's map the landscape a bit. Broadly, streaming platforms fall into a few categories:

SVOD (Subscription Video on Demand)

Filmmakers license films for lump-sum fees or per-view royalties via distributors or sales agents, as streamers rarely accept unsolicited films. They favor festival hits or buzz worthy titles. With streamers prioritizing

self-produced content, indie films need strong appeal or established channels to secure deals.

Netflix and Hulu are highly selective, prioritizing films with festival
buzz, star power, or niche appeal (e.g., horror documentaries). For example, Netflix's $17M acquisition of *It's What's Inside* at Sundance 2024 shows
their focus on high-profile festival hits, but most indie films don't achieve
this level of attention. Hulu, owned by Disney, often acquires films with
mainstream or awards potential (e.g., *CODA* for $25M in 2021), but such
deals are rare.

For indie filmmakers, Netflix or Hulu acquisitions are also rare, with
only standout films securing deals. Small films may fetch $10K–$500K licensing fees[2], but after sales agent (10–20%) and aggregator fees (15–20%),
breaking even is tough, especially for budgets over $200k. While a Net-
flix deal boosts notoriety, enhancing future opportunities, profits are often
slim due to high costs and limited backend. Focus on festival buzz or niche
appeal to maximize chances.

TVOD (Transactional VOD)

TVOD is the digital equivalent of a rental or purchase. Audiences pay
per title to rent for a limited window (usually 48 hours) or own digitally.
Platforms like iTunes, Amazon, and Google Play operate under this model.
TVOD is best suited for films with strong genre appeal, a recognizable cast,
or a built-in fan base willing to pay for early access. The best time to launch
TVOD is early in the release window—ideally alongside or shortly after a
theatrical debut—to capitalize on release excitement and offer an option
for viewers who prefer not to go to the theater. While the per-unit revenue
is higher than AVOD or SVOD, volume is the challenge. Unless you drive
demand with aggressive marketing, piggyback off theatrical momentum,
or ride the shirttail of an established fan base, TVOD often underperforms

---

2   Licensing fees, like MGs, are based on how much profit a platform estimates they
will earn during the licensing term, not how much you think it's worth.

expectations.

AVOD (Advertising VOD)

AVOD has become a rising star in indie film distribution. Platforms like Tubi, Pluto TV, Roku Channel, and YouTube let audiences watch for free with ads, generating revenue for filmmakers based on ad impressions or hours watched. While the payout per view is lower than TVOD, volume can make up for it if your film finds traction.

AVOD audiences tend to be value-driven, often opting to wait until a film is available to stream for free rather than paying to rent or subscribe. While there is some overlap with TVOD and SVOD users, AVOD generally doesn't noticeably cannibalize those revenue streams. However, if AVOD is introduced too early or without strategic timing, it can fragment the audience and reduce potential earnings from paid windows. A six-month hold back on AVOD after theatrical is generally good timing, because it allows TVOD to run its course (typically the first 2-3 months).

Importantly, AVOD is often non-exclusive, and many aggregators (like Filmhub, which takes 20%) specialize in placing indie films across multiple platforms. Some filmmakers report making more money on Tubi over a year than they ever did on iTunes—simply because access was frictionless. While success on AVOD can be unpredictable, it's now a key component of most indie distribution plans, often following or running alongside a short TVOD window

Cable/Satellite VOD

Cable/satellite VOD (e.g., Comcast Xfinity, Spectrum) offers on-demand rentals, accessible via aggregators like FilmHub or Quiver, which handle delivery and quality control. TV networks (e.g., Showtime, AMC) or foreign channels (e.g., BBC, ZDF) license films for flat fees, often requiring sales agents for pitching, as DIY submissions are rare. Documentaries or genre films fit well, but exclusivity clauses may limit availability on other platforms for 1–5 years. Track placements via aggregator dashboards, as some distributors under report earnings from smaller outlets. Persist with approvals, as platforms have backlogs and strict content standards.

Technical requirements

Each platform requires specific video encoding, subtitles, and artwork. Aggregators handle most deliverables, but you must provide quality files. For direct uploads (e.g., Amazon Prime Video Direct), ensure QC-approved closed captions and formats and budget time for technical onboarding—it's not drag-and-drop.

AVOD streaming offers long-tail revenue. Initial earnings may be modest ($1K—$5K), but steady viewership or sudden relevance (e.g., a pandemic film in 2020) can boost income for years. Promote periodically across platforms ("Now free on Tubi!"), as each audience differs. Availability doesn't guarantee visibility, so plan and market persistently to stand out.

Film Festivals: Hype vs. Reality in Distribution

Festivals are fantastic for celebrating your work, meeting other filmmakers, and maybe nabbing some laurel leaves for your poster. However, film festivals do diddly squat for securing distribution deals for most films. They can be a distraction that delays your release and drains your resources.

The fantasy goes something like this (fed by those high-profile Sundance acquisitions you read about in the trades): You get into a top festival, you have a packed premiere, a bidding war erupts in the lobby, and you sign a big distribution deal before the after-party is over. Boom – instant career, money, fame. But then reality pops your balloon. Out of thousands of films on the festival circuit, only a handful get significant distribution offers at festivals, and nearly all of those are at top-tier festivals like Sundance, SXSW, Tribeca, Cannes, Toronto, or maybe Berlin. Sales agents and distributors attend the majors, but they're not trolling Podunk Regional Film Fest, looking for the next hit. So, if you're pinning your distribution hopes on getting noticed at Joe's Indie Fest in Nowheresville, the chances of that happening are slim to none.

The odds are slim even at Sundance, the mecca of indie deals. In recent years, Sundance has premiered around 100-120 feature films. A tiny percentage captured a distro deal. The rest may get minor offers or end up self-distributing. Notably, Sundance 2023 highlighted a trend: It's becoming less about acquisition frenzies and more of a prestige showcase. Following that year's festival, in a guest editorial on *The Park Record*, Keith Ochwat noted that Sundance is "becoming less and less relevant as a marketplace for distribution. It's a distribution delusion to think that a filmmaker's best path to success is to premiere at Sundance."

Those are strong words, but the streamers have pulled back after years of Netflix and Amazon throwing money at festival darlings. They're now choosier, favoring sure-fire content (true crime docs, celeb-driven projects) Ochwat went on to say, "Only a few filmmakers will ever get a big deal from a streamer, and even if they do, the filmmakers often don't receive the lion's share of the money once agents, lawyers, and distributors take cuts."

Ouch.

We mentioned in Chapter Two that we had a film submitted to us that won the Narrative Feature Grand Jury Prize at Slamdance. Talk about hardware! We don't know the specifics of any offers they received or if they received any, but we got a taste after offering a minimum guarantee, and they declined. They may have mistaken the festival win for commercial viability and set their expectations accordingly.

We've painted a dismal picture, but festivals are not *entirely* worthless for distribution. Top-tier fests like Sundance or Cannes *can* put your film on the radar in rare cases. A film that might've been ignored can attract distributor interest simply because it carries a laurel.

Festivals are also a hunting ground for sales agents, but ideally, you should already have one before you arrive. Sales agents pitch your film to buyers in different territories, but this mostly happens at major festivals. Mid-tier fests are better for audience feedback or an award.

The real danger is the festival bubble where filmmakers chase the next laurel, postponing release for a year or more. Momentum fades. The press loses interest ("Wait, didn't that premiere last year?"). By the time the festival run ends, some distributors may see the film as stale. We've seen filmmakers finish an 18-month tour only to self-distribute a movie that's no longer market fresh. In hindsight, they would've had better results by leveraging early buzz and striking while the fire still burned.

So, how should indie filmmakers approach festivals?

Strategically.

Aim high, but set a time and money limit. For example: "We'll submit to festivals for six months. If nothing happens, we pivot to release." Use the hype of selection for marketing. Send links to distributors, invite sales agents to screenings, and don't just wait to be discovered.

Be honest about which festivals matter. Winning Best Feature at a small regional fest is a nice ego boost and adds some credibility, but it won't attract a Netflix call. That money might be better spent on deliverables or marketing, especially if your film isn't the next *Moonlight*.

Just remember the mantra: Festivals are a means, not an end. The goal is to get your film in front of real audiences and make money. Don't chase the laurel if a festival doesn't move you toward that.

That said, festivals can be great for building buzz. A decent review from *IndieWire* or *Variety,* or an award you can feature in your trailer, can boost credibility. But beware the "all festival, no release" cycle. Getting hooked on applause and Q&As is easy because it feels like success. Meanwhile, the real distribution work is harder, lonelier, and full of rejection. But it's how you get your film out.

Bottom line: Festivals are great for celebrating your film and opening doors but are not a distribution strategy. If you get into a top-tier fest, use it. If not, don't stall. The real audience is out there, and they won't wait forever.

And remember back in Chapter One when we joked about not banking on a "Sundance miracle"? We kinda weren't kidding. If it happens, that would be awesome. Buy a Powerball ticket while you're at it. If it doesn't happen, at least you planned like a pro.

Seasonality and Market Cycles

If you're going to major festivals or aligning with them, that's great. If not, be aware that if you send a screener to a distributor in late October, some companies might be busy with AFM, or if you send them in December, people are on holiday. There are also better and worse times to release certain films. For example, if you have a horror movie, many distributors aim to release it around October to tie into the Halloween season, so they'd want to acquire it by spring to set that up. Awards-bait films are often released in the fall. Family films in early summer, etc. As an indie producer, you might not have much say or need to worry if you self-distribute (you'll pick a date that suits you), but if a distributor is interested, you might ask, "When do you see this being released?" to gauge if they have a plan or are just hoarding content.

Lead Time for Release

Once a distribution deal is signed, or once you decide to self-release, it can still take 6-12 months before the film is available for the world to see. Why? Deliverables (which we'll cover next) can take a few months to prepare and get approved. Distributors also slot your film into their calendars. They might say, "We love it, but our next available slot for a marketing push is next April." If they're a small company, they might only release a few films a month, and you have to wait your turn. If you're self-distributing, you might set a release date several months in advance to give yourself time to build buzz (e.g., announce the film, drop a trailer, do a pre-order campaign on iTunes, etc.).

Rushing a release is generally not wise; you only get one "debut," and you want some eyeballs. Don't go to the other extreme and let years slide by. We've encountered filmmakers who finish a film, then spend two years tweaking small things or waiting for the "perfect" moment to release, by which time the film's relevance has faded, and the team has moved on mentally. Momentum is critical. Use the energy from your festival premiere or your finishing process to propel you into distribution. If you're self-releasing, set a date and stick to it. If you're seeking a deal, set internal deadlines like, "If we don't have a solid offer by X date, we pivot to Plan B (DIY)."

Another timeline to consider is submission to platforms if you're self-distributing. For example, Amazon Prime Direct might approve within days or weeks, but it's unpredictable. If you want a coordinated multi-platform launch on July 1st, you might need to start the ingest process in May or April. Also, if you're planning any public relations or press, they'll want a screener and info at least a month before release and major outlets even longer. So, plan in reverse: pick a release date and work backward to schedule press outreach, platform submission, asset creation, etc. We know scheduling isn't fun, but it's part of the game.

A special mention on "submission windows" for specific platforms or distributors: Some companies, like certain streaming services, might only take submissions or meet new filmmakers at particular times, often around film markets or via periodic open submission calls. Always read up on the latest info. There have been initiatives like Amazon's Film Festival Stars program (now defunct) or Netflix's penchant for picking up a couple of festival docs each year. Know what the targets are and time your approach accordingly. If you miss one cycle, you might have to wait months for the next one.

Finally, patience vs. proactivity: It's a balance. Don't sit idle, thinking a distributor will eventually knock on your door; be proactive in chasing opportunities. But also, once you've done your part by submitting and following up, be patient because these processes take time. It's okay to nudge politely ("Just checking if you had a chance to watch our film; we're aiming to make decisions soon on our distribution path") but recognize everyone is juggling projects. If you haven't heard back from a distributor in a month, chances are they're not interested, or your email got buried. It's fine to ping again, but have your Plan B on standby. The worst feeling is losing time. Time is a currency for indie filmmakers; every month your film isn't released is a month of no revenue and lost potential audience awareness. You don't want your movie to become yesterday's news before it even comes out.

In summary, distribution should be treated like another production phase with its schedule and milestones. As we've hammered throughout this book, plan early – ideally while you're in post, start mapping out these timelines. So many things in this industry are slow until they're not, so a little foresight goes a long way in avoiding those "Why is everything taking so long?!" panics.

The Hidden World of Deliverables
Paperwork and Pitfalls

Deliverables are the materials you must deliver, hence the name, to your distributor or platform to consummate the deal and release your film. It's more than just handing over a hard drive with the movie. It's the phase where countless indie films hit a wall because deliverables are detailed; some are technical, some are legal, some are procedural, and some can be expensive. Screw them up, or run out of money for them, and your whole distribution can implode at the finish line.

Here are just a few of the costs you can expect. And again, if you're a first or second-time filmmaker, consider hiring someone to help you through the process:

$5-15,000 for legal

$4,000 - 5,000, E&O insurance. We've seen it as high as $15,000 in one case (it was a high-risk film).

$750 - 5,000 for key art design (find a qualified graphic designer who specializes in key art)

$1,500 - 5,000 for trailer edits (optional, but trailers are tricky to edit yourself)

$1,500ish, quality control (QC) lab + delivery

$800-2,000 for closed caption files (unless you create them yourself)

$60 or so per theater if you're delivering DCP

Up to $5,000 for Chain of Title

Let's not forget music licensing. If you're using a song you heard on the radio, expect $50,000 - $100,000 for the rights to use that song or any part of it. That's well out of range for most indie filmmakers.

And most distributors will not pay for deliverables. *You* do.

Distributors don't just buy movies; they buy packages. And if your package is missing critical elements, you're not getting through the door—or paid. Some distributors will drag out that first check until you've delivered everything. We had a movie in theaters, and the first check was held for weeks because of ONE minor agreement that wasn't in their Google Drive. They didn't let us know until we asked about the holdup. Talk about stress!

So, while you're obsessing over lenses and locations, someone on your team needs to obsess over deliverables and collect them as you go. Start now. Create a Google Drive or Box folder for your movie, plus an offline backup. Get the documents, assets, and permissions gathered during pre-production and production, or they'll disappear like grip tape on wrap day. Start with a fully executed deal memo for everyone on set, even your unpaid PA who only wants an IMDb credit. If they're not under contract, they can potentially claim authorship of the film (no, we're not kidding. This is real).

Let's pause a moment so you can catch your breath. While this seems overwhelming, the process happens relatively smoothly if you plan for it. It can be tedious, but the process is generally painless if you're organized and know what you need.

Next, collect location agreements for every space you shoot in, even if they're free. Get life rights under contract if your film is based on a real person or event, vendor contact lists with names, emails, service details, and any agreements signed for everything from camera rentals to catering to the restaurant that brought free donuts to set just to be nice, and insurance certificates showing coverage for gear, liability, and locations. You'll also need talent releases, crew releases, extras releases, appearance releases for non-actors appearing on camera, and minors' permission forms with guardian signatures.

Document music contributions, even temp tracks or "friend deals." Have written permission or license language on file. Capture on-set production stills, BTS photos and footage, and a daily log of locations, shots, and call sheets. It matters later when someone asks, "Do you have proof you were allowed to shoot that?" or "Who provided this gear, and what's their contact for billing?" You might not remember, but fortunately, your deliverables folder will. The more you collect now, the less you'll pull your hair out later. Paperwork is part of the process. Respect it, because your entire release depends on it.

Below is a list of a few common deliverables that most distributors require once the film is completed. The full list is far more extensive; these are a sample (most of these also apply if you're self-distributing):

Picture Master Files, AKA Printmaster Files

Typically, a high-resolution digital printmaster of your film in ProRes 444 file, but most platforms will accept ProRes 422 HQ. Most distributors want 4k with 5.1 surround and stereo mixes. Plus, a textless master is your film without any on-screen text, like location labels or credits, so distributors selling in territories that speak different languages can add their language text (which is becoming obsolete with real-time AI transcription solutions). Most distributors will allow beginning and ending credits, if they occur over images and not black, to be included textless at the end of the printmaster, eliminating the need to encode and upload a second enormously large ProRes file. For an international release where redubbing of the dialogue will occur, you'll need to send separate tracks, or "stems," including dialogue only (DX), a stereo M&E (music and effects only, no dialogue), and all 5.1 tracks separated in mono stems (SFX L, SFX R, SFX ls, SFX Rs; music L, music R, music Ls, music Rs, C (dialogue), and LFE (low-frequency effects for subwoofer boom-boom)).

Closed Captions & Subtitles

Closed captions (CC) for the hearing impaired in your film's original language are mandatory for any streaming platform or TV. These must be perfectly formatted to spec. Some distributors only want CCs formatted to 608 standards (for the old 4:3 aspect ratio) but may also want a separate 708 file for widescreen. CC files must be embedded into the ProRes printmaster and separately as "sidecar" files. If you haven't created the CC files already, expect to pay a professional service to create these at a rate of roughly $8-$10 per minute of runtime, so around $800-$1000 for a feature. Be careful who you choose when creating closed caption files. They're not always accurate; some use AI tools, so you'll need to proofread their work. You can make closed-caption files yourself. That's our preferred method in-house, and Adobe Premiere has the right tools. Premiere is great for transcribing and creating closed caption text, but it formats text inconsistently, and it's not 100% accurate, so you must proofread and fix weird things. That's time-consuming but doable for building 608 and 708-compliant closed captioning. If your film has bits in a foreign language, you'll need translations or an English subtitle track if it's mostly not in English.

Trailer and Promo Stills

These include a high-quality trailer and maybe a teaser in similar formats, a set of high-resolution screenshots from the film, and a set of high-resolution still pictures from set. You will likely have these, but ensure they meet the requested technical specs. Multiple versions of your trailer are a bonus, but each must be in powerhouse form.

Metadata and Synopses

You'll need to provide written synopses for platform metadata—short, long, cast/crew lists, genre tags, etc. Compiling this is easy but time-consuming.

Chain of Title Documentation

We'll talk in-depth about chain of title in Chapter Eight, but this is where many indies face trouble. "Chain of title" means all the legal documents proving you own all the film's rights and can license it.

Music Licenses and Cue Sheet

Every piece of music and sound effects in your film must be cleared for the territories and platforms you're releasing on—SVOD, TVOD, etc.—for at least the full term of your distribution deal. If you have a composer, you have a composer agreement and an ASCAP/BMI cue sheet listing all the cues. If you use stock music or songs, you'll need master and sync licenses. You must have those licenses covering all applicable media rights, not just festival rights. Many indie filmmakers make the mistake of getting "festival only" music rights for a smaller fee, thinking they'll upgrade later. The problem is that you can't legally deliver without clearing those thoroughly. If you didn't, you may have to either renegotiate with the music rights owners, which can be pricey, or replace the music in the film. It's painful but sometimes necessary. Also, any stock footage or images in the film need licensing. The deliverables usually consist of copies of all those licenses and a cue sheet listing all music timings.

Licensing only for the territories you know you'll use can save money upfront, especially on a tight budget. Expanding later is possible, but it often comes at a higher cost because licensors may charge more when they know you're committed, and you lose the advantage of bundling multiple rights in a single deal. There's also the added time and complexity of renegotiating. If the cost difference is minimal, securing broader rights from the start is often smarter, especially for music, where territory and duration can heavily impact pricing. When in doubt, weigh your distribution plan carefully, but lean toward securing what you'll likely need. It's cheaper than circling back later.

Out-of-Context Music and Visual Rights

Licensing a song or visual clip is not just about how you plan to use it in your film. Rights holders are increasingly protective of how their content is portrayed, especially if it is out of context.

Out-of-context use refers to the song or visual appearing in a manner not initially approved, such as a scene from your film in a trailer, promo, or social media clip, where the music or visual was licensed initially only for in-film use.

To avoid legal headaches, always secure broad usage rights upfront, which means negotiating permissions that cover trailers, social media, and other promotional uses. If you're on a tight budget, prioritize licensing tracks with more flexible terms or consider royalty-free music to eliminate the issue.

If you don't plan ahead, you might find yourself stuck with a soundtrack you can't legally promote or, worse, facing a lawsuit.

Error & Omissions (E&O) Insurance

E&O insurance is a liability policy that protects the distributor and you if someone sues, claims the film libels them, infringes copyright, etc. Every reputable distributor will require you to have an E&O policy in effect. They also often require you to maintain it for the first 3-5 years of distribution. Getting E&O isn't hard; you apply through an insurance broker, and they'll want to see your script and maybe the chain of title docs to underwrite it.

For an indie film, E&O insurance costs $2,500–$5,000 for a 3-year policy with $1M per claim/$3M aggregate limits and a $10,000 deductible. Low-risk films (e.g., nature documentaries) may cost $2,000–$3,000, while higher-risk projects (e.g., corporate exposés or films with extensive human footage) can reach $15,000.

Many indie filmmakers get to this stage and say, "Wait, I bought production insurance, now I need THIS? And it costs HOW much?!" Yes, and it is expensive. So, if you don't budget for it, you're in trouble—no insurance, no distribution. In Chapter Two, we warned you to set aside finishing funds – this is a prime example of why.

Credits & Compliance Documents

This is a copy of the final credit roll text and a billing block (the text block on posters with credits). Many times, distributors want that separately. Also, any guild required documentation: e.g., if you had a SAG-AFTRA actor, you may need Taft-Hartley approval or a final cast list from SAG. If you use union writers or directors, the guilds might require certain things like WPA for writers or ensuring the credits match what was arbitrated. For most non-union indie films, guild deliverables might not apply. But if you did use union talent, be prepared to have those obligations squared away, like all dues paid, residuals set up if applicable, etc. Distributors often ask for a Paid Ads statement/credits summary, which is a document that outlines everyone's contractual credit obligations and any restrictions like "Actor X must be in first position in all advertising." Yes, they check that stuff.

Marketing Assets

These are oftentimes listed as deliverables, too: key art (poster) in layered Photoshop or Illustrator format, behind-the-scenes photos, an EPK (Electronic Press Kit) with the director's statement, bios, etc. You likely have much of this, but ensure it's organized and presentable.

How to win the deliverables maze

Looking at this list, you might think, "That's a mountain of stuff." You're not wrong. A distributor will usually give you a multi-page deliverables schedule that is contractually required. Many indie films are wrecked at this stage. We know of a filmmaker who got a decent distribution offer. When the distribution company saw their deliverables files, they found he hadn't cleared two songs and didn't have E&O. The cost to fix all that basically equaled the advance he was offered. The deal fell through. The film eventually went out via self-distribution, but without those popular songs (he had to replace them) – a compromise that somewhat dulled the film's impact. Another case: a doc filmmaker had tons of archival footage they claimed under "fair use," but no lawyer's opinion letter backing that up. No distributor wanted to touch it until they paid an attorney a few thousand dollars to verify the fair use claims, which is costly and time-consuming. These are the hidden dragons in the distribution dungeon.

So, how do you survive the deliverables gauntlet? Start early. During production and post, keep records and copies of every agreement. As soon as you picture lock, begin the process of securing E&O insurance. The best strategy is to get a quote for your E&O policy early, then bind it once you have a confirmed release date. If a distributor pushes for E&O before that date, negotiate for the release-date start. Show them the quote to prove you're ready, but explain that starting the policy on or just before release maximizes your coverage window.

You have the option to get your film QC'd before you sign a distribution agreement to help you deliver professionally. And get those copyrights registered. It's cheap, $65 each, and you can do it online, but you need to allow up to 3-4 months to get your registration certificate.

Some deliverables can be negotiated or waived. For instance, maybe a small distributor won't require a textless master if they don't plan any foreign dubbing. Or they might advance you the E&O cost and recoup it later (a few sympathetic distributors do that). If you can't deliver something, discuss it upfront and see if there's a workaround. Don't sign a deal and then admit later you can't provide something essential; that's how you burn bridges. Transparency can save you: Distributors may have solutions, such as cheaper in-house services or alternate arrangements.

In short, deliverables are the bureaucratic side of getting your film out, but they're crucial. Treat it like a final exam you must pass to graduate into distribution. And like any exam, preparation is everything.

Our rule is that when we sign a film for sales and distribution, we will not make platform or co-distribution deals until all deliverables are in place. It's best for everyone involved; the filmmaker is still pressed because they want the film released, but they're not scrambling. When you make professional deliveries, the platforms know you can be trusted. We learned that the hard way with a film that almost cost a relationship with two exhibitors. Many deliverables were improperly submitted, and the filmmaker had difficulties fixing the issues.

Go to our website, **Profoundstudios.media**, and click the DELIVERABLES tab. There, for a small fee, you'll find a sample delivery schedule and templates for some of the more commonly misunderstood paper deliverables. You're welcome.

Quality Control: The Final Hurdle Between You and Distribution

As we've alluded previously, you will be required to quality control (QC) your film. QC is a thorough technical check of your master video/audio files. Some distributors will handle QC, but many require you to furnish a Master QC report from an approved lab, such as DCU or Digital Blu.

Most legitimate distributors, especially those placing your film on platforms like Apple TV, Amazon, Netflix, or any cable VOD, will require a professional quality control report, not to critique the content, but to go uber geek on the technical elements of the film. And not the "looks fine to me" pass from your buddy who watched it on a laptop. We're talking about a frame-by-frame, audio decibel-by-decibel forensic dissection of your film by a certified facility.

QC is where robots and nerds judge your life's work. And they do not care that you made the whole thing with duct tape and dreams. They care if your audio peaks at +3 dB instead of under -2. They care if your black levels are off, your title-safe margins are sloppy, or your final fade is jittery. They care if one frame — one single, stupid frame — goes south of acceptable. Kirk recalls a filmmaker who, after failing QC, argued, "My film won first place at a festival; the quality was fine!" Unaware of technical standards, he dodged feedback, later claiming, "Where I'm from, QC means something else." The filmmaker was just embarrassed that they didn't understand. Don't let ego block the progress of learning; QC ensures your film meets platform standards, protecting your release's potential success.

If you want distribution for your film, know that:

- Most distributors require a qualified, third-party lab to do the QC.

- It costs around $1,500 for a 90-minute feature.

- If your film fails QC, you must fix the issues, resubmit, and pay again. With a failed QC, you'll typically pay a discounted re-test fee. And failure is common. We've seen a film fail QC five times. FIVE. The filmmakers thought they were done but missed fixing a weird artifact or audio issue. Each time, they paid. And most films we've distributed have failed the first pass. QC is as serious as a tax audit.

Common reasons films fail QC:

- Levels are off: peaks too loud, dialogue too soft.

- Audio channels not correctly mapped (e.g., stereo instead of discrete 5.1).

- Dropped frames, flickers, or sync drift.

- Closed captions not timed correctly or missing altogether.

- Inconsistent black levels or over-peak highlights.

• Title cards not within safe margins.

• Foreign object in frame (boom mic dipped in on frame 43521).

• Frame shift, meaning a one-pixel-wide black line is on one side of the frame.

• Glitches introduced during final export — the DCP looks fine, but the ProRes has a corrupted frame.

Most filmmakers don't know this process exists until it's sprung on them late in the game.

Then it's a mad dash for time and cash. You're staring down a deadline, your composer is on vacation, your colorist is ghosting you, and the lab says your film is "out of spec." You panic and bleed more money. You wish you had read this book six months earlier.

Here's what you do:

• Budget for QC. With the high likelihood of at least one QC failure, bump that up $600-$800 per re-test. Hopefully, it will not fail, but plan as though it will.

• Do your own relentless QC before sending it out. Watch your final master on a calibrated monitor. Listen for minuscule issues with headphones and overall sound on speakers. Watch with subtitles on. Check the whole thing twice.

• Ask your post supervisor or editor to walk you through a QC checklist. Most know what to expect, or they can refer you to someone who does.

So, don't blow your last shot. Plan and budget for QC. Nail it the first time and move on with your life.

Preparing for Distribution: Next Steps

By now, you've seen that distribution is complex, often unfair, and requires as much hustle as making the film, if not more. But knowledge is power. One of the reasons we took the time and expense to write this book is to arm you with that knowledge so you don't walk blindfolded into distribution or other arenas in the business of film.

We've decoded how money flows, what paths to release are open to you from old-school theatrical to DIY digital, how to navigate the modern streaming jungle, and why you shouldn't drink the festival Kool-Aid too heavily. We also spotlighted the deliverables monster lurking at the end of the road.

Make smart choices about distribution models that fit your film. Empower yourself to get your movie out there, budget real money and time for distribution tasks. And never forget why you made the film in the first place; to share a story with the world. Keep that as your north star. Distribution is just the means to that end.

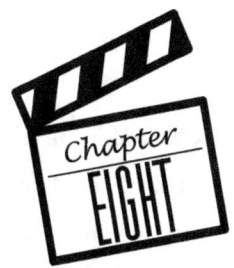

Legalese Made Fun

"The law is the law, Nicholas. It's not subject to negotiation."

— Inspector Frank Butterman, *Hot Fuzz* (2007)

O K, we admit, the chapter heading is sarcasm; there is nothing fun about legal unless you're an attorney. And even then, we have our suspicions. Still, we'll do our best to make it less painful—maybe like ripping off a Band-Aid.

This chapter is all about legal CYA. As you know, we care about your film being seen and accepted by an audience. But honestly, a brilliant movie can die on the vine because of paperwork screw-ups. Boring, seemingly insignificant forms can stop your masterpiece from ever being seen.

Although we are not attorneys, we will help simplify the legalese for filmmakers who have zero legal knowledge. We'll walk through the essential documents and issues you must handle, but you'll learn to do it with style. Remember when we talked about budgeting for everything, including legal expenses? We advised you to plan and budget for a lawyer, contracts, marketing, and insurance. This is where that advice pays off.

Copyrights and Trademarks

Protect Yourself (and Your Stuff)

Copyright is a Big One for filmmakers. It defines the ownership of your creative work including your script, film, footage, poster art, all of it. When you create something original and fix it in a tangible form (like writing a script or shooting footage), it's automatically protected under copyright law in most countries through the Berne Convention. So why bother doing anything more? Because in the U.S., and many other jurisdictions, you must register your work to fully enforce your rights.

In the United States, registration with the U.S. Copyright Office is required to sue for infringement and to claim statutory damages or attorney's fees. Without it, your rights exist, but your legal remedies are severely limited. The same concept applies in Canada, the UK, Australia, and many other countries that are signatories to the Berne Convention: You automatically own the copyright once your work is fixed in a tangible form, but registration can strengthen your legal position.

Most indie filmmakers delay this step until they smell a distribution deal, which is a mistake. Don't wait. Register your screenplay early. Then register your film. Then consider registering your trailer, poster, and any other creative asset you plan to exploit. If it's worth making, it's worth protecting.

When copyrighting your film, there are two schools of thought. 1- Register before filming, and 2- Register after picture lock. Which is better? Doing both is the smart move.

Register Before Filming

In America, registering your script with the U.S. Copyright Office or the WGA (Writers Guild of America) before filming does a few essential things:

- Establishes authorship and ownership from the start.

- Protects you legally if someone tries to steal, claim, or copy your work (yes, it happens).

- Shows investors, producers, and legal teams that you know what you're doing.

- Allows you to enforce copyright in court if things go sideways.

Check your nation's laws if you live outside the United States.

If you're seeking financing, attaching producers, or doing a co-production, you'll need proof of registration, so don't skip this step. Think of it as insurance for your intellectual property.

Register Again After Picture Lock

Your shooting script and finished film are rarely identical.

- Scenes get cut.

- Dialogue gets reworked.

- Characters shift.

- You rewrite on set.

- You improvise in editing.

The final version, which matches what's on screen, should be registered as the "literary work" based on the final cut. This ensures your copyright covers the actual work that was publicly released, not the version that lived on paper six months and twelve breakdowns ago.

Also, once you register the film itself (the audiovisual work), the copyright office prefers a version of the script that reflects the final cut for documentation purposes.

The Smart Move

So, smart filmmakers play it like this:

1. **Register your original script before filming** (WGA, U.S. Copyright Office, or your nation's equivalent agencies) to establish protection early and build credibility.

2. **Register the final, screen-accurate version after picture lock**—either as a revised script (literary work) or as part of your film's complete copyright registration (motion picture).

The All-Important Chain of Title

A clean chain of title is essential for a valid distribution agreement, ensuring clear ownership. Issues can delay or void the contract.

If you plan to license, sell, or distribute a film internationally, having all your copyright registrations buttoned up (script + finished film) becomes part of your chain of title documentation, which buyers, distributors, and E&O insurance providers will absolutely want to see.

Protect your film's chain of title by registering the final script, or the shooting script, with the Copyright Office, not the WGA. Combine the final film copyright registration with the shooting script. Distributors require a clean chain to validate agreements, including the shooting script's ownership. Early registrations strengthen legal protection.

Registering a finished film with the Copyright Office is standard. In the U.S., it costs $65 (electronic filing), but a rush processing request costs an additional $800 on top of the base fee.

So, for a rush registration of a completed film, expect to pay:

$865 total ($65 + $800 rush fee).

Rush processing must be formally requested and justified (e.g., pending litigation or distribution deal), and approval is not guaranteed.

But that paper is worth far more than its weight in gold if someone claims they wrote your story or if a distributor wants proof that you own the film. Don't rely on the old "poor man's" mail-yourself-a-copy trick or just a WGA registration – those aren't substitutes for a real federal copyright. As we warned in an earlier chapter, skipping this tiny task can cause massive headaches later when trying to prove you own your work.

Trademarks

Trademarks protect titles, names, logos, brands, and slogans that might get you thinking, "I'm an artist, not a soda company; why do I care?" Say your indie film's title or production company name starts getting buzz. If you haven't secured a trademark and that name is catchy, someone else might slap it on their stuff (a film, merch, whatever), and suddenly you're in a fight. Trademark rights in the U.S. come from using the mark in commerce, but getting a federal registration from the United States Patent and Trademark Office (USPTO) is how you tell everyone that "this is mine." Unlike copyrights, trademarks do not exist automatically; you must apply and be approved. Many filmmakers ignore trademarks because not every film needs one. Indeed, single movie titles usually aren't trademarked (there's a whole thing about titles of single works not being eligible). But it's worth considering if you plan a series or have a unique production company name or logo. Big franchises like *Jaws* or *Star Wars* have trademarks up the wazoo, which is why you don't see knock-off toys using those names. For your indie film, the most common pitfall is infringing someone else's trademark. Check your title before you lock it. A quick Google and IMDb search can save you from naming your drama *"Avengers"* and getting a cease-and-desist letter from an angry lawyer. If your title accidentally includes a trademarked term (say, your rom-com is called *Starbucks Lovers* – bad idea), you might need to change it or get permission. The bottom line is that copyright protects your film's content, and trademark protects its branding.

Contracts 101

Sign on the Dotted Line, Even for Freebies

Contracts are the nerve-wracking paperwork that defines who gets to do what, who gets paid what, and who owns what in your production. Indie filmmakers often skip contracts because "we're all friends working for free" or "we have no budget to hire lawyers." That mentality has sunk more than a few films. Even if everyone is volunteering, you need paperwork. When there's no money upfront, clear agreements become your only protection against confusion or later disputes. In fact, the "friend trap" – working with buddies on a handshake – is the #1 reason indies neglect proper contracts[1]. It feels awkward to ask your pal to sign an agreement when they do you a favor, right? But it's a lot more uncomfortable when, say, your film gets into a festival or, holy crap, becomes successful, and that friend suddenly says, "Where's my share?" If you don't set terms at the start, people's memories and expectations can drift. If your indie does blow up, those old friends might expect a piece of the pie, and without a contract, you're setting your-self up for conflict. You can burn bridges and risk your movie's release in one fell swoop. Not worth it. So, let's talk about the key contracts you need in place, *especially* for freebies.

Actor Agreements

Every actor on your set, from your lead star to the extras, should sign a talent release or acting contract. This spells out the basics: the role they're playing, the compensation, even if it's no money upfront, the credit they'll

---

1   MortenForland.com March 26, 2025 "The Unsexy Truth About What Makes or Breaks Your Film Distribution"

receive, work dates, and the fact that you can use their performance in the film. It includes a work-for-hire or licensing clause, so you own their performance footage. Without this, an actor could theoretically object to you using their scenes. It's rare, but it can happen. So, to distribute a film, you'll need this paperwork. Write it down if you promised your actor anything such as deferred pay, profit share, a copy of the film, a puppy – whatever. This manages expectations. We know an indie director who lost a distribution deal because one of his lead actors refused to sign a retroactive release; the actor suddenly wanted more money once the film was poised to make money. We've also experienced this in a past movie, with an actor who didn't want his face on the poster. Honestly, we think it was his agent more than him. So, why wasn't this in writing? Because "He's a friend." Get it in writing on day one.

Crew Deal Memos

Deal memos are like actor contracts, but for your crew: cinematographers, sound recordists, PAs, drivers, everyone. A simple deal memo can outline their job, any pay or deferment, and importantly, that the project owns their contributions. For example, your cinematographer is creating footage; you need that to be owned by the production outright. Same for editors, composers, etc. Many indies operate super informally with the crew, which is fine until someone feels short-changed. Even if a crew member is a buddy doing you a solid for free, a deal memo clarifies volunteer status, and they won't claim ownership or wages. It also covers credits, meal breaks, and other basic working terms. If later a crew member claims you promised them X or that they are a co-owner of the film, your paperwork shuts down that discussion. It happens, mainly if they worked on the script or as a producer without clear definitions. It's not about mistrust; it's about everyone understanding the deal upfront.

1099 or W-2 forms

Anyone working on your film must be classified correctly for tax purposes. In the U.S., independent contractors—those not on payroll and with no taxes withheld—must receive a 1099-NEC if paid $600 or more during the year. These forms must be sent to the contractor and filed with the Internal Revenue Service by January 31.

Employees, who have taxes withheld for Social Security, Medicare, and income tax, must receive a W-2, also due to both the employee and IRS by January 31. Misclassifying workers can lead to serious IRS penalties.

If you live outside the United States, most countries have similar distinctions between employees and independent contractors, with different tax reporting and withholding rules. Check your national tax authority's guidelines to avoid misclassification, fines, or legal issues.

Location Releases

You found a perfect diner for a scene, and the friendly owner says, "Sure, film here, no problem!" Great – now have them sign a location release. This permits you to use the property in your movie and to show it in any media. The legal phrase is usually "throughout the universe in perpetuity" – attorneys love cosmic language. Without a signed release, that owner, or a future owner, could object to their property being shown, possibly blocking your film from being displayed or forcing you to edit that scene out of the movie. At a minimum, an unsigned location can give a distributor cold feet; they don't want to risk a lawsuit from someone claiming invasion of privacy or property rights. Also, consider permits (more on that later). The location release is the owner saying, "You can film my private property." Permits are often–but not always–required for public spaces or city property. Both matter. Common pitfall: You film in a friend's apartment without paperwork. Two years later, you're ready to release, and that friend had a falling out with you, or someone else is living there now. They could make trouble. A simple one-page release avoids that drama.

Music Licenses

Music is another Big One. Using music in your film without proper rights is like playing with fire while drenched in gasoline—it will burn you rather quickly and ferociously. This includes songs and background scores.

For any music you didn't compose and perform yourself, you need a license from the copyright holders—usually the songwriter/publisher and the owner of the recording (if it's an existing track).

If you have a composer friend scoring your film, that's fantastic, but you still need a contract—either a work-for-hire agreement or a license that clearly grants you the exclusive, perpetual right to use the music in your film.

Even if you wrote and recorded the music, you'll license it to your film entity (LLC, for example) to avoid future legal ambiguity. If you ever assign or sell your music rights—to a label, publisher, or even your heirs—those new rights holders could revoke your film's use if there's no written license in place. You could also miss out on royalties or backend payments if the rights aren't properly assigned. Licensing your own music to the film ensures that, regardless of future ownership changes, your film retains clear, perpetual rights to use the music without dispute and that you still benefit financially from its use.

No distributor in their right mind will touch your film if you have unlicensed tracks. A typical distribution deal killer is when filmmakers fall in love with a popular song, include it without clearance, and can't afford the license later. The result is either you lose the deal or you spend frantic weeks re-editing scenes with new music. Even stock sound effects or library music need proper licenses. So, do it right the first time. If it's free music (public domain or Creative Commons), double-check that it's genuinely free. And if a friend says, "I'll make you a song for free," you still get a license agreement *and* a composer agreement; otherwise, that friend still owns the music and could pull it or demand payment later if your film blows up.

Chain of Title: Proving You Own Your Film

As Chapter Seven mentions, "Chain of Title" is the legal paper trail proving you own what you say you own. Just like you can't sell a house without a clean title—no liens, no disputes, no missing sig-natures—you can't sell, license, or distribute a film without show-ing you've secured the rights to every element in it: the script, the performances, the music, the footage, the artwork... *everything*. It's your movie's receipt, deed, and proof of ownership all rolled into one. If any part of that chain is missing or broken—like forgetting a signed actor release or failing to clear a music cue—distributors will back away faster than a cat near a vacuum. From their perspective, they can't buy what you don't legally own.

Chain of title includes copyright registrations for the script and the final movie, all the contracts with the cast, crew, locations, etc., proof of owner-ship for any story rights (e.g., if it's based on a book, the option agreement), releases for any real people depicted, and so on. Often, a distributor will want a lawyer to provide a Copyright and Title Report and Legal Opinion letter attesting that the chain of title is clean. You must pay an entertain-ment lawyer to review your paperwork and write the letter. If you didn't have a lawyer during production and you cobbled together contracts from the internet, that's when flaws show up. The cost for a chain-of-title re-view and opinion can run as much as a few thousand dollars (estimated $3,000–$5,000 just for the legal work). You can't do chain of title review and opinion yourself, unfortunately.

A strong chain of title makes your film a legitimate, sellable asset. A weak one is a lawsuit waiting to happen. Don't guess. Lock it down early and thoroughly.

We've seen projects fall apart—not during development or financing—but right before production, with real money on the table, A-list actors attached, and a greenlight within reach.

One of the worst examples was a big, broad A-list comedy. A well-known executive producer handed Kirk the script over lunch in Toronto and said, "This is the one." And for a while, it was. Within weeks, Kirk had two A-list actors attached and a fully committed investor ready to finance the entire film. He was flying between LA and the investor's city, with meetings scheduled and a January shoot on the horizon.

Then came the cracks: delays around budget sign offs, confusion over who the lead producer was, posturing over credits, and the biggest red flag of all: the director didn't have rights to the script. Whenever asked about the chain of title, he dodged the question. Eventually, it came out that the writer hadn't signed anything—no option agreement. No contract. Nothing. The A-listers backed off. The project slowed down. The window closed. The movie never happened.

A year earlier, it happened again on a prestige drama. We had a major actor excited to take on the lead. However, when we requested the chain of title from the producer, it took four months of stalling. When the paperwork finally arrived, it was a one-page letter of intent dated the night before. LOIs are non-binding. It confirmed what Kirk feared: they were bluffing. And years later, that same actor did a similar film based on the same public domain source material, but with a different script.

Don't trust handshake deals, even with your best friend. If you don't legally control the script, you don't control the project. That's when investors, actors, and distributors vanish. Get it in writing. Get it early. No paper, no movie.

A clean chain of title means no gaps in the record. At minimum, it should include:

- Copyright registration for your script and film

- Writer agreements granting you rights, even if you're the writer yourself

- Co-writer or story contributor agreements

- Option or purchase agreements (if based on someone else's work)

- Actor and crew contracts, talent releases, and work-for-hire clauses

- Location releases, music licenses, and any other IP clearances

By the time you're done, your chain of title folder might include dozens of documents. It's a lot, but don't panic. If you've been following along and doing the contracts covered earlier, you're already building it piece by piece.

Why does this matter so much? Before a film is sold, buyers want assurance that no one will pop out of the woodwork claiming, "Hey, that's my footage/music/story/face!" If you can't prove you own the film, you effectively don't in the eyes of the industry. Imagine spending years making a film only to discover you can't release it because a co-writer never signed over character rights. Or a documentary subject changes their mind and sues because you didn't get a life-rights agreement. One missing document can derail everything.

Here's a common scenario: You adapt a short story by a friend. The film is great; festivals love it, and a distributor is interested. During due diligence, they ask, "Do you have the rights in writing?" You say, "Uh... my friend said it was cool in an email." Deal killer. A simple rights agreement upfront would have saved you. Or your editor drops in a funny viral YouTube clip. You forget about it. That clip belongs to someone else. Without a license or rock-solid fair use defense (more on that later), that 5-second joke could wreck your chain of title.

The goal is zero questions and zero loose ends. When it's time to deliver your film, you should be able to hand over a clean PDF bundle showing every link in the chain. Distributors often require a chain of title affidavit or opinion letter from an attorney confirming you own all necessary rights. You can't get that letter without having all the documents anyway.

In short, if Contracts 101 is about getting people to sign, chain of title is about organizing those signed papers to prove your ownership. Start a folder—physical *and* digital—and save everything; every release, license, agreement, and registration receipt. Think of it as an insurance policy for your film's future.

Title Report

This is slightly different but related. It means checking that your film's title doesn't infringe on another title. You can't copyright a title, but you can trademark and wordmark it, and even without those, if your title is too similar to a famous one, it could cause confusion or legal claims. Distributors often ask for a title report, a search to ensure your film's name won't trigger a lawsuit. For example, if you call your movie *The Fast and the Furious: Dallas Drift*, you'll hear from Universal's lawyers. *Star Wars Within* would attract a letter from Lucasfilm because of the famous words in the title. If you have a working title that conflicts, be flexible to change it. You don't want your film held up because of a title dispute at the last minute.

In summary, a chain of title = prove it or lose it. Keep it clean and you'll sail through this part when opportunity knocks. Overlook it, and your film could sit on a shelf indefinitely while you scramble to fix the paperwork, which, trust us, is ten times harder after the fact. Get it in order now; in the future, you (and your distributor) will be eternally grateful.

The Copyright Report: The Overlooked Twin of the Title Report

A copyright report is a formal, third-party search that verifies that your film, or any elements within it, does not infringe on existing registered works. It's essentially a deep dive into the U.S. Copyright Office and sometimes international databases to ensure that no one else already holds rights to something you're using. That includes titles, music, artwork, footage, and even the name of your movie. Check local laws if you live outside of the United States.

It's not about whether you think you came up with everything. It's about whether someone else has registered something similar enough to cause a legal nightmare.

Distributors, sales agents, and especially E&O insurance providers love to ask for this report because they hold the legal bag if something goes wrong after release.

What It Covers

- Conflicts with your film's title (there are rules about this)

- Existing registered characters or storylines

- Unlicensed source material or adaptations

- Any third-party materials embedded in your project (stock footage, graphics, etc.)

- Even your business name or logo, if used in connection with the film

When You Need It

You should commission a copyright report:

- Before you go to market

- Before applying for E&O insurance

- Before signing distribution agreements

- Especially if your film has any commercial exposure

Who Performs It

It's typically conducted by specialized legal clearance firms or entertainment law offices with access to copyright databases and the experience to flag possible infringements. This is not a DIY Google search. Spend the money.

Put It in Writing, or It Doesn't Exist

That's the legal mantra. It might feel overkill when you're running on passion and cold pizza, but every signature you gather is one less worry later. When everyone knows the deal, there's nothing to fight about later. So, do your future self a favor: get those agreements signed before anything happens. Contracts aren't about mistrust; they're about clarity. A friend of Roger's once said, "Contracts help friends remain friends."

E&O Insurance

We discussed Errors and Omissions insurance in the last chapter. No indie filmmaker ever got excited about buying E&O insurance, but it's a necessary evil if you want your film widely distributed. Many distribution deals have been delayed or nearly killed because the filmmaker looked like a deer in headlights by this requirement and tried to avoid it. Budget for it, shop around and get quotes. Some insurers specialize in indie films, have decent rates, and treat it like a standard part of finishing a movie. After all, you insure your car or home, hoping never to need it; the same goes for E&O; you hope no one ever sues, but if they do, you'll be quite happy that you have a policy.

Fair Use: Not a Magic Wand

Ah, fair use – that mystical, oft-misunderstood concept that many creators invoke like a spell in a vain attempt to ward off legal responsibility. Fair use is not a magic wand you can wave to stop people from suing you[2]. It's more like a *potential* defense shield that may or may not hold up when someone throws a fireball at you. In other words, just claiming "fair use" doesn't immunize you from legal trouble. Even if you genuinely believe your use of copyrighted material is fair, you can still get dragged into court and have to prove it, at great expense.

Fair use, in U.S. law, allows you to use limited portions of copyrighted material without permission under certain conditions, typically for purposes like commentary, criticism, news reporting, education, or parody. It's analyzed using four factors: Purpose of use, nature of the work, amount used, and effect on the market for the original. But fair use is subjective and decided on a case-by-case basis, usually by a judge in court while you're being sued. There's no easy formula like "under 30 seconds is automatically fair." That's a myth. (We should have added that to the 2nd chapter. Maybe in the next printing.) There's no official fair use license you obtain; you use the material and hope it qualifies. It's a risk calculation.

For example, you're making a documentary and including a 15-second clip from a TV newscast to provide historical context. That could be fair use, especially if you're commenting on or analyzing the clip. Documentaries do this often. Or maybe you have a scene in your narrative film where characters briefly sing a line from a famous song as a joke. That could be fair use as a parody or incidental use. However, the content owner might disagree and send you a cease-and-desist or file a lawsuit. Even if you eventually win on fair use grounds, the legal process could cost you more than a license would have.

So our strong advice: Don't lean on fair use unless you have to, and

---

2   "How to Legally (and Genuinely) Use Other People's Content in Your Own" Pat Flynn 8/2/2022 SmartPassiveIncome.com

involve a lawyer when you do. An experienced entertainment or clearance attorney can analyze your scenario and give an opinion on whether it's likely to be fair use. They might suggest tweaks to strengthen the fair use argument, such as adding commentary or using less of the clip. And, as mentioned earlier, if you're going for distribution, an insurer or distributor will often require a formal Fair Use Opinion Letter from a lawyer if any unlicensed material is in your film. This letter says, "In my professional opinion as an attorney, this usage should be considered fair use." It's not a guarantee, but it satisfies insurers that you did due diligence.

A common pitfall is thinking that fair use is a blanket exemption. For instance, some filmmakers think, "Well, I'm not making money off this film (yet), so it's fair use," or "It's under 10% of the source material, so it's fair." Nope. Non-commercial use can help your fair use argument, but if you later monetize the film, that changes. And there's no 10% rule; context matters more. Others say, "I'm adding commentary, so it's automatically fair use." Adding commentary helps, but what if you still used too much of the original or the heart of it? It's tricky.

Another scenario: You include copyrighted music in a scene because it played in the background during filming (e.g., the radio was on during a take). You might think it's background noise, so it's fair use. That's usually not fair use; that's "you failed to turn off the radio and now captured music you don't have rights to." There are ways to handle that with re-dubbing audio, getting a license, stripping it with AI tools (although AI sound cleaning tools are not 100%), or arguing it's de minimis if it's super faint, but ignoring it is dangerous.

Fair use is often invoked in documentaries and video essays criticizing the media. Satirical films that riff on pop culture clips use it. But even big companies sometimes err on the side of caution. Do you ever notice that biopics or docs sometimes recreate a famous TV clip rather than use the original? That's because getting sued, even if you might win, is a hassle they'd rather avoid.

If you have unlicensed footage or music and you're thinking of calling it fair use, consider the worst case: you get sued by a giant corporation with lots of lawyers. They can outspend you easily. Even if you are 100% in the right, you could go broke winning.

Consult a lawyer when you realize you want to use someone else's material and can't or won't get permission. Get a professional opinion on record. Talk to a clearance attorney if it's a short bit of copyrighted video or audio, and you believe it's crucial and under commentary. They will likely charge a fee for a consultation or that opinion letter, but it's far cheaper than a lawsuit. Also, a lawyer can sometimes negotiate a license for less money than you'd expect, making the whole fair use question moot.

Also, keep in mind that fair use is a U.S. concept. If you plan to distribute globally, other countries have different rules. Some are narrower, and some don't have fair use at all but have something called "fair dealing," which is stricter. Your distributor will consider that, too. They might say, "We don't want to deal with this clip for international distribution; please remove or license it." Again, fair use isn't a bulletproof shield.

In summary: Don't treat fair use as your get-out-of-jail-free card. It's more like a maybe-you-won't-go-to-jail card. If you're not well-versed in the doctrine, get advice from someone who is. Always have Plan B: What will you do if someone challenges it? If the correct answer is, "I'd have to remove the clip or pay up," maybe do that now instead of gambling. We're not saying never use fair use; some films must include third-party material to tell the story. For example, a doc about the history of *Star Wars* has to show clips, or it's pointless. Just be thoughtful and cautious. Or, as we like to say, fair use is a shield to use carefully, not a sword to swing wildly.

Guild Compliance

Navigating the Union Maze

You might think, "Unions? My film's so indie it's just me and my friends—do I need to worry?" The answer: maybe. And you should at least understand the basics. You must play by guild rules, even on a micro-budget, if you work with union members, such as a SAG-AFTRA actor, WGA writer, DGA director, or IATSE crew.

SAG-AFTRA (Actors)

This is the guild most indie filmmakers will face, especially if you want to cast a recognizable actor or a friend who happens to be in a union. SAG-AFTRA offers low-budget agreements, from Micro-Budget to Modified Low, designed for indie productions. These deals make it feasible to become a SAG signatory, even on a small scale. SAG Indie exists specifically to help you through it.

But you can't go rogue. If you use a SAG actor "off the card"—meaning without filing the proper union paperwork—you put both yourself and the actor at risk. Unless the actor is not a full SAG-AFTRA member and has formally registered as Financial Core (Fi-Core), they cannot work on non-union projects. SAG's Global Rule One strictly forbids members from accepting non-union work. If they're caught, they can face fines, suspension, or expulsion. That's why most SAG actors won't touch your project unless it's officially signed with the union.

Submit paperwork, agree to minimum rates or deferred pay under specific agreements, follow labor rules like breaks and meals, and possibly post a refundable deposit to guarantee payment. All cast, union or not, must be listed on SAG reports. You may also need to contribute to health and pension funds based on payments made.

Where this matters most is distribution. If your film includes SAG actors, you'll need:

- A letter of compliance

- Final cast list

- A Distributor's Assumption Agreement.

You will sign the DAA if your distributor will not, but they may still agree to pay residual obligations. Many distributors, especially in the indie and ULB space, have policies against signing a DAA—but will still service residuals for you. This can include ongoing payments, residual tracking, and even set-up fees required to establish your residuals account with the union.

SAG considers the producer liable until a distributor formally assumes those obligations in writing. Without that written assumption, SAG can place a lien on your film to enforce payment. So plan ahead. If your distributor refuses to sign the DAA, make sure you have a binding clause in your distribution agreement that requires them to handle all residuals administration. Without that safety net, you could face unexpected costs—or worse, delays in your film's release.

Pro Tip: **When Your Distributor Won't Sign the DAA**

Some distributors—especially in the indie and Ultra Low Budget (ULB) space—have strict policies against signing SAG-AFTRA's Distribution Assumption Agreement (DAA), even for wide release projects. This isn't personal; it's a legal and risk-management choice.

If you hit that wall, you can still protect yourself and satisfy

SAG:

• Negotiate residual servicing into your distribution agreement. Require the distributor to process and pay residuals, track obligations, and cover union set-up fees—just like a payroll house would.

• Keep yourself off the default list. Structure the deal so you aren't placed in SAG default status if the picture hasn't recouped.

• As the producer, you can still sign the DAA yourself. The distributor handles the payments, but you remain the official signatory with SAG, keeping the release moving forward.

This hybrid approach gives SAG the assurance it needs, keeps your distributor happy, and avoids last-minute legal roadblocks. Always get the servicing terms in writing inside your distribution contract.

If you did not use SAG actors, you're mostly off the hook but still be ready to provide written proof that no union performers were involved. Some distributors require this as a deliverable.

WGA (Writers)

If your writer is a WGA member, different rules apply. WGA writers typically only work for signatory companies, but the guild has a low-budget agreement that allows participation in lower-budget indies. You'll need to:

• Contact WGA for the right contract

• Handle writing credits through their process

• Honor any deferred or minimum pay terms

• Plan for possible residuals (especially for TV or international sales)

Most early-stage indies don't involve WGA writers unless you bought a script from a pro or you yourself are WGA. If the guild isn't involved, no action required. But don't slap a WGA logo on your credits unless it's legit.

DGA (Directors)

The Director's Guild is harder for small indies to work with. Unlike SAG, DGA doesn't actively court low-budget projects, although a DGA director will benefit your project if you can work it out. If your director is DGA, and you'll know if they are, you must sign a DGA agreement, likely triggering requirements for hiring DGA crew such as UPMs (unit production managers) and ADs (assistant directors), following turnaround times, and paying residuals.

DGA does have some low-budget tiers, but the minimum budget levels are higher than most micro-indies can handle. If DGA is involved, bring in an entertainment attorney; don't try to wing it.

Most indies will not involve the DGA. But you may trigger their rules if your film grows or brings in a DGA director for reshoots or second unit.

Crew Unions (IATSE and Friends)

While not part of the leading trio, crew unions like IATSE, Teamsters, and the International Brotherhood of Electrical Workers (IBEW) can matter, especially in cities like NYC or LA, where union rules govern who can work in specific locations. Most ultra-low-budget shoots use non-union crew, which is fine. Just don't mis-classify labor by labeling someone as a "volunteer" if they're working full-time—that can violate labor laws. If you bring on a union crew member, expect to meet union pay and benefit standards, including pension, health, and turnaround rules.

Don't Fear the Forms

Think of guild compliance like following a recipe: it's a bit of prep, a few forms, and respect for the craft. Picture your SAG rep as a no-BS teacher; do your homework, and you get a gold star and your film gets to go on the field trip, aka distribution. Cut corners and you might end up with fines, legal trouble, or a blocked release.

Even if you're non-union now, plan with future growth in mind. One day, you might be in one of these guilds and appreciate producers who did things right.

Permits and Clearances

Film Like a Rebel, But Stay Legal

Indie filmmakers often pride themselves on being guerrillas, breaking the rules, and shooting run-and-gun. That energy is awesome until the po-po shows up. Shooting without permits or failing to get necessary clearances can lead to fines, shutdowns, or even arrests. Yes, *arrests*.

Filming without a permit is illegal in places like Los Angeles, where it's been a misdemeanor offense since 2009. The LAPD has arrested producers, confiscated gear, and slapped fines on anyone bold or naive enough to roll without one. Getting hauled off set in cuffs because you thought you could "just grab a few shots" on Hollywood Boulevard is not precisely the kind of behind-the-scenes story you want in your press kit. And it's not just LA.

One night in Minnesota, thank God Kirk had secured a permit... but at 12:01 a.m., chaos erupted. Furious about their generator noise, a local woman had been waiting for hours. When the permit expired, she rushed in and tried to tip 12-foot lights over a cliff, right into a waterfall where the film's actors were swimming. Kirk said, "We struck the set just in time. She knew the law better than most and timed her move down to the minute. We might have ended the night with lawsuits and deep-fried talent if we hadn't been permitted." Get your permits. Always.

Many cities require a film permit for any commercial filming, and yes, if you plan to sell or distribute your film, it's considered commercial, even if you're not making money yet. New York City, for instance, has specific rules. You might be okay without a permit if it's just a camera on sticks and a small crew, but you need one when you have props and equipment or are asserting control of public space. Other cities have small permit fees for indies. Chicago has a discount permit for indie/student projects, for example. The process usually involves showing proof of insurance and agreeing to specific guidelines like not blocking traffic without permission, noise limits, etc.

Shooting in the Wild: When the Town Has No Idea What a Film Permit Is

So, you've scouted the perfect small town for your indie masterpiece. Quaint streets. Rustic barns. Zero parking meters. You call the city office to ask about a film permit... and they say, "A what?"

In small-town America, filmmaking isn't exactly a weekly event, but just because a place doesn't require a formal "film permit" doesn't mean free sailing. You still need to engage the right people and do your homework because even the most chill town can come after you with pitchforks if you block traffic or run a generator outside someone's house at 2 a.m.

Cities and towns that don't require formal film permits are often the easiest to overlook but the hardest to manage when things go pear-shaped. Do the due diligence. Be respectful. Communicate clearly. You're not just representing your production; you're laying the groundwork for the next filmmaker who comes through.

Act like a pro, even when no one's asking you to.

And hey—if you leave a good impression, you might find yourself in a quiet, affordable location that welcomes you back next time with open arms and coffee.

What exactly is a film permit?

A film permit is an official approval from a local authority that lets you shoot in public spaces like streets, parks, sidewalks or private property that affects the public, like loud generators or nighttime lighting. It usually involves notifying local police or film offices about when and where you're shooting. Permits often come with conditions: you might need to hire off-duty officers for traffic control or notify nearby residents with flyers. Think of it as a contract; you agree to specific terms, and in return, you get to film without interference.

Yeah, we get it. Most indie filmmakers have done a stealth shoot; grabbing a quick scene on a subway or sneaking a shot on a busy street. You can get away with it if you're small, fast, and lucky. But know when you're likely to get flagged:

- **Visible gear**: Tripods, lights, booms, or reflectors scream "film shoot" and attract attention. A phone? Probably fine. A RED on a dolly? Uh, no.

- **Public alarm:** Prop guns, fake violence, chase scenes— anything that might trigger a 911 call is a hard no without a permit and police coordination. Real cops have shot people with fake guns.

- **Obstruction:** Blocking traffic or sidewalks—even with a tiny crew—can result in complaints and shutdowns.

- **Sensitive locations:** National parks, government buildings, and transit hubs require permits. One filmmaker was fined

(and nearly jailed) for shooting in a national park without one
after the footage was monetized.

One filmmaker challenged national park permit rules as
unconstitutional. He lost. The ruling clarified that you need
a permit to shoot commercially on federal land, even a
monetized YouTube video. There are no exceptions. Uncle
Sam will fine you, and jail is on the table.

Get the permit if you're drawing attention, blocking anything, or staging anything risky. It's cheaper than a fine, safer than a lawsuit, and less
stressful than explaining yourself in cuffs.

If someone on your set screws up and damages property, or a neighbor
gets upset with noise, authorities will be involved and ask for your permit.
No permit could mean immediate shutdown and a fine.

Sure, permits sound like a hassle, as do forms, fees, and red tape. But
many cities want filmmakers and are indie-friendly. Places like Austin,
Texas, or Portland, Oregon, often keep costs low or waive them entirely for
student or ultra-low-budget projects. The key is to contact the film office
early, be honest about your shoot, and stay professional. They might say,
"You don't even need a permit for that," or "Just pay $50 and carry this
document." Then, if a cop shows up, you flash the permit and keep rolling.

Production Insurance

Most film permits require general liability insurance (not to be con-
fused with Errors & Omissions). A $1 million policy is standard. Short-
term policies are available; some cities offer blanket coverage for small productions. But if you can't afford basic insurance, you shouldn't be staging
risky public stunts.

> *Pro tip:* Team up with a nonprofit or school. They may be able
> to extend their coverage to your shoot or secure the permit

under their name.

Clearances (Beyond Permits)

This is about content, what ends up in your frame.

- **Brands & Logos:** If you film in public and catch posters, artwork, or logos in the background, it's usually fine unless the brand is shown negatively or looks like an endorsement. Still, some filmmakers blur or avoid trademarks altogether just to be safe.

- **Example:** Shoot a gritty scene outside a Coffee Bean and Tea Leaf and someone gets shot—yeah, they'll have a problem with that. Technically, visible brands fall under your chain of title, and a Coffee Bean and Tea Leaf logo could be considered product use or even trademark infringement depending on the context. Distributors and insurers may ask whether you've cleared all visible brands, especially if they're shown in a negative or controversial light. When in doubt, blur it or get permission.

Artwork

- Paintings, posters, and prints—even inside someone's home—are usually copyrighted.

- You'll need to either:
    - ✓ Get written clearance from the artist or rights holder,
    - ✓ Or blur it in post.

- Museums and galleries almost always require permission to film any displayed art.

- Even documentaries have had to blur artwork when they

couldn't secure rights.

People in the Background

- If you're filming in a public space, you generally don't need releases from passersby who appear incidentally.

- But you should get a signed release if someone is recognizable, featured, or identifiable.

- **Best practice:** Post visible signs saying, "By entering this area, you consent to being filmed." Reality shows use this all the time. It's not foolproof, but it helps.

- Interviewing someone on the street? Always get a release.

- The legal concern here is the right of publicity, especially for private individuals. Crowd shots? Usually fine. Solo FaceTime? Get the paperwork.

Permits for special cases

If you're using a drone to film in the United States, you must follow FAA regulations. Often, those are local rules. That means you'll need a Part 107 licensed drone operator and FAA clearance to fly for any commercial purpose within U.S. airspace. If your film is intended for a paying audience, it's considered commercial use, no matter how indie your production feels. You may need Part 107 certification for flying in certain restricted areas, regardless of whether the shoot is for commercial purposes or recreational. Drone shots without proper certs can lead to fines. If you live outside of the U.S., check your country's requirements for drone use.

Animals

Know the rules for working with animals, especially wild ones, or doing significant animal action. The "No animals were harmed" credit isn't automatic. You must invite the American Humane Association (AHA) to monitor the shoot. Some locations also require special permits for animal use. Check early, and don't wing it.

Locations

For every scene, ask: Is this public or private property?

- **Private?** Get a signed location release.

- **Public?** You may need a permit.

A low-key shoot—say, two people talking in a park with a hand held camera—might slip by. But getting a permit is smart once you add lights, tripods, or attention-drawing setups.

The point is that a single disgruntled neighbor can derail the mood—and possibly the permit. So, get out of it. Be polite. Be prepared. And understand that some people want leverage.

If You Insist on Going Guerrilla

If you can't afford a permit and want to go rogue (and we strongly advise against that), be smart about it.

- **Have a plan.** If approached by authorities, be respectful, apologize, and walk away if necessary. Arguing escalates the problem.

- **Know the risk.** If caught mid-scene, your footage could be unusable, or worse, confiscated.

- **Have a safety plan.** Permits exist for safety, too. Even if you're guerrilla shooting, brief your crew, check your surroundings, and make sure you're not accidentally trespassing.

- **Choose your time wisely.** Early mornings and late nights have fewer bystanders, but watch your noise levels. Night complaints can shut you down fast.

Fun fact: Robert Rodriguez shot *El Mariachi* without permits and nearly got busted more than once. His advice is be fast: get the shot and get out. That might have worked then, but today's world, post-9/11, full of phone-wielding bystanders, going guerrilla comes with new levels of risk. People call the cops on anything suspicious.

The Takeaway

Permits and clearances are protection. Getting shut down mid-shoot kills morale. Getting fined or dragged into court is worse. A little planning can save your film and your sanity. You don't have to abandon your indie spirit; you must respect the game. Consider permits as creative constraints, not creativity killers.

No one wants their filmmaking story to end with "...and then we got arrested."

Save the drama for the screen, not the courtroom.

Chapter
NINE

So... You Wanna Produce?

"With great power comes great responsibility."

— Uncle Ben, *Spider-Man* (2002)

This chapter does two things. First, it unpacks what a capital "P" Producer, the Big Cheese, truly means; a ton of responsibility most underestimate. Second, it aims to scare you off slapping "producer" on your title and risking someone else's money without knowing how to pull it off. We have decades of scars shouting this warning, so ignore it at your peril.

If you want to step in as a producer, let's demystify the role. The Producers Guild of America (PGA) defines a producer as someone who makes regular, continuous, and substantial decisions regarding production, budgetary, and legal concerns across all stages of production, from development to post-production and marketing, and who is primarily responsible for managing a project's production and delivery. In other words, the producer ensures that the movie, in the director's head or the writer's script, becomes a reality on screen. That involves everything from hiring the team to managing SAG agreements, scheduling and budgeting, handling crises, and overseeing distribution. If that sounds like a lot, it is. On the professional level, producing is not a fresh-out-of-film-school position. It requires creativity, business savvy, people skills, industry relationships, thick skin, a deep commitment, and experience.

Why do so many people call themselves producers when they have little to no experience in the role? And why do so many new filmmakers think they will "roll up their sleeves and figure it out as they go?" Brain surgeons don't have this dilemma. No one pitches them their best ideas. "Hey Doc, I have some lobotomy ideas; lemme take a whack at this. I've read a couple of books and watched a YouTube video, so... yeah, take the day off." Of course, no one would dare suggest this to a Neurosurgeon because it's so outlandishly silly. But why, then, with no experience, would you try to produce a film with an investor's money involved if you've never done it before? We're asking you especially, the writer-director or actor who "wants to get it done."

If you jump into the producer's role without real experience, you'll quickly discover how much you don't know. A commercial producer with over a decade of ad work came to us to co-produce his first feature. He had solid credentials in that world but no clue how narrative filmmaking works. He assumed producing a commercial was the same thing. It's not.

He didn't understand the chain of title, had never dealt with deliverables, didn't realize casting impacts foreign pre-sale estimates, and had zero grasp of how to develop a film for recoupment and investor profit. He was used to handing off a polished 30-second spot to an agency, not defending a $500,000 investment to backers who want a return on their money or at least not lose it.

Instead of focusing on the business mechanics, he obsessed over gear and "cool stuff." He was excited about shooting on RED, scoring a free jib arm, and getting a discount on a virtual wall studio. The film looked decent and had a couple of semi-recognizable actors. However, the script had core issues that the investor-writer refused to fix. The producer didn't care. "My client gave me the money, and it's their script—let's just make it and have fun." Translation: I'm here to pad my resume.

The film flopped, and now that producer will struggle to get another shot. It may recoup some money eventually, but the odds are slim. The cake is baked.

Why the fail? Because he misunderstood the job. He thought producing meant assembling gear and hiring a crew. He missed everything else; the market, the strategy, the recoupment path, and stopping a weak script from going to the camera.

Look, we've been there; sometimes, you follow the money. But if the person steering the ship doesn't know how to build a product that sells, you're all but ensuring an unprofitable film, and your reputation will be on the line as well.

The Many Hats of an Indie Producer

On a typical independent film, a producer might fill multiple roles. On paper, titles such as Executive Producer, Line Producer, and Associate Producer are outlined in Mistake #9 of Chapter Three. Still, none of these roles qualify for the "Produced by" credit. Here are the key tasks you'll handle or supervise as a producer:

Development

If you're the writer or already have a script, development means refining it until it's bulletproof, not "my friends think it's great." Get professional script coverage. Three separate critiques will reveal patterns like structural issues, flat arcs, and pacing problems. A quick online search will turn up plenty of professional script coverage services. And when the notes come in, don't take them personally. You paid for the truth, not a pat on the back.

Feedback isn't there to feed your ego; it's there to fix your story.

Development means finding a concept worth betting on if you're not the writer. Maybe it's a book or a true story, but if an author pitches their novel, your first question should be: "How many copies have you sold?" Nine times out of ten, the answer is, "Not many, I just published it." Translation: no audience.

No built-in audience means no built-in value unless the story is extraordinary enough to stand alone, which is rare. A bestseller with buzz gives you leverage if you can convince the author to license the rights to you. The same goes for life rights: A guy who rescued a child on national news has momentum. The hermit in the woods who found inner peace might be inspiring, but it's hard to sell.

Often, development means working with a writer to option, refine, or commission a script. Your job is to find a great story, but it must be a story that has a solid marketing hook and one you can make. A brilliant, high-concept epic might read like a hit, but if it needs a $100 million VFX budget, you're chasing fantasies.

That's why so many festival-winning scripts never get produced; they're brilliant but difficult or impossible to shoot. A one-location thriller is straightforward from a logistics perspective. The story might be complex, but the UPM will love it. Smart producers develop with logistics in mind from the start. Every location adds cost, complexity, and risk: Fewer locations = fewer chances to crash and burn.

You're in for a reality check if you've never planned a ten-hour day with twelve pages of dialogue and a company move at lunch. Even on a pre-lit sound stage, shooting twelve script pages a day is demanding. Add camera builds, lighting tweaks, wardrobe changes, setup changes, holding the roll until a dog quits barking, striking locations, a cross-town move, and pray the grip truck doesn't break down. It's a time bomb. And even with flawless planning, the first frame usually rolls 90 minutes after call time. That leaves 8.5 hours to shoot. You can go over but kill crew morale with overtime often enough, and you will quickly lose the respect of your team.

Script decisions are location decisions. You survive production by simplifying it in development.

Financing

Arguably, financing movies is the producer's most misunderstood role in filmmaking. Usually, that's the Executive Producer's world. This brings us to a critical point: define the roles.

A single film can have anywhere from 13 to 50 people with "producer" in their title; Executive Producer, Co-Producer, Line Producer, Associate Producer, or some custom-made title you invent to keep someone happy. The screen credit doesn't matter nearly as much as the responsibility behind it.

What does matter is who is actually in charge.

So, as an indie filmmaker, if you're the "*Produced By*" producer—the lead producer driving the project—you'll almost certainly spearhead the fundraising. Not a hired gun, *you*. It's a common misconception that hiring a producer means they'll magically secure funding. Most for-hire producers are focused on raising money for their slates and likely won't be incentivized to do it for you. Fundraising is your job. That said, an experienced producer can boost your credibility, which helps when pitching investors. They often have sharper instincts for high-net-worth conversations and may even speak directly to your investors to help close the deal.

Another common myth is that someone with an Executive Producer (EP) credit will ride in with a bag of money. Maybe. Maybe not. The EP title is broad. It's often given to someone who writes a check, introduces an investor, or helps unlock access to funding. It doesn't mean they're running the show. EPs don't typically handle development, logistics, production, or deliverables. That's the lead producer's job. Your job. You're holding the reins. Raising money is your job unless you explicitly bring someone on to do it, and even then, you're still the one accountable. You'll pitch investors, explain the recoupment waterfall, and defend the creative choices that make the film marketable.

Film is a director's medium, but the lead producer is the engine behind the entire machine, from concept to cash flow to release.

Titles are cheap. Accountability is not.

This misconception that producers automatically come with money is so prevalent that it seems to be embedded in the DNA of most filmmakers, so let's put this to rest once and for all. A huge frustration for us is devoting time to discussing with filmmakers how we add tremendous value to their film and manage it across its entire lifespan, only to hear, "Hey, we've got our money, so we don't need you." They still needed a seasoned, capital "P" Producer, not just a line producer, to help manage the enormity of turning their film into a marketable product. Still, because they dismissed us from the producing role after securing funding, the unspoken message was that they only expected us to raise money for them. The reason we were in talks in the first place somehow escapes them.

And then, their film fails.

> *Pro Tip:* Be very careful with finder's fees. In the United States, offering someone a percentage or commission for introducing an investor or helping you raise money is illegal unless that person is a registered broker-dealer. The SEC (Securities and Exchange Commission) has strict rules: Only licensed brokers can legally take a cut of raised funds. If you pay someone a "finder's fee" without proper licensing, you could invalidate your entire financing structure, and it could bite you during

due diligence, distribution, or in court.

Even worse, if your investors lose money, they could claim the raise was illegal and demand their investment back, and the SEC will enforce that call. That puts you, your company, and the film's rights, at risk.

If someone helps connect you to an investor, thank them. Give them a producer credit. Buy them a nice dinner. But unless they're properly licensed, don't promise or pay them a percentage of the raise. Always consult an attorney when structuring deals involving someone else's money.

Funding sources vary, including private investors, crowdfunding, which builds awareness, grants, especially for docs and cause-driven films, pre-sales, co-productions, tax credit loans, product placement, or friends and family. The rule is the same for all industries: Investors back people *first*, ideas *second*. They want to know you have the team, the plan, and the skills to execute.

To earn that trust, remember:

1. You must demonstrate that you know what you're doing.

2. You must demonstrate a clear pathway to profitability.

Start with a modest budget. Build a high-concept story that travels well with manageable production logistics. Leverage state incentives. Show them you've thought it through.

Know that you'll spend more time pitching than shooting. You'll feel like a blend of entrepreneur, evangelist, and salesman. And that's okay. Without the money, nothing else happens.

Great indie producers are the ones who find creative ways to stretch dollars and source capital. If finance isn't your strength, partner with someone who thrives in that lane because "I hate finance stuff" is not a valid excuse for losing other people's money.

Pre-Production (Planning and Team Building)

Pre-production can begin once a meaningful portion of the money is in place; not all of it, but enough to get moving. As a producer, you are the project manager. That means hiring key crew alongside the director, often starting with a line producer or production manager to help shape the budget and shooting schedule.

You'll coordinate hiring department heads: cinematographer, production designer, editor, and more. You'll oversee casting by hiring a casting director or running auditions yourself. Location scouting will likely fall on your plate, including securing permits and negotiating deals once locations are selected. You'll also handle insurance, which is non-negotiable; one accident can bankrupt your project and maybe you personally. You'll set up the production entity (usually an LLC in the US), open a bank account, and manage the flow of funds.

Bottom line, your job is to build the system that lets everyone else do their jobs.

The complete pre-production workload means locking the schedule, often with an assistant director (AD) or line producer creating a day-out-of-days schedule (DOOD) and stripboard, finalizing a department-by-department budget, securing locations, arranging travel or housing, and prepping cast with table reads or rehearsals. You'll rent gear, assign call times, and hold production meetings. Communication becomes your superpower; checklists, calendars, updates. Your job is to make sure no one's guessing. If unions, such as SAG, are represented on set, you'll be navigating their paperwork and keeping the production compliant to appropriate guild rules.

By the time cameras roll, you should be able to confidently answer questions like, "Where's Scene 42 being shot? Who's bringing the police uniforms? Do we have a permit for that alley?"

If not, you're not ready.

Managing the Budget (and Saying "No" When Necessary)

Budget control is one of your most critical responsibilities during pre-production and well beyond. You are the guardian of money. That means tracking every dollar and making tough calls. If the director wants a Jimmy Jib or an extra shoot day that isn't budgeted, you'll have to say, "We can't afford it," cut something else, or find more cash.

If you're also the director, objectivity becomes harder to maintain. That's where creative problem-solving comes in. As lead producer, you should know the script inside and out. Your value often lies in creatively solving financial issues with smart script adjustments that preserve the scene's intent. Ask first: "What is the purpose of this scene?" Clarity here opens the door to cost-effective solutions.

Can't afford a rain machine? Cheat it with sound design and a quick exterior shot from stock footage. Or make rain with a firetruck. Reach out to your local fire department. Some are open to helping low-budget productions if you're respectful and file the correct paperwork.

In indie filmmaking, spending less while still getting what you need is a priority. Savings can buy you an extra day or a cushion for the inevitable emergency. Treat every dollar as sacred. Will the audience or investors notice if someone wants to blow 10% of your $50K budget on a fancy camera rig? Or would that money be better spent on marketing or an experienced AD who keeps the shoot from derailing? A $50K film can be shot on a DSLR and the results look solid in the right hands. Unless someone offers you a high-end rig for free, don't blow your cash by chasing gear envy. Rookie filmmakers often splurge on the wrong things and then run out of money for post. Your job as a producer is to prevent that from happening.

Scripts often carry dead weight—lines, moments, or setups that seem essential in writing but don't serve the story. Writers and directors may miss it because their attention is elsewhere. You can't afford to.

Kirk tells a story from a consulting gig where he found seven separate moments in the script: "A car drives up to the house. Someone gets out. Walks to the door. Knocks." Why? Just cut to: Knock knock. "Hi, what took you so long?" "You know me, I'm a slow driver." You don't need to show everything, especially not seven times.

Roger learned this lesson with Della Reese on *Meant to Be.* Della was one of those actors who had the ability to memorize lines on the spot, scene by scene—an incredible talent. But that skill was challenged when it came time to shoot an extended scene with too much dialogue. When Roger suggested posting her lines with cue cards, Della wouldn't have it. So, Roger and producer Bradley Dorsey worked with the dialogue to cut her lengthy monologue down to its essence.

The lesson was hammered home on *Taken by Grace.* Angus McFadyen had a scene with way too much dialogue. The crew taped the sides in his eye line, but in the end, most of the scene was deleted in post. It was a waste of time and money. Learn to trim before you roll.

Production (The Shoot) – Field General & Problem Solver:

When cameras finally roll, your job as a producer shifts into full-on crisis management. Ideally, you handled most logistics during pre-production: crew hired, schedules locked, locations confirmed, but once you're on set, reality mocks your plans with casual glee. Every day will bring problems, and everyone will look at you for answers.

If an actor calls out sick, you reschedule. If a location falls through, you sweet-talk the owner or find a new one. If the crew is behind, you cut shots with the director, negotiate overtime (if budget allows), or bribe the team with a Starbucks run. You are the air traffic controller, keeping the production from face-planting in the dirt.

Your job is leadership, not just logistics. Keep the cast and crew fed, hydrated, and sane. Enforce safety. No shot is worth an injury, or worse. Dealing with guests, investors dropping by, or local media sniffing around. The director stays focused on the film. You handle everything else.

If you have an assistant director, and you should, they run the set. You back them up, protect the schedule, and adjust the plan when it breaks.

Expect 12+ hour days of putting out fires, hopefully not literal, while juggling questions like, "Where's the fake blood? Did we pay for the hotel? Why are we out of water bottles?" It's stressful, intense, and unforgiving.

But if you do your prep right, production becomes less about panic and more about pivoting. And *if* the plan works... That's victory.

Post-Production Oversight

Once the shoot wraps, celebrate, throw a wrap party, and take a breath. But the job is far from over. Post is where the truth shows up. You either shape a film that works, or realize what you didn't get. As the producer, you're still on the hook: managing the post schedule, budget, team, and deliverables.

Suppose you hired an editor, someone other than yourself. That's great, but consider bringing on a post supervisor or post-co-producer, someone who handles logistics and finances in the post the way your line producer did on set. You still oversee everything. Keep the timeline moving. Nothing slips. One of the biggest indie mistakes is relaxing after the shoot and letting post drag on for months or even years. Not on your watch.

Create a clear post-plan: Start and end dates for editing, deadlines for picture lock, music, sound design, color, etc. You'll be hiring or playing the composer, mixer, and colorist roles, and make sure they get done.

Utilize test screenings. Show your rough cut to a small, unbiased audience, people who don't know you and have no reason to lie. Use tools such as SurveyMonkey to ask tough, specific questions about clarity, pacing, and emotional impact. Ask: "Which character did you hate the most, and why?" or "On a scale of 1 to 10, how engaged were you by the second lead's arc? If under 5, what lost you?" Generic questions won't help you re-edit.

In one case, Kirk surveyed 100 random people in a real theater. It was fun and eye-opening and gave him data he could show buyers. In another, feedback about a bloated second act helped him tighten the film. Some filmmakers hate hearing the truth, but it makes their movies better.

If the budget allows, consider hiring an outside PR or marketing firm to conduct your test screenings and analyze results. Real data leads to real improvements.

Budget-wise, make sure you reserve money for post-production. You'll need to back up all media on separate hard drives, do audio mixing (stereo and 5.1, including the correct stems for foreign sales), close captions, quality control, and handle licensing for any music in your film and trailer(s). Didn't get that signature on a release form? Now's the time to track it down.

Also, start thinking about festival submissions. How do deadlines affect picture lock? You'll likely be the one prepping screeners, submitting online, managing tracking spreadsheets, and paying submission fees. Build it into the budget and calendar because the post isn't just editing. It's delivery. And delivery is everything.

Distribution and Marketing (Producer as Salesperson)

Traditionally, producers handed off the finished film to a sales agent or distributor and walked away. That's not how it works in indie filmmaking anymore; not often enough, anyway. Today, innovative indie producers stay in the game through distribution, becoming key players behind their film's release.

That could mean attending film markets, hitting festivals, pitching directly to distributors, and negotiating deals, ideally with an entertainment attorney. But if money's tight, you'll be in those meetings yourself.

But you'll also be instrumental in coordinating the marketing, especially early on. That might include social media, press outreach, trailers, key art, festival PR, and audience engagement. If you have a dedicated marketing or distribution lead, that's amazing. But even then, stay involved. Magnify the reach. Coordinate with your distributor to stay on-message and on-brand.

Brothers in Blues is a great example. Producer Kirby Warnock personally worked to drive the film's visibility. Long after release, he contacted newspapers, TV editors, bloggers, radio stations, and influencers. He had something to say. He knows Jimmie Vaughan and has personal Stevie Ray Vaughan stories from his days as a writer for *Buddy Magazine*. With all that firepower, he became an expert in marketing his film, and it made a huge difference. That level of promotion, if paid for, would've created unmanageable costs for the size of the film. For him, it only took time and hustle.

The takeaway: *Brothers in Blues* is a prime example of how producers can exponentially enhance release strategies. You may not have the same experience as Kirby when promoting your film, but never expect your distributor to do all the work; you'll leave money on the table. This is indie filmmaking. Help your distributor maximize your film's potential. That's smart business.

Producing indie films will test your nerves and reveal some you didn't know you had. It takes grit, vision, and a skill set that spans everything from finance to fire safety. You'll likely work without a paycheck, ride on gut instinct, and hustle until something finally breaks through. It's like joining a band on tour, except you're the roadie, tour manager, bus driver, and bankroller.

We admit it's a lot. That's why we recommend hiring a seasoned producer for the first couple of films you make and why we say don't try this alone. You'll still wear a lot of hats, but you shouldn't try to wear them all.

It's thankless and exhausting but oddly rewarding work. You could have the producer gene if you have the stubborn fire to will a film into existence no matter what.

The Brass Teapot Case Study

One of the smoothest packaging and financing experiences Kirk was on "The Brass Teapot," which he produced, starring Juno Temple. At the time, she wasn't a household name yet, but she was an exciting, up-and-coming actor with momentum. Once she was attached, we put together a package and brought it to Cannes Film Festival—not to screen it, but to shop it. That's an important distinction. People often assume that if you "go to Cannes," it means your film has been selected for competition. The truth is, Cannes is also one of the biggest film markets in the world. Many producers attend not with a finished movie, but with a package they're hoping to pre-sell, promote, and finance. That's exactly what we did.

The strategy worked. With Juno in place, we secured a foreign sales commitment at Cannes that covered roughly a third of our budget. Combined with the New York tax credit—which we knew could be cash-flowed—we suddenly had a financing structure that made the equity piece much easier. It was a textbook example of how debt, incentives, and presales can combine to de-risk a film and give it momentum before a single frame is shot.

From there, our casting choices became just as important as the financing. We decided not to chase one massive "name" actor who might have been too expensive, nor to stack the cast with unknowns who wouldn't move the needle. Instead, we filled out the ensemble with young, up-and-coming actors like Michael Angarano, Alexis Bledel, and Billy Magnussen—people we believed were on the rise and would be more recognizable by the time the movie hit audiences. That approach didn't instantly skyrocket our pre-sales, but it created a wave of momentum. Other actors wanted to join, sales agents liked the energy, and investors could see that the film was stacking up in a smart way.

That's the bigger point: In independent filmmaking, it's not always about one magic ingredient—script, director, or budget. It's about the cocktail. "The Brass Teapot" had a sharp script and a strong and motivated director, but having a curated cast of rising talent gave it the attention that moved things forward. They brought energy to the set, helped us stand out on the festival circuit, and gave the project a "cool factor."

The lesson is: If the big-name star you're dreaming of is out of reach, don't just give up and fill your cast with friends or unknowns. Look for the actors who are about to break out. It's okay to take your time. Be strategic. That can often be smarter than swinging for the biggest name you can't afford, and it can make all the difference in the packaging and financing process.

The *American Herro* Case Study

Kirk recalls a time in his career when he had to take a bigger swing. He had previously done commercials, a few features, some theater, and even sold a *Lewis and Clark* docuseries, but he didn't feel challenged. Then one night, he saw his childhood friend Herro Mustafa, an American-Iraqi Kurd, on television, serving in the George W. Bush administration on the National Security Council, focusing on Middle East affairs. They hadn't spoken for a while, but he sent an email asking, "Would you consider a documentary?" To Kirk's surprise, she replied: "Of course. Come meet me at the White House." He had no budget, no plan, just a gut feeling that this was going to be a great story.

That project became *American Herro*. When Kirk and Herro reunited in

Washington. She agreed to do the project under one bold condition: "Only if you come with me to Kurdistan, Iraq." He had never previously left the continent, let alone considered stepping into a war-torn region. His family thought it was crazy. But Herro's confidence and courage were contagious, and she challenged Kirk to rise to the moment. So, he scraped together his own money, along with financial help from friends and family, and relied on numerous volunteers and a great deal of faith. He even convinced his dad to come with him to Kurdistan (which is probably an entirely different book). What unfolded was not just a film, but an adventure that tested everything Kirk thought he knew about filmmaking, risk, and himself.

Kirk describes countless moments when he wasn't sure they could push forward. "We had almost no budget, endless logistical hurdles, lost footage, and more than once, it felt like the whole thing might collapse." But Herro led with steady conviction, reminding him through her actions what diplomacy, determination, and dedication really look like. That lesson was as valuable as any piece of footage he captured.

Three years later, the film premiered to a sold-out audience at the Kennedy Center in Washington, D.C. Kirk had interviewed Secretary of State Condoleezza Rice, Under Secretary of State Nicholas Burns, and countless members of the Kurdish community. The film appeared on PBS and Netflix back when they still mailed DVDs. They did a few film festivals and were honored by the International Documentary Association with a prestigious award. It didn't make a fortune, but it made Kirk a better filmmaker. From financing to filming to marketing and distribution, they had to do a lot of the work themselves. Who was "They"? Not only Herro and Kirk, but his then business partner Chad Spokely, Kirk's late wife Bryn and many of their families and friends. It was the ultimate team effort.

The film also brought new opportunities. The exposure from the film was humbling. Kirk was invited to speak at schools, conventions, festivals, and events as a keynote speaker. He began receiving offers from other filmmakers and potential investors. Kirk often credits that period as the opportunity to launch Northern Lights Films, which was another phase of his career that helped him level up.

American Herro wasn't as much about financial success as it was about the courage to "greenlight" himself without permission. It was about following intuition, taking the risk, and discovering the rewards that only come when you leap before you think you're fully ready. The film gave him lifelong memories, new friends, and a reminder that this type of work can be rewarding but requires serious long-term commitment.

Rising Above as a Producer

Embrace Ruthless Organization. Spreadsheets, calendars, and task lists are standard kit. Keep meticulous records: cast and crew contacts, budget breakdowns, shooting schedules, call sheets, and contracts. Every cell on a spreadsheet represents something tangible, such as a costume, a location, a meal, that could cause chaos if mishandled. Keeping things organized is your armor against entropy.

Be a communicator. You're managing people. Everyone's looking to you for clarity: Cast, crew, vendors, investors. That means proactive, consistent updates. Don't assume people know things, even if they say they do. Tell them. Keep investors informed. Manage expectations. Be honest when something changes. Listen when someone raises a red flag. When your AD says the schedule is tight, listen to them. Great producers don't bulldoze;

they adjust.

And remember, you are the production's general manager and CEO. You shouldn't do everything yourself, but you do have to know what's going on. You are the decision-maker, the delegator, the cheerleader, the good cop, the bad cop, and the face everyone turns to when the plan falls apart. So be prepared to answer complex questions, solve messy problems, and keep moving.

Know When to Say No (and Yes)

As a producer, you'll constantly field requests for more time, money, and resources. You must know when to put your foot down for the project's health. But also know when to say "yes, let's do it" to support the director's vision in critical moments. It's a balancing act between the practical and the creative. Suppose the director passionately needs an extra hour at a location to get a crucial scene, and you sense it's essential. In that case, you might negotiate overtime and cut something else later. Pick your battles. Protect the film from foolish indulgences, but don't be a penny-pinching tyrant who squashes all creativity. If you're not filling the same roles, you and the director are like partners; build trust such that when you say no, they understand it's for a reason, and when you say yes, they know you moved mountains for them.

Keep Your Eye on the Finish Line

While others focus on their immediate tasks, such as an actor on their performance or a DP on the shot, the producer must keep the whole picture in mind and the end goal; a fully completed film presented to an audience. This means thinking about things like deliverables during production and pre-planning for post-production by noting the pickup shots still needed. You're like the shepherd guiding the project from script to screen. Always ask, "How does this decision affect our ability to finish and sell this film?" That will guide you in making the right calls.

Now, a reality check:

You might be reading all this as a first-time filmmaker or a writer/director who must produce out of necessity. You might be thinking, "This sounds overwhelming. I just wanna make my movie!" It *is* overwhelming if you do it all alone and without forethought. Many do, and many fail. But detailing all these helps you anticipate the responsibilities and either take them on methodically or share the load. If you can, find a producing partner. Many great indie films are born from a director-producer duo where the director focuses on creativity and the producer on logistics/business (e.g., think of partnerships like Darren Aronofsky and producer Scott Franklin or the Coen Brothers, who produce their own stuff but with the help of line producers, etc.). If you don't have a partner, maybe you can recruit a highly organized friend to be a production manager or a business-minded colleague to help with fundraising.

Producing, like any skill, improves with practice. You will make mistakes on your first go, hopefully not the catastrophic ones we warned about in Chapter Three. Learn from them and keep going. Producers often work up the ladder by producing shorts, micro-budget features, bigger features, etc., and building experience and contacts. If this is your first feature, keep it simple with contained locations and a minimal cast. Not only will that make producing manageable, but it'll also make it easier to get made at all. Prove you can deliver a small project, and it'll be easier to attract support for a bigger one next time. For larger projects, it's best to hire a seasoned producer. Not a line producer, but an actual producer.

As this chapter implies, producing requires many skills, a boatload of industry knowledge, and key relationships. Nobody may ever fully appreciate how much you did. When you make it *look* easy, everyone thinks it *was* easy, but that's okay. The results speak for themselves. The skills you gain, such as leadership, negotiation, budgeting, etc., will serve you in all areas of life and future projects. So, if you wanna produce, now you have a clearer sense of what that means.

Building a Sustainable Career in Filmmaking

"Hope is not a strategy."

— Doug Carlin, *Déjà Vu* (2006)

Many newbie filmmakers operate with what some call the Hail Mary mindset: "If I can just make this *one* feature and get it into a big festival, my career is set!" It's the one-shot dream, the addiction to the hope that your film will be the miracle that launches your career into the stratosphere. It's seductive, sure. We all grew up on stories of overnight successes and breakout hits, but banking your future on a single project is like putting your life savings on one spin of the roulette wheel. It's a sucker's bet.

A sustainable career is a marathon, not a sprint.

If you treat your first or any film as the end-all, be-all, you're gambling with terrible odds. The "all or nothing" approach leads to mostly nothing. Even if that one project hits big, and we genuinely hope it does, what's next? Always think several moves ahead. A filmmaker with a career mindset is plotting a trajectory, not a one-time fireworks show.

Shift your perspective to the long game. Instead of asking, "How can this film make me famous?" Ask, "How does this film fit into my 5-, 10-, or 20-year plan as a filmmaker?" This means setting both creative and business goals for the long haul. Maybe your first feature only breaks even financially, but it could help you build relationships with actors or crew who'll join you on future projects. Perhaps it showcases your style and lands you some directing gigs for hire, giving you income and clout to get your next passion project made. Maybe it teaches you invaluable lessons, the kind you don't learn in film school, that save you money on film number two. All of that has immense career value beyond immediate dollars.

It's been said that it takes ten years to become an overnight success. The greats, even the "overnight success" stories, usually have a trail of smaller projects, failures, and learnings behind them. Quentin Tarantino didn't go straight to *Pulp Fiction* without first working in a video store, making a scrappy debut *(Reservoir Dogs)*, and writing scripts for others. Ava DuVernay started in film publicity and produced short documentaries and a micro-budget feature before her breakout. These filmmakers treated each endeavor as part of a continuum, not a one-off gamble.

The long-term mindset also means being okay with incremental progress. Hits don't happen often; not every year will bring an award or a fat paycheck. Some years, you're grinding, planting seeds that don't sprout until much later. That's normal in any career, especially a creative one. If you expect constant explosive success, the first quiet period will shatter your confidence. Instead, view your career like an investment portfolio: you're in it for steady growth, diversifying (more on that later) to weather the downturns, and playing the averages for long-term gain

When you think long-term, something magical happens: You start making smarter decisions. You won't throw your entire budget at flashy gimmicks to get noticed; you'll allocate resources wisely to ensure you can make the next movie. You won't sacrifice your reputation with shady deals or burned bridges because you know you'll work in this industry for decades, and relationships matter. You'll take care of your health and sanity (we'll address burnout in a few pages) because you can't run a marathon on caffeine and adrenaline alone.

Taking the long view turns you from a desperate noob swinging for a home run into a savvy filmmaker consistently hitting singles, doubles, and a few triples. Those add up. You stay in the game and eventually score a home run by combining skill, persistence, and strategy. Plan long-term, not a moment, and you'll get to enjoy many moments over your career.

Diversify Your Creative Hustle

The secret sauce behind many sustainable film careers is diversification. The indie film world rewards those who wear multiple hats and know when to swap 'em. Suppose you're only ever willing to write and direct art house features. In that case, you might find a lot of downtime between passion projects, with years where you're hunting for funding or waiting on festival notifications with no income and growing frustration. The solution is to broaden your skill set and expand how you can work and earn in the film industry.

Think of yourself as a creative entrepreneur with multiple streams of income and experience. Sure, maybe you're a director, but perhaps you're also a writer for hire, a producer on someone else's project, a consultant, an editor, a cinematographer, or even (gasp!) a teacher. Not only can these other roles pay the bills, but they also sharpen your craft and increase your value in the marketplace.

Let's break down some ways to diversify your skills and hustle.

Write

If you have writing chops, consider writing screenplays or punch-ups for others. Many successful directors started as writers. Writing gigs such as feature scripts, TV episodes, web series, or commercials can bring in money and connections. Plus, writing regularly keeps your storytelling muscles in shape, a strength every director needs.

Direct for Hire

Not every directing job has to be your magnum opus. Direct music videos, commercials, short films, TV episodes, web content, or anything that pays you to do what you love in a slightly different flavor. Each format teaches you something. Spike Jonze made innovative music videos before films; many filmmakers do commercials to finance their indie projects. There's value in that game. Work is work; you're leveling up your skills whenever you direct anything.

Produce

Producing *your* film is obvious, especially if you're initiating projects, but try making someone else's film occasionally. If you have a knack for organization or fundraising, it can be both a revenue stream and a way to build credibility. Producing others' projects also expands your network like crazy and earns you goodwill that might be returned when it's your turn behind the camera. It teaches you the nitty-gritty of the business side, including contracts, logistics, dealing with unions, distribution deals, and everything that will inform how you handle your films.

Consult

You can consult or coach other filmmakers if you're knowledgeable in a specific area, maybe story structure, editing, VFX, crowdfunding, film festivals, or whatever. For example, perhaps you've become a whiz at crowdfunding after running three successful campaigns. New filmmakers would pay, or at least barter, for your guidance. Consulting earns extra cash and positions you as an expert, raising your profile.

Mentor/Teach

This might come later in your journey, but teaching a workshop, speaking at panels, or mentoring an up-and-comer can reinforce your knowledge. There's a saying: To teach is to learn twice. When you articulate your experiences to others, you understand them more deeply. And practically, teaching gigs at a community college, film school, online course, etc., can provide steady income between projects. Mentoring others also strengthens the community. A rising filmmaker you helped might become a future collaborator or even produce your film.

Adjacent Creative Work

Storytelling skills translate to other media. Some filmmakers write novels or comic books. Some direct theater. Some do photography or design. Diversifying doesn't mean abandoning film; you're feeding your creativity from multiple angles and possibly finding additional income. Just keep these side pursuits balanced to support, and not derail, your main filmmaking goals.

By diversifying, you're essentially bulletproofing your career. When one avenue slows down during lean periods, another can pick up the slack. Instead of waiting for years for a $5 million budget to materialize for your dream project, you're busy working on a short-term gig that pays rent and might teach you a new camera technique or introduce you to a new actor or investor. It's all connected.

Importantly, being multi-skilled makes you more resilient and less desperate. If you know you can fall back on an editing job or a writing assignment, you won't feel like your life is over if a directing opportunity falls through. That steadiness will keep you from burning out or selling out. It also makes you a better leader on set; you understand your crew's jobs because you've done many of them in some form. A director who's also an editor knows how to get enough coverage. A producer who's been an actor knows how to treat talent respectfully.

Think of career diversity like a tree: Your primary identity, say, writer-director, is the trunk, and the branches are the related skills that support that identity. Just don't grow so many branches that your trunk can't support them. Pick complementary skills that interest you and strengthen your core goals. The point is to enrich and stabilize your main journey, not distract yourself from it. s

So, ask yourself, what other talents could you develop? How else can you contribute to a project besides your primary role? The more valuable you become in multiple areas, the more opportunities will open, and the less likely you'll ever be stuck anxiously waiting for a miracle job. Hustle smart, diversify, and keep the income—and inspiration—flowing.

Burnout Stops Here

So Does the Drama

Have you ever ridden a roller coaster that left you in equal parts exhilarated and nauseous? That's the emotional journey of an unprepared filmmaking career. The extreme highs like festival applause, a great review, or funding secured! Followed by devastating lows such as when the money fell through, an actor dropped out, or a rejection email came from that grant you prayed for, can make even the most passionate filmmaker want to curl up and sleep for two weeks. Burnout and anxiety are real, and they're a career killer if you don't deal with them correctly. The key to avoiding that fate is to treat this gig like a marathon and a profession, not a thrill ride or a roll of the dice.

Let's acknowledge that filmmaking is inherently an emotional venture. You pour your heart into a project, so you feel it in the gut when things go wrong *or* right. We're not suggesting you become a robot, but you *do* need to find balance. If you let the ups and downs toss you around like a rag doll, you'll flame out or become bitter and cynical. Who wants to work with that person? Building a sustainable career means learning to ride the waves without losing your center.

Avoiding burnout and drama begins by injecting some professional discipline into your routine. We're talking about basic lifestyle and mindset habits:

Set a Schedule

Keep some regular hours and routines during pre-production, production, and even downtime. This is about giving yourself structure without constant chaos. You could write every morning from 8-10 or dedicate afternoons to business tasks such as emails, budgeting, and networking. Treat it like a job. A flexible, fun job at times, but still a job. Having a schedule means you have time to rest, recharge, live your life, exercise, and keep your relationships solid. Your family needs you more than your career does.

Manage Expectations

Roger once heard a saying that stuck with him; "Every day is a good day, but some days are better than others." We don't know who originated that saying, but it simply means that not every day is going to be a blockbuster day. Some days, just answering a few emails or tweaking your script is all you get done, and that's fine. By setting realistic daily and weekly goals, you avoid the constant feeling of failure that many over-ambitious creatives battle. It's great to have lofty long-term goals, such as "I'll finish the screenplay by next month" and "I'll raise $50k by the end of the year." That drives you, but break those into bite-sized tasks. When you steadily check things off, you feel progress, and that momentum carries you through the dreary days.

Take Care of You

Sleep enough. Consume something other than coffee and craft service snacks. Make time for regular exercise. Move your body, even if it's just walking the block while you brainstorm. Don't overlook your personal balance because it doesn't just affect you. It shapes how others experience working with you. Kirk once heard a story where two equally talented directors were up for the same gig. The deciding factor was that one was easier to be around, steady, self-aware, and had no drama. In this industry, talent gets you in the room, but positive energy keeps you there. If you know how to take care of yourself, stay grounded, and handle pressure without turning into a walking emergency, people will notice and keep calling.

Prioritize Mental Health

Filmmaking is pressure-packed. You're managing deadlines, egos, budgets, and perfectionism, and if you're not actively tending to your mental health, you're setting yourself up for collapse. Anxiety, depression, and impostor syndrome aren't "part of the gig." They're signals that something isn't tracking with your state of mind. Pay attention. Therapy is maintenance. Find your outlet, whether it's a licensed therapist, a peer support group, or a trusted friend who will call you on your BS. Normalize check-ins with yourself: Am I okay? Do I still love this? What do I need right now? You'd reshoot a scene if it weren't working; do the same with your mental patterns. A clear, cared-for mind will make better creative decisions, handle setbacks with more resilience, and ultimately, help you lead more gracefully.

Nourish Your Spiritual Core

At some point, you'll face a crossroads where talent and hustle aren't enough, where the only thing keeping you going is a deeper "why." Don't ignore your spiritual compass. Make space for prayer, reflection, stillness, whatever reconnects you spiritually.

The industry doesn't discuss this much, but it's vital. Your soul is not a side hustle. If your spirit dries up, your work becomes hollow. Filmmaking is a calling, not just a career. Keep that sacred fire alive, and your voice will carry further than any marketing budget ever could.

Mental, emotional, and spiritual health are your survival tools, so they aren't negotiable in this game. Find what recenters you, whether it's prayer, meditation, journaling, therapy, or just blasting your guitar in the garage. Your mind, body, and perspective must stay in harmonic tune. Burnout sneaks in when you ignore the basics, telling yourself, "I'll sleep when I'm dead" or "Just one more all-nighter." You might think that Red Bull-fueled 16-hour days make you look hardcore, but you're heading for a crash, creatively, physically, and emotionally.

Another key to long-term sustainability is separating your identity from your work if only a little. It's tough, we know; filmmaking feels like *who you are.* But when your entire self-worth hinges on the success of your latest project, every rejection lands like a personal betrayal. That's not just unhealthy; it's unsustainable. You must remember that you are more than your last film. You need a life outside of production meetings and gear. You need hobbies and friends who don't care what you're shooting.

Getting caught in a cycle of stress, self-doubt, and burnout is easy when the pressure is relentless and the results feel elusive. Depression doesn't usually hit like a lightning bolt; it creeps in gradually and can start with prolonged exhaustion, frustration from setbacks, or feelings of isolation when your vision isn't catching fire. Over time, these feelings can snowball into hopelessness or worthlessness, especially when constantly pushing forward without seeing progress. Depression doesn't mean you're weak or unfit for this path. If you find yourself in that space, know this: You have *far* more value in life than you may realize at the moment. Feeling overwhelmed, stuck, or hopeless doesn't make you broken, it makes you human. And just like you'd seek help for a broken bone, there's no shame in reaching out when your mind needs care. Depression isn't a flaw in your character. It can stem from many sources—chemical, emotional, circumstantial—but none define *who you are.* Whether talking to a trusted friend, seeking professional support, or simply pausing to breathe and recharge, taking care of your mental health is a strength. You can't pour from an empty cup and build a sustainable creative career if you're running on fumes. Take care of yourself first and always.

A reminder that there's a whole world outside your next deadline. And there is a paradox here; the more balanced you are, the more your work strengthens.

Take Kirk, for example. He's a producer, but his life isn't just film sets and final cuts. His hobbies, fantasy football, tennis, hiking, and poker, are intense, competitive, and oddly therapeutic. Poker sharpens his negotiation instincts. Hiking clears his mind and gives him space to reflect; plus, he snaps tight nature pics that can make Instagram jealous. Tennis pushes him physically, but it also teaches finesse and strategy. Fantasy football is portfolio management in disguise, predictive thinking, team dynamics, and resource allocation. All of it makes him sharper as a filmmaker. When he hits a wall in one area, he shifts gears into another and often comes back with fresh insight. That kind of balance is a force multiplier. He once read a quote about improving just 1% a day. It stuck. Because 1% daily is 365% in a year. Do the work and remember to live in the process.

Also, let's talk about the drama addiction some filmmakers have. You know the type; if things are going too smoothly, they manufacture a crisis to feel normal. Panic is their baseline; they think it's part of the "showbiz" culture. But it's not a good look, especially for a *producer.* Over time, that chaos takes a toll on your team, family, and reputation.

Drama is usually a sign of poor planning, self-control, or both. If you're always in emergency mode, ask yourself: is this a real crisis, or did I create it by procrastinating or winging it? Yes, surprises happen on every shoot. But the common denominator might be *you* if every production meeting ends in shouting or tears.

Harsh? It is if that shoe fits. Professionalism is how you treat others, but it's also how you manage your energy, emotions, and expectations.

Again, one way to reduce drama and burnout is to share the load. By building a strong team and delegating, you avoid burnout from trying to be a one-person army. One of the smartest ways to lighten your load and boost your project's success is hiring the right people, starting with a seasoned producer who's been around the block.

Hire Smart, Hire Early

The Seasoned Producer Advantage

This might be some of our most important business advice: BUILD YOUR TEAM. Do it early; on your first feature, hire a seasoned producer before hiring anyone else. If you are that producer, great, then, build a team that complements your strengths, covers your weaknesses, and gives you something worth leading.

When you're new and riding high on indie DIY spirit, juggling 1001 jobs feels bad ass. "I wrote, directed, produced, scored, and catered the film myself!" Congrats! But now you're exhausted and probably missed a few critical things in the process. Filmmaking is a collaborative art for a reason. One filmmaker we worked with insisted it wasn't. "It's one person's vision," he said. "Everyone else just works for him." That mindset didn't end well. Later, he admitted he couldn't do it without a team. He wasn't being arrogant by dismissing us, but he had convinced himself the "one vision" was the entire supply chain of creative juice.

The real magic happens when several creative people magnify their talents into something larger than the sum. Then it's not about one person doing everything, it's the right people doing the right things together. And when it comes to the business side of this art, a good producer is worth their weight in gold.

A seasoned producer brings experience, connections, and foresight, everything you typically lack when starting your career. A veteran producer has made and learned from mistakes, so you don't have to. They know the pitfalls, the legal gotchas in contracts, the realistic costs that first-timers underestimate, the festival strategies that don't work, and the distribution traps to avoid. They've managed films from idea to release, which means they can anticipate problems way down the road while you're still fussing over cameras.

Crucially, a seasoned producer often has a network. That means crew, distributors, sales agents, and even name actors. Doors that once were closed to you can magically open when an industry veteran calls on your behalf. It might feel unfair that who you know matters so much, but that's the game, so recruit people who know people, and suddenly *you* know people. It's a force multiplier for your project. It's not just "who you know," but if they are also a valued relationship where they've earned someone's trust for years. The cliché phrase, "It's all about who you know," should be something like, "It's about who TRUSTS you and vice versa." That can take years to earn. Having someone with a trusted relationship on your team is a gift. So, "Don't look a gift horse in the mouth!" Translation: accept the gift without nitpicking.

Now, you might be thinking: "How do I convince an experienced producer to work with me, a newbie with nothing but a script and a dream?" Good question. They're professionals, so you must pay a retainer for their services. You wouldn't ask your dentist to work for free, and it's not a good idea to ask your producer to work for backend points only. Be open to their bid. Be fair and respect their value.

To find producers, network at industry events, ask for introductions and use social media or filmmaker groups to find producers interested in new talent. Or reach out to us at ProfoundStudios.media. When approaching a producer, don't just say, "Help me, I'm new!" Pitch your project professionally and highlight why it could be exciting for them, too.

A reminder that a producer-for-hire will not be your source of funding, but they can add value to your funding process. There's a difference. They add a lot of credibility when you pitch to investors, but as we said earlier, real producers are trying to raise money for their projects. Unless your film blows them away and you're open to a true partnership, they won't be amenable to the marginalized role of "finding money for you." So, if you can access development funds from family or early investors, spend that money on an experienced producer. They'll open doors that will be very difficult for you to open on your own.

But that doesn't mean the lazy definition of a producer, as some might describe it. A producer isn't an editor, sound recordist, gaffer, 1st AD, line producer, or DP; those are all separate positions.

Bringing on a heavyweight means sharing control and even deferring to their advice. But that's wisdom. A smart relationship is a partnership of complementary strengths. If you're the director, that frees you to focus on creative vision and execution; the producer focuses on making that vision feasible and financially sensible. You want someone to challenge your choices if it's going to save the film or make it better. You want someone who isn't afraid to tell you, "We can't afford that crane, but here's an alternative," or "Your third act is weak; we need to workshop the script before pitching to investors." This kind of push back early on can be the difference between a project that flounders and one that flies.

And if you want to produce for a living long-term, you'll learn the ropes by osmosis when working alongside an experienced producer.

To be clear, not every project or every filmmaker will immediately snag a super-experienced producer. But even finding a producer just a few steps ahead of you on the journey can be immensely helpful, even if it's delegating duties by "divide and conquer." If you're fresh out of film school and making your first short, maybe the producer you bring on has done a few shorts and worked on a feature as an Associate Producer. They may still know more than you do in certain areas. Or, if you're gearing up for your first feature, partner with a producer who's made one modest feature or worked in development at a production company.

Once again, a line producer isn't what we're discussing here. As a reminder, the producer we're describing to you is the one defined by the Producers' Guild of America. You don't always need a decades-old veteran, though if you can get a seasoned old hand interested, go for it! The point is to know you do not need to be, nor *should* you be, the most experienced person in the room in every aspect of your film. Many have said it, and it's worth repeating: If you're the smartest person in the room, you're in the wrong room. Hire up so you have room to grow.

There's a real-life example of this principle where an indie filmmaker wrote about how he hired two experienced producers to mentor him through the process after raising some initial funds for a film. They became partners on the project, and he "humbled himself, listened and learned[1]." The result was a far smoother production and a filmmaker who came out much smarter on the other side. The cost of bringing them on was an investment in his education and the film's success. That's a winning mindset.

In practical terms, a good producer will cost upfront money and a share of your budget and profits. But they're the insurance policy you need to prevent costly mistakes and increase your film's chances of making money or at least finishing and reaching an audience. What's expensive, giving up a percentage to a producer or not finishing your film because you ran out of funds due to mismanagement? Or finishing the film without knowing how to sell it, leaving it to die on a hard drive?

If you can't find or afford a seasoned producer for your current project, at least seek advice from one. Don't operate in a vacuum. Some producers are willing to consult or offer pointers for free or a modest fee, especially if you approach them respectfully, with clear, thoughtful questions, and without assuming one favor opens the door to five more. The wisdom of experience is out there. Tap into it.

We mentioned this at the beginning of the book but it can't be said often enough: *Most indie filmmakers don't know what they don't know, and that becomes the root of all their problems.* That includes *you*. Take that to heart not as an indictment but as a warning. Ignore it, and the fallout is yours to manage.

The Takeaway

Bring on people who know more than you do, especially in the areas of business and finance. Adding a seasoned producer to your team early is like strapping a rocket to your indie film plans; suddenly, you have knowledge, credibility, and connections you wouldn't have alone. It's not

---

1   "The Importance of Finding an Experienced Film Mentor" Tom Malloy 3/31/2022 FilmmakingStuff.com

selling out; it's setting yourself up for success. Work with the pros, learn from them, and before long, you'll be the seasoned vet helping the next generation, and reaping the rewards of well-produced films.

Lead Like a Pro

Know Your Strengths, Hire Your Weaknesses

If you're serious about a long-term filmmaking career, there's one role you must embrace: Leadership. That means knowing your vision, guiding the team, and building a crew that complements your strengths, not mirrors them.

You're not great at everything. Maybe you're brilliant with actors but clueless about budgets. Your visuals might pop, but pitching terrifies you. That's normal. The sooner you admit your blind spots, the sooner you can hire people who thrive where you struggle.

Start with a self-audit: What are your superpowers? Be honest. Ask trusted collaborators if needed. This is Leadership 101; keep your ego out of it.

Bring on a seasoned line producer if you're strong creatively but shaky with logistics and money. Find a filmmaker who can bring your project to life if you're a producer but not much of a director. Leadership means doing what's best for the project, not clawing after titles.

Let the experts you hire be experts. Guide the vision, then step back. Micromanaging professionals only breeds resentment and inefficiency.

Why hire a great DP if you'll hover over every shot?

Roger says that a film is a living thing; let it breathe, nurture it with proper guidance, and help it blossom into what it's supposed to become (That's a great way to raise children, by the way). But if you hold on too tightly, you're in danger of choking your film to death.

Communication is everything. Set the tone. Clear, calm, honest communication builds loyalty. Secrecy and chaos don't. Be transparent about challenges—creative, financial, or logistical. Problems don't get smaller when you hide them.

Your leadership will evolve. The team you need now may not be the team you need in five years. That's just fine. But ask, "Do I have the right people surrounding me for this project?"

Confidence means knowing when to say, "I don't know." It builds trust, while ego kills growth.

So lead boldly, but not alone. Surround yourself with people better than you in their zones. Your job is to steer the ship, not row it. And when your team feels valued, they stick around. That kind of loyalty is platinum.

Scorsese didn't build a career alone. Neither will you.

Hire your weaknesses. Amplify your strengths. Deliver great work. That's how you lead, and that's how you last.

Always Be in Learning Mode

Stay Hungry and Keep Evolving

The film industry loves fresh talent but has no problem tossing aside those who stop evolving. If you want a career that lasts, you must be a lifelong student of the game.

The most dangerous mindset in a fast-moving business is, "I have it all figured out." The moment you believe that, the industry will humble you. Beginners *usually* assume they have filmmaking figured out, or worse, believe it. If you've never made a feature film, you don't have it figured out. Some who've made two or three don't. That's why continuing education is essential.

Technology, distribution, audience behavior, and market dynamics are constantly shifting. Stay sharp, curious, and adaptable.

Continuing education for indie filmmakers can take many forms, formal and informal. Here are some ways to ensure you're always learning and staying ahead of the curve:

Follow Industry News & Trends

Subscribe to the trades *(Variety, Hollywood Reporter, Deadline)* and indie film sites *(IndieWire, Filmmaker Magazine, No Film School, etc.)*. Make it a habit to skim the headlines daily or weekly. Learn to analyze the news and ask, "Why?" Who got a big distribution deal, and why did they get it? What genre is hot in the streaming market, and why did certain films excel in the genre while others failed? Which indie just broke out at the box office unexpectedly? Why? This is market research. If you know what buyers and audiences are responding to, you can make more informed decisions about what projects to pursue or how to position your own. Staying informed about industry shifts like a new streaming platform launching or theatrical indie successes in foreign markets can spark ideas for your next move.

Learn New Skills & Tech

The tools we use to make and sell films evolve. One year is all about shooting digital vs. film, and another year is about virtual production with LED walls. Next, everyone's using some new editing software or a game engine to pre-visualize scenes. You don't have to chase every trend, but you do need to update your technical knowledge. Take a workshop on that new camera or spend a weekend learning the basics of Unreal Engine or whatever is buzzing. At the very least, you need to understand technology enough to discuss it and decide if it's useful for your work. The same goes for distribution tech; know how streaming algorithms work, how to navigate a crowdfunding platform, etc. Each skill you add makes you that much more self-sufficient and confident.

Study the Masters (and the Newbies): Keep watching films and content, both classic and contemporary. It's easy when you're busy hustling to stop watching movies for inspiration; don't fall into that trap. Make time to see what other filmmakers are doing, especially the upcoming generation, not to compare or get jealous, but to learn. Every film, good or bad, has lessons. If it's excellent, find out why it works. If it sucks, ask what could have been done differently. Read books or listen to podcasts by filmmakers you admire. There's a wealth of knowledge in interviews and director commentaries that can give you insight into both the craft and the business.

Engage in Workshops, Classes, or Labs: This could mean applying to a Sundance Lab, attending a weekend producing workshop, or even enrolling in an online course for writing or marketing. The structured environment can force you to grow in areas you might neglect alone. And don't scoff at film education just because you're out of school—the industry pros teaching these things often have up-to-date real-world experience. Plus, workshops and labs are networking opportunities in disguise; you might meet a future collaborator or mentor there.

You'll be in great company; Javier Bardem returns annually to Juan Carlos Corazza's acting school in Madrid for a month of training. He values the opportunity to challenge himself and reconnect with the fundamentals of acting, stating, "It's a place where I can go to do it wrong, and after the others see me fail onstage, they say, 'He's got the same [issues] that we do.'" Sigourney Weaver credits her expanded acting range to ongoing sessions with coach Jack Waltzer. Introduced to Waltzer by Roman Polanski in 1993, Weaver engaged in his master classes to deepen her craft. Pro golfers practice daily and hire coaches to improve their skills. The list of professionals from many industries who routinely attend classes and labs for continuing education is almost endless.

Network and Listen

Sometimes, education is just shutting up and listening to people who know things you don't. Attend film festivals, not just to hawk your film but to go to panel discussions, Q&As, and mixers. When you meet other filmmakers, ask about their experiences. How did they land their distributor, and how did that relationship work out? What's the biggest lesson they learned on their last shoot? You'll pick up so much by being curious and letting others share their war stories. And again, you expand your network, often leading to more learning opportunities. Maybe someone mentions a great entertainment lawyer; file that away. Perhaps a conversation alerts you to a grant you never heard of. It's all proper intel.

Stay Humble and Adaptable

The overarching mindset here is humility, admitting you don't know what you don't know and need to keep learning. The industry will evolve with or without you; it's better if you to grow with it, simultaneously. In the early 2000s, many old-school filmmakers resisted digital cameras and online distribution. Some adapted late and survived; others became irrelevant. In the early 2030s, maybe it's AI, interactive content, blockchain, or global streaming dynamics. We don't know exactly what tomorrow's game-changer will be, but we do know that those who stay curious and flexible will ride the wave instead of drowning.

Remember, continuing education is an investment in your longevity. It keeps you from becoming that grumpy veteran who's bitter that "nobody watches movies in theaters anymore" while the world moves on. Instead, you'll be the savvy creator who saw and leveraged the new trend while still doing what you love.

Staying educated also loops back to keeping your passion alive. Learning new things can spark creativity. A course on VR storytelling may give you an idea of a traditional film that is told from a different point of view. Maybe reading about international co-productions plants a seed to shoot in a country you never considered, with funding from abroad. When you keep feeding your mind, you prevent stagnation. And a filmmaker who's constantly growing is far less likely to burn out because there's always a new challenge to ignite that original passion.

In short, never stop being a student. The great thing about this industry is that it's an endless playground of knowledge. You cannot learn everything there is to know about film, and that's beautiful because it means you'll never run out of things to discover. Embrace that. The most impressive filmmakers aren't those who think they have all the answers but those who are always asking questions. Stay hungry, keep learning, and you'll keep finding new ways to build and sustain your career.

Careers Are Built, Not Born

By now, the message should be loud and clear: Sustainable careers are built, brick by brick, day by day, through intention, discipline, humility, and collaboration. It's about playing the long game with eyes wide open, balancing your artistic soul with your business brain.

Building a sustainable career in independent filmmaking is not an easy path. But the beautiful payoff to doing it is you get to wake up every day and live the life of a filmmaker on your terms. It is not a one-hit-wonder, not a "remember that guy who made that thing once?" but a true professional storyteller with a body of work and a wealth of experience to show. You'll have ups and downs, hits and misses, sure. But you'll also have the confidence that you're in control of your trajectory, and the respect from others knowing you're the real deal.

And perhaps most importantly, you'll contribute to an industry culture where success is routine rather than accepting a 97% failure rate. Imagine a world where independent film isn't seen as a wild gamble but as a viable, vibrant alternative asset class in the eyes of investors because filmmakers like you consistently deliver quality and demonstrate sound business practicies. That's the world we want to help create, and you have a role in it.

So, go forth with intention in your plans, discipline in your work, humility in your attitude, and collaboration in your heart. Build that sustainable career brick by brick. One day, you'll look around and realize you've constructed something far more rewarding than a one-time jackpot – you'll have built a life in film, on solid ground. And that, dear filmmaker, is a legacy worth chasing.

Mastering In-Person Networking

"The world is run by those who show up."

— President Andrew Shepherd,

The American President (1995)

In a world obsessed with likes, follows, and digital clout, it's easy to forget the oldest truth in showbiz: Nothing beats showing up in the room. You can tweet with producers or DM actors all day, but if you want real industry connections, *be* there. Shake hands. Make eye contact. Be *present*.

There's a saying in the biz: Network or no work. Most film gigs aren't on job boards but are passed along through relationships. So yeah, put on some nice threads and go meet people.

If networking makes your skin crawl, you're not alone. Most filmmakers would rather be behind the camera than working a room. But you don't need to be slick or extroverted to be great at it. This chapter is your guide to real-world networking; where to go, how to build genuine rapport without being a desperate puppy dog, and what *not* to do.

Networking is about showing up, staying curious, and building relationships over time. Let's go.

Why Face-to-Face Still Matters (More Than Your Follower Count)

These magical in-person opportunities happen anywhere filmmakers gather to screen, learn, or celebrate.

Film Festivals – Obvious but essential. From Sundance to your local indie fest, festivals are full of filmmakers, producers, actors, critics—your whole ecosystem. Attend screenings, Q&As, mixers, and after-parties. Spark a convo with, "What'd you think of that last short?" Easy. Can't afford a pass? Volunteer. Instant access and street credibility.

Workshops & Panels – Industry masterclasses and Q&As are gold. You learn something, and you're shoulder-to-shoulder with fellow filmmakers. Talk to the person next to you. Thank the speaker afterward—instant connection.

Mixers & Meetups – In most cities, clubs, groups or individuals host casual film meetups in bars or creative spaces. Everyone's there to talk, so lean in. Don't see one near you? Start your own. A weekly film night can grow into a powerful circle.

Local Screenings & Events – Support indie screenings, student films, film clubs, Oscar parties—anything film-related. After the event, congratulate the filmmaker. It's genuine, easy, and opens the door.

Markets & Industry Conferences – If you're a little further along, hit events like AFM. They're more business-driven but still all about face time. Just being there regularly signals you're part of the tribe.

Show up, consistently. Don't hit one mixer a year and call it networking. Go often, build face familiarity, and before long, people will greet you with, "Hey, good to see you again." That's when the real magic kicks in.

How to Build Real Rapport Without Being The Desperate Puppy Dog

Alright, you made it to the event—*now* what? How do you connect without appearing like a needy vampire? Be human first, filmmaker second.

Show up without an agenda. Yes, you might be looking for a producer, a job, a collaborator, or a buyer for your script, but if that need radiates off you like a fire alarm, people will turn away. Nobody wants to feel like they're being targeted for a transaction. So, relax. This isn't *Shark Tank*. It's just people who love film and hanging out. Sometimes, there are events at festivals and conferences where you can sign up for a pitch-a-thon or other opportunities to pitch a producer, script, or finished film for distribution. We often attend those events as producers looking for projects, and that's an excellent opportunity to build relationships. But it's in an environment designed *precisely* for building relationships whether you're extroverted or introverted. Deals are never made on the spot, but they open the doors to that possibility.

Outside of that structure, it's perfectly fine to approach an industry professional. Smile. Say hi. Ask something easy: "What did you think of the keynote?" or "That shirt's amazing—Hitchcock fan?" But read the room; professionals are radar-tuned to spot agendas and sleight-of-hand. They're always pitched by people who don't know what they don't know, and the second they smell an agenda, they'll clam up. Build friendships first. Business will flow out of that friendship. It takes time, but that's how the game is played on the indie playground.

Listen more than you talk. The fastest way to get ignored is to dominate the conversation. Ask what they're working on. Be curious. Engage. That alone will make you memorable.

When it's your turn, have a clean, 20–30-second answer to "What do you do?" That's not your cue to launch a TED Talk. Something bite-sized and fun: "I'm finishing a short comedy about a time-traveling barista—it's been wild. How about you?"

And don't force your pitch. Wait for a natural segue. If they say they need a sound designer and you know one, perfect. If not, leave it at a good first impression. That's the win.

Networking should feel like making a new friend, not a backroom deal. Laugh. Share. Connect.

Be the version of yourself people want to talk to again, which translates to *being yourself*. That's the *entire* game, right there.

By the way, that's the same way you build relationships with investors. Let that sink in. If you read a fundraising book or paid thousands of dollars to attend a capital-raising workshop, building relationships with investors before pitching will be the #1 takeaway. Makes sense, right? Investors invest in people first.

Following Up: From Handshake to Lasting Connection

So, you had some great chats and swapped info. Now, the real work begins. Events plant the seed. Follow-up is the sunlight and water that make it grow.

Don't wait three weeks. Within a day or two, send a short, friendly message; email, DM, text, whatever makes sense based on your connection. Remind them who you are and where you met, and reference something specific. Example:

"Hey Jane, great meeting you at SXSW. Loved hearing about your doc—your desert story cracked me up. Let's keep in touch. I know someone who would be great if you need a sound editor. Good luck with your festival submission!"

That shows you listened. It's flattering, adds value, and is not a thinly veiled ask.

Personalize It

No copy-paste "nice to meet you" spam. Mention that raccoon-on-set story or shared love of sports. Real details make you memorable.

Don't offer a gift basket, just something helpful. Recommend a contact, a location, a film, or an article. Small, useful gestures build trust. Networking is trading.

Keep It Short

No monologues. No 120-page scripts. You're building rapport, not closing a deal. Think friendly thank-you note, not "Please review my life's work."

From there, feel it out. If the vibe's good, suggest a coffee sometime or say, "See you at the next event." Follow through on anything you promise. Do what you said you'd do. That's how trust starts.

Stay lightly on their radar: Comment when they post big news, share an opportunity, tag them on something relevant. Keep it warm. Keep it real. That's how a quick convo at a mixer turns into a real industry relationship.

Planting Seeds and Adding Value Before You Ask

Networking is a long game. The connections you make today might not pay off for months or years. That's normal. That's how it works.

Think like a farmer, not a hunter. You're planting seeds by showing up, being cool, and offering value. Keep watering. Check in, stay supportive, and be helpful. One day, one of those seeds will bloom: A casual chat at a workshop becomes a job offer a year later, or a friend-of-a-friend drops your name to a producer. You never know which relationship will bear fruit, but the more you plant and nurture, the better your odds.

Most people make the mistake of rushing it. They meet a producer at a panel and ask for script coverage the next day. Slow down. Build trust before you ask for anything. Be supportive. Volunteer. Offer a useful intro. Add value first, then ask later.

Think of it like social credit. Every positive interaction builds a bridge. Build the relationship, then make your ask. It works way better and won't feel gross.

If you want to be taken seriously, show up consistently. Don't be that person who only appears when they need something. Show up when there's nothing in it for you. That's how people remember you and trust you.

Play the long game. You'll build a real network, not just a contact list. And when the time comes to ask for something, it'll feel like asking a friend. That's how careers are built.

Networking Hall of Shame

What Not to Do

Nothing kills a connection faster than rookie mistakes.

Don't Be the All-About-Me Megaphone. If every sentence starts with "my film, my script, my genius," you should seriously consider a career in politics, not filmmaking. Networking is a dialogue, not a monologue. Share briefly when asked, then pivot. Show interest in the other person. Nobody wants to help someone who only talks about themselves.

Don't Pretend to Listen. If you wait to talk instead of listening, people can tell. Your eyes glaze, you interrupt, and you miss their point entirely. Be present. Ask for a follow-up. Make them feel heard. It's basic, but it's powerful.

Don't Pitch Cold. This is not your pitch meeting. Don't ambush people with your logline mid-convo. If they didn't ask, don't offer. And for the love of humanity, don't carry scripts or DVDs to parties. It screams amateur. Build rapport. If they're interested, there's time later.

Don't Launch With "Should We Hop On a Call?"

Ugh. The LinkedIn message that asks, "Does it make sense to hop on a call?" No. It doesn't. That question is just a polite vampire bite. We give an hour of free advice and eat wasted time for lunch, because nothing productive emerges from those calls. Please don't do that to anyone.

Don't push vague calls unless there's a clear reason and mutual interest. Most of the time, filmmakers are just fishing—trying to hook an industry executive into legitimizing a half-baked idea. Instead, follow up with a credible and professional purpose. Later, if the email conversation evolves, you can say, "Would love 15 minutes to ask your advice on X." Specificity earns the ask. And remember, industry professionals are busy, so asking for valuable time on the phone without clarity or value to do so is an amateur move. "Hey, Roger, I was at your seminar today and have a script I've been working on. I really felt the synergy between us, so when would be a good time to hop on a call?" That's the fastest road to Ghostville. Vs: "Hey, Kirk, Great news, we got the deck together, and I would welcome your feedback and learn more about your process. Thanks!" That's much more precise, and it doesn't feel like a trap, especially if Kirk previously advised you to get a proper deck together. We'd likely open the deck to look at it and maybe discuss the next steps. You get the idea.

The problem is that filmmakers can easily fall into the trap of familiarity. They meet an industry professional at an event, engage in a "promising" conversation, and think the connection is an open door through which to charge. Don't be the sleazy salesman who shoves your foot into the crack of a barely opened door. Unless the invitation has already been extended, begin the follow-up with a polite knock and a professional and legitimate reason to come to the door in the first place.

Don't Be Fake or Clingy

Forced flattery and overly formal vibes are a dead giveaway for something less than sincere. And if someone's disengaging, let them go gracefully. Don't chase VIPs to the bathroom with your pitch. Social cues matter. Read the room. Respect goes a long way. Avoid these traps, and you'll be ahead of 97 percent of the room.

Shift Your Mindset

Networking = Genuine Curiosity and Value

A significant part of networking the right way is re-framing your thoughts. Real networking is about curiosity, consistency, and mutual benefit.

Think of it as making friends in your professional world. Go into each interaction asking, "Who is this person? What can I learn?" not "What can they do for me?" You listen better, connect deeper, and stand out naturally when genuinely curious.

Adopt a mindset of adding value. This could mean sharing information, offering encouragement, introducing yourself, or listening well. People remember those who contribute, not just those who take.

Consistency matters. Networking is a regular part of your creative life. Show up, stay connected, and trust that it builds over time.

And above all: be real. Don't create a fake interest just to fit in; never inflate your credits. Be honest, humble, and confident. You're not begging for a shot; you're offering your talents, and that's valuable. Treat people with respect, and they'll remember you.

Reframe networking as building genuine relationships around the work you love. That's how opportunities find you and where the playground feels much more fun.

Networking Is a Skill – And You Got This!

By now, you might be thinking, "I'm not naturally good at this." Networking is a skill to learn, not a personality trait. No one's born great at it. Every successful filmmaker started awkwardly, nervously, and unsure. If it doesn't go well the first time, they do it again. They got better with practice. You will, too.

Mastering networking opens doors you didn't even know existed. Projects, referrals, and real opportunities flow through relationships. It's not just what you know or who you know. It's who knows you and thinks well of you.

You don't need to be extroverted; introverts network just as successfully. Just be honest, prepared, and present. Know your intro. Show up ready and listen. That's it.

If you're shy, set small goals: Talk to one new person per event. Prepare a few icebreakers. Remember: You don't have to impress to connect. Good questions go further than good stories. Many investors and other producers are introverted, too. Kirk sees himself as an introvert until he's asked to speak publicly; then, it's like a switch flips, and "it's on." Imagine that many folks you're approaching likely have much in common with you. How will you know unless you find out?

Not every interaction will click. That's normal. Success is staying consistent without getting discouraged.

And celebrate the small wins: Showing up when you're nervous and having one real conversation adds up. Kirk met a new investor at a film festival, making small talk and jokes about asking if the punch was spiked. One thing led to another, and that friendship grew without expecting anything further. Kirk didn't even know the guy was an investor until a year later. That led to a long relationship and multiple films.

Networking, done right, doesn't just fuel your career. It fills your life with real allies and friends. Work the rooms with confidence. And remember, no one makes it alone.

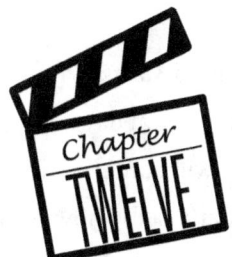

Eyes on the Horizon

So here we are, Chapter Twelve! What a ride. If you've made it this far, you've been through insights that might have embarrassed you because you are guilty of one or more of the mistakes we wrote about. All good, no shade, and you bought this book to learn how to do it better than you thought you ever could.

You absorbed the hard lessons and stuck with it. In this final chapter, we're going big-picture: wrapping up the core lessons from this guide and then peering into the near future of what independent filmmaking could look like, grounded in everything you've learned.

Recap

Core Lessons from the Journey

Before we bust out the crystal ball, let's recap the key takeaways you need to tattoo on your brain:

Treat Your Film Like a Business

Approach your film as an entrepreneur would with a startup. Budget realistically, plan for revenue, and strategize distribution from day one. Indie filmmaking doesn't work with a "build it and they will come" mindset. You're creating a product you must finance, market, and sell. Show business is two words; the second matters just as much or more than the first. Develop a business mindset, so you're not just making art but making a living from it.

Don't Skip Proper Development

We know you're itching to grab a camera and start rolling. But rushing in without solid development is an amateur's mistake. The development phase—writing, revising, budgeting, scheduling, and planning distribution and marketing—is where you bulletproof your project. It's the foundation of the success or failure of your film. Every hour refining the story and planning the production will save you ten hours and countless dollars. The best directors and producers sweat the small stuff early so the shoot and post-production work. Your story is your foundation, so make it rock-solid before production.

Know Your Market

Your film might be your baby, but it's also a product for an audience. Who are they? Faith fans, art-house aficionados, rom-com date night couples? Identify your target market and tailor your approach to them. It's not selling out – it's making sure your film connects. Whether you're gunning for the festival circuit, niche streaming platforms, or a YouTube fan base, knowing where your film fits is half the battle. Do your homework: what similar films have succeeded, and how? If you can't describe your audience beyond "It's for everyone," you're not ready to spend one dollar on production.

Raise a Marketing Budget

One of the cruelest truths in filmmaking is that a great movie can die unseen if nobody knows about it. By now, you know to stash cash for marketing as surely as you budget for cameras or catering. Smart indie producers treat marketing as essential and don't expect a distributor to figure it out. It's a line item as critical as the camera department. Remember, Hollywood studios often spend 2x or 5x of the cost of production on marketing and advertising. Isn't that the stereotype you've heard, "Hollywood is all about marketing?" Uh… yes. If you're an indie filmmaker and not a big fan of "Hollyweird," you can probably still respect that they know how to market. Use what works. An effective ratio might be less than 1:1, but you need a war chest to get your film in front of eyeballs. Plan how you'll promote before you raise funds, and then fuel the hype machine.

Build a Team

Independent doesn't mean alone. You might wear twelve hats to get through pre-production, but no one makes a film solo. Assemble a killer team of people who share your vision and complement your skills. That means crew, cast, mentors, and champions. Hire people better than you in their specialty; an experienced cinematographer, a savvy AD, an editor with storytelling chops, a lead producer. Leadership in indie film often means being the chief recruiter of talent. So, cultivate your tribe: Find folks who will go the extra mile on a shoestring because they believe in the project and you. Treat them well, inspire them, and work your collective butts off together.

Invest in Relationships

Beyond your core crew, this business runs on relationships. Filmmaking is a long game; every connection can spark the next opportunity. Think about all your contacts at workshops, film festivals, on set, and even on social media. Stay in touch, support others, and build your network. These ties matter to the distributor you met at a festival, the line producer who offered advice, or the director you exchanged notes with. Doors open because of people, not just projects. Who you know won't replace talent, but it multiplies your chances to succeed. Put genuine effort into networking and helping others; over time, you'll have an army of allies in your corner.

You Don't Know What You Don't Know

The indie filmmakers who crash and burn often can't admit, or identify, their gaps in knowledge. Be humble and curious. If distribution isn't your forte, find someone who knows it. If you're clueless about sound design, consult a sound editor early. There's zero shame in asking questions or bringing on advisors; it's precisely what a smart producer does. By admitting that you don't know what you don't know, you position yourself to learn and avoid nasty surprises. This book gives you a great foundation, but the learning never stops. Continuous improvement is your secret weapon. Armed with that mindset, you'll navigate pitfalls that swallow up less prepared filmmakers.

The biggies are the core principles we've hammered on through this book. If any of these still make you flinch, re-read the chapter that tackles it. Truly own these lessons. They are the bedrock of your strategy as you venture forward.

With these fundamentals in your toolkit, let's turn our gaze to the horizon. The world of filmmaking is evolving faster than ever. For scrappy independents like you, that means opportunity. Time to dive into the trends and tech that are shaking up the game and how you can leverage them without losing sight of those old-school fundamentals.

The Future of Indie Filmmaking
New Tools, New Terrain

"We are at the crossroads between art and commerce."

– Kirk Roos

Most artists don't fail because they lack talent. They fail because they don't understand *business*. They don't study the market. They don't build infrastructure. They wait for permission. And by the time the world finally notices them, they're often dead broke, or just plain dead.

That's a tragic pattern stretching from Edgar Allan Poe to Van Gogh; brilliant creators who lived in obscurity because they weren't wired for commerce. They were wired for beauty, but beauty, unfortunately, isn't enough to move units.

If you're an independent filmmaker, or any kind of creative professional, you are standing at a new kind of crossroads. One even more complex than before.

The Crossroads Has a New Name: Tech

The next 5 to 20 years will see a seismic shift in how art is created, distributed, monetized, and owned. And if you're still thinking like it's 2015 (or 2005, or 1995), you're going to get left behind.

AI Integration: Your New Assistant (Not Your Replacement)

Artificial intelligence is the buzzword du jour. Maybe it's more accurate to say it's the buzzword of the millennium! And unlike a lot of hype, this one's making a difference on set and in post-production. But technology is a tool, not a savior. A great story and a savvy filmmaker are still the driving forces of a film; AI helps you execute faster and maybe cheaper. So, how can artificial intelligence fit into your indie toolkit?

No, a computer isn't going to spit out a Tarantino-level screenplay on its own, and who would want it to? Think of it as a super-charged script consultant: It won't replace your creativity but can kickstart ideas when you're staring at a blank page. Feeding your outline into an AI might reveal patterns or provide prompts – "80% of thrillers have a twist by page 30, did you consider doing that?" That's information you can use or ignore. The control stays with you, the writer; AI offers a fresh lens. Shortly, you might verbally pitch a scene to your laptop and watch as an AI drafts a version in seconds, ready for you to refine. It's like having Robo-caffeine for your creativity; great for a creative jolt, but you still have to do the real writing.

Next, let's talk about production and post, where AI is coming in hot. We're already seeing AI-driven tools handle grunt work that used to eat days of an editor's life. Need to sync a ton of audio and footage? Balance color between shots? An AI-powered editing software can crunch through those repetitive tasks in a snap, freeing you up to focus on the creative edits. AI can automate tedious post-production chores like color grading and sound sync with astonishing speed. Fewer late nights for your editor means more time polishing the cut.

And how about visual effects on an indie budget? Welcome to the era of AI-powered VFX. Machine learning can analyze your footage and generate CGI elements that blend shockingly well with real shots. Like that sci-fi short you want to make, with creatures or futuristic cityscapes you thought were out of reach. You can pull off respectable effects with AI assistance without a $100M ILM budget. We're talking about AI that can erase the water bottle you accidentally left in a frame or populate a crowd scene with virtual extras who don't demand lunch breaks. AI can remove most background noise that would otherwise have to be fixed with ADR. It's democratizing CGI for filmmakers who have big visions but tiny wallets. One filmmaker recently experimented with AI tools like RunwayML to create a fantasy battle scene by mixing AI-generated elements with practical footage, and the results were surprisingly solid for a one-person VFX team. Shortly, you might design entire locations or even minor characters using generative AI art and animation. AI avatars for low-budget VFX are on the horizon, too.

Do you need a futuristic soldier or an alien in the background? Instead of hiring an actor and costly makeup/prosthetics, you could generate a photorealistic digital character and composite it in. Early adopters are already playing with this; in a few years, it could be as normal as using After Effects.

Imagine it's three years from now, and you're making a gritty detective thriller. You write the script with help from an AI that suggests a few clever red herrings. You then feed rough storyboards into an AI tool that instantly creates a 3D preview of your scenes. Now you know exactly how the car chase will look before you hire the stunt drivers. During production, an AI camera assistant auto-adjusts your shots for perfect exposure and focus (goodbye, reshoots of out-of-focus takes). In post, you realize one pivotal scene would hit harder at sunset instead of noon – no problem, an AI program changes the lighting in your footage to golden hour, and it looks real. You didn't have the budget for a helicopter to shoot skyline footage, but you typed a prompt and generated a few seconds of gorgeous aerial city shots to use as transitions. Finally, you use an AI marketing tool to cut a dozen trailer variants and see which one an online test audience responds to best.

Sci-Fi is here. It's a looming reality for Indies. AI is not here to take your job; it's here to take some of the drudgery out of your job so you can focus more on creative.

AI is as significant as the discovery of fire; it's *that* profound. You can fight, ignore, or call it the devil's work, but it's not going anywhere, and it will only get more powerful.

But remember, without a solid story, no amount of AI will save you. A terrible script with perfect color grading and slick AI monsters is still awful. Use AI to amplify your skills and do what you can't do alone, but don't let it lull you into thinking you can cut corners on storytelling or human insight. At the end of the day, audiences want compelling characters and emotions, not just stunning imagery. You could gain an edge if you embrace AI as a clever assistant. If you rely on it as a crutch... You will make very fast, efficient, polished garbage.

Blockchain and Decentralized Film Financing: Fans as Investors, Films as Tokens

Blockchain technology underpins Bitcoin and other cryptocurrencies, and it's beginning to make waves in film financing and distribution. At its heart, blockchain is about secure, transparent transactions and decentralized control for filmmakers, which translates to new ways of raising money and reaching viewers without always relying on traditional gatekeepers.

One significant innovation here is the tokenization of film assets. In plain English, you can represent ownership or investment in your film through digital tokens on a blockchain. Imagine selling off 20% of your film's future revenue as 1,000 digital tokens. Fans and investors worldwide could buy these tokens and thereby fund your production. It's like crowdfunding 2.0: Instead of a T-shirt or a thank-you credit, backers get a token that might earn them a tiny slice of the profits if your film takes off. This approach democratizes investment, opening the door to a global pool of micro-investors who believe in your idea. You're no longer limited to begging a few deep-pocketed patrons or chasing studio execs; you can rally a community of true believers who want you to succeed.

It's already happening. Films have been funded through cryptocurrency ICOs (Initial Coin Offerings) and NFT sales. In 2021, an indie film called *Zero Contact,* starring Anthony Hopkins, no less, was released as an NFT, treating the film itself as a digital collectible. And more projects are flirting with these models every day. You have platforms specializing in blockchain-based film financing, allowing creators to mint tokens or NFTs tied to their project's revenue or ownership. Early adopters are navigating some legal gray areas here (securities laws are no joke), but the momentum is real.

Let's break down a speculative scenario: You have an excellent concept for a thriller, but traditional fundraising isn't going well. So, you create KillerCoin, a custom token for your movie, *Killer App.* You outline that 10,000 KillerCoins will collectively be entitled to 20% of the film's gross profits. You sell these tokens to the public – maybe film fans, crypto enthusiasts, whoever, to raise $500,000 for your budget. Each token holder now has a stake (small, but meaningful) in your movie's success. The blockchain automatically records their ownership. Production happens, you finish the film, and you self-distribute online. Through smart contracts (self-executing programs on the blockchain), whenever your film earns money – a rental, a sale, whatever – that 20% designated for token holders automatically gets split and sent to their digital wallets. No middlemen, no accounting shenanigans, no waiting months for checks. It's instant, transparent payment to your backers. Essentially, you've turned your die-hard fans into investors and then into your marketing squad – because you better believe they'll tell everyone to watch *Killer App* since they have "skin in the game."

Beyond financing, blockchain could shake up distribution, too. Decentralized distribution platforms might allow you to release your film directly to viewers and get paid in cryptocurrency, with every transaction recorded transparently. This could reduce piracy and ensure you see every cent you're owed. It's like putting your movie on an indestructible ledger where no more studios cook the books, or mysteriously make profits "disappear" through Hollywood accounting. For indies, that clarity is a revelation; you can instantly know if your film is making money and automatically ensure the team gets their share.

Technology is not magic. There are challenges: Crypto markets are volatile. Your $500K could be worth half if the token value crashes, and not everyone trusts NFTs yet (lots of scams and hype to sift through). Regulations are still catching up; you might accidentally create tradable security and run afoul of the law if you're not careful. Crucially, using blockchain doesn't guarantee people will want to watch your film; you still need to make something people care about. However, as part of a smart strategy, these tools can give the little guys some advantages that were once reserved for the big studios and financiers.

At its best, blockchain tech promises empowerment and transparency. You get to keep more control over your work, and your supporters get to participate in your success tangibly. It flips the script on the old power dynamics. We're not saying NFTs will fund every future indie film or that you should drop everything to learn Solidity coding. We are saying that understanding these trends could open opportunities for you. In an industry notorious for opaque deals and creators getting screwed out of profits, a world where code automatically enforces fair payouts is quite attractive.

Your next project could get a boost by selling a limited-edition NFT that grants super fans behind-the-scenes access and a vote on the key art design. You could distribute via a blockchain-based platform that reaches a niche audience globally without intermediaries. Stay flexible and watch this space. The indie filmmakers who embrace these tools wisely might find themselves ahead of the pack. The hustler who adapts is the hustler who survives.

New Distribution Windows and Platforms: Beyond Theaters and Traditional Streaming

Distribution used to be a straightforward sequence; theatrical release, then DVDs, then pay TV, then maybe late-night cable. Those days are as gone as Blockbuster Video. The modern landscape is a wild, fragmented world of possibilities, especially for indie films that might not sniff a wide theatrical run. The good news is you have more ways than ever to get your film in front of an audience. The challenge is that you must be savvy and strategic to make any money or impact amid the noise. Here's what's up in distribution:

Streaming rules the day. Netflix, Amazon, Hulu, Apple TV+, Disney+… the list is long and growing. Theaters are still a thing, but their heyday is long gone. Getting your indie feature onto a major streaming platform is the holy grail for many indie filmmakers. But many streamers now focus on their productions or high-profile acquisitions, putting most indie films out of reach of those options. But the digital revolution has other doors open for you:

Niche Streamers and Platforms

Your film may be very specific, such as a basket weaving documentary or a neo-noir Filipino thriller. The good news is there's likely a niche platform for that. Filipino filmmakers target the SVOD channel, iWantTFC. Documentary makers might hit Docurama or CuriosityStream. There are platforms for shorts, black cinema, and indie darlings like IFC's streaming arm. These smaller services may not pay huge licensing fees but seek indie content to please their dedicated subscribers. Being a big fish in a small pond can be more attractive than being plankton in the Netflix ocean.

Hybrid and Event Distribution

Another emerging idea, especially after the pandemic era, is treating distribution like an event or interactive experience. You could do a live-stream premiere on YouTube or Twitch, where you, as the filmmaker, do a Q&A before/after, turning it into a special night.

Live streaming your film globally in real-time can create urgency and a communal feel. Imagine this: "Tune in at 8 pm Eastern Friday to watch with us." Some filmmakers sell tickets to online premieres on platforms like Moment or Veeps, essentially running a virtual theater. And, of course, there's still the good old film festival circuit, which has partly moved online, too. Festivals sometimes geo-block a selection of films for virtual attendees. The point is to think beyond the obvious. A limited theatrical release in 2 cities might get you 2000 views, whereas a digital event could get you 20,000 if you've built an online following.

Windowing is Flexible Now

The sequence in which you release things can be non-traditional. You could drop your film online worldwide, then later do special theatrical event screenings once buzz has built (the reverse of the old way). Or release episodically in short chapters on a platform, then compile into a feature for sale. Maybe you put a film out free for a limited time to build word-of-mouth, then later put it behind a paywall. There's no one-size plan so that you can be creative with distribution.

Key Advice

Educate yourself on distribution or get a mentor who knows it. Distribution changes every year. What stays constant is the need for hustle. To get onto platforms, you opt to self-distribute, which many indie filmmakers do now via aggregators like FilmHub or Quiver. In that case, you'll need to be your own marketing department. That's why we keep yammering on and on about a marketing budget! Getting onto a platform is one thing; drawing viewers to click on your film is another. That's why building an audience on social media, having a great trailer and poster, and timing your release smartly, maybe you can ride a trend or theme. All of it matters.

The Takeaway

Today, you have unprecedented power to get your work in front of a paying audience. You don't have to wait for a studio or distributor to "give you permission" to be seen. The flip side is if you dump your movie online without a plan, it'll vaporize without a trace. The new platforms reward those who come prepared and treat distribution as an extension of the creative process. So, plan your festival run, VOD debut, social media blasts, and collector's edition Blu-ray if you have super fans – plan it with the same care you did your screenplay or your shots list. Indies find their audience in the modern era by being tactical, flexible, and audience-savvy. The tools are in your hands; use them wisely.

The Future Will Reward the Business-Minded Artist

Andy Warhol understood the audience. He understood attention. He understood that commerce shapes culture, and he leaned into it.

"In the future, everyone will be world-famous for 15 minutes."

– Andy Warhol

Was he right?

Were his soup cans less 'art' because they sold well? Or were they art because they understood the world they were made for?

So, What Should You Do Now?

- **Study tech.** Know what blockchain, Web3, and AI can do for you.

- **Build community.** Fans are more valuable than festivals.

- **Control your rights.** Think long term.

- **Think beyond "release day."**

- **Collaborate smartly.**

- **Create systems.**

The Short-Form Storytelling Resurgence

Big Impact in Small Packages

Some of the most exciting indie creativity happens in short-form content like short films, web series episodes, and 60-second micro-movies, bite-sized storytelling that fits the online era. Once upon a time, short films were mainly calling cards for directors to prove their stuff or bonus features on DVDs that almost nobody watched. But today, the short form is having a renaissance, thanks to digital platforms and audiences' insatiable appetite for quick, engaging content. As an indie filmmaker, this is a trend you can't afford to ignore. It's both an opportunity and a testing ground.

Consider the Landscape

TikTok and Instagram Reels have trained a generation to devour stories in under a minute. Remember when "short" meant a 15-minute festival piece? Now, a 15-minute video online feels like an epic. Audiences are scrolling, swiping, and watching on phones, hungry for content that grabs them fast. Far from dumbing things down, this has given rise to incredible creativity under time constraints. It's the haiku version of filmmaking— you need to evoke emotion, tell a story, maybe land a twist, all in the time it takes for someone to wait in line for coffee. And people are pulling it off! There are horror shorts on YouTube that are three minutes long and scarier than entire feature franchises. There are one-minute dramas on TikTok that have made millions of viewers cry or laugh. Audiences are consuming content in bite-sized pieces, with TikTok leading the charge, and that presents a massive opportunity for you to build an audience and hone your craft.

Why Short Form is a Goldmine for Independent Creators

It's faster and cheaper to produce. You can shoot a five-minute film over a weekend with friends, edit it in a week, and have it online, getting feedback immediately. Compare that to the year(s) of labor and fundraising a feature requires. This low barrier to entry means you can experiment more. Try bold ideas in short form; some will flop, but others might blow up big. The financial stakes are lower, but the rewards in exposure can be high.

It can go viral, but that's a bonus. You can't build a business plan around "maybe." Platforms like TikTok, YouTube, and Reddit have produced overnight sensations, but the reality is that algorithms now favor frequent output over one-off hits. Every so often, a short will catch fire—David F. Sandberg's *Lights Out* or the proof-of-concept that became *Saw*—but those stories are the *exception*, not the rule.

Today, the smartest use of a short is as a strategic proof-of-concept for a feature you're already developing, a teaser to excite investors, or part of a series that builds your audience over time. Chase the lightning strike if you want, but make sure it's connected to a bigger plan. It's a lab for your ideas. If you have a feature script you're unsure about, make a short set in that world or a scene from it, and see how audiences react. Short-form content can be a proof-of-concept for your bigger projects, e.g., Angel Studios' Torch[1], a prototype video that is at least five minutes long and accurately represents what the final production looks like.

Short form is a way to test the market and your execution. If the short leaves people begging for more, you know you're onto something. If it falls flat, it's better to learn that in three minutes than after spending $500K on a feature. Studios are doing this too: Notice how Pixar releases short films to test tech/characters or how *Kung Fury,* a crowdfunded 30-minute insanity homage to 80s action, became a cult hit, leading to a feature-length sequel with Michael Fassbender attached. In indie land, your short could be your calling card and focus group.

Shorts build your portfolio and your skills. Each short project is a chance to practice storytelling, refine your style, and populate your You-Tube or Vimeo channel with content. It keeps you in the conversation and maintains momentum between larger projects. Also, you never know who's watching. Your next collaborator or investor might first encounter you through a two-minute film on Instagram that some mutual contact shared. Stay visible by consistently putting out quality short content, and you'll slowly but surely grow a following.

All that said, short form isn't a panacea. It won't directly make you rich – monetizing shorts is tricky because ads on YouTube pay pennies unless you have huge view counts, and TikTok's creator fund is infamously stingy. But exposure, networking, and skill development pay off in other currencies. It's also increasingly respected. Festivals like Sundance and Cannes

---

1   **Angel Studios' Torch:** A short proof-of-concept film produced for Angel's Torch platform, where filmmakers present their vision, tone, and story potential. These videos are used to rally audience interest and attract early backers, giving Guild members a preview of the creative direction before a project is greenlit.

give high honors to short films, and there are Oscar categories for them. And online, there's no distinction to the audience; a gripping story can be three minutes or three hours.

The resurgence of anthologies and series is another angle. Short-form content has made conceptualizing stories told in episodes or pieces easier. Maybe you don't have the budget for a feature, but you can produce a five-part web series with ten-minute episodes. Release them weekly on YouTube or a custom site, promote them on social media, and you've essentially distributed your mini-Netflix series. If it gains traction, you could compile it and sell it as a feature or pitch it as a show to a bigger platform. Studios are also eyeing short content for IP – look at how the web series *High Maintenance* got picked up by HBO or how Comedy Central scooped the YouTube series *Broad City*. Shorts can be a scouting ground for the industry. Playing in that space, you're essentially auditioning your ideas for a global audience.

International Co-productions

Go Global to Level Up

All around the world, there are vibrant film industries with talented professionals, equipment, locations, and money. Sometimes, one of the smartest moves an indie filmmaker can make is to think beyond borders. Enter the realm of international co-productions, where you partner with producers or companies from other countries to get your film made and distributed. It's not just for big-budget art house films or Oscar-bait dramas; it's a strategy that can benefit you, the scrappy indie creator, by unlocking resources and audiences you might never reach otherwise.

Our colleague lives in Houston and produces and releases in Argentina. Production costs are a fraction of those in the US, and he carved out a nice living in the process.

Different countries have different funding pools, such as government film grants, tax incentives, and regional funds that might become available if your project is structured as a partnership with a local entity. By partnering with a foreign production company, you could tap into their home turf advantages: Maybe France, Germany, South Africa, or wherever will chip in funding because now it's partly their film, too. Co-productions can unlock additional funding sources and subsidies in the partner's country. It's like having multiple patrons instead of one.

Perhaps the story you wrote is set in part overseas; a co-production can give you boots on the ground there, local crews, and maybe even a known actor from that region to boost international appeal. You're pooling resources and sharing the load, which can make a huge difference when every dollar counts.

Then there's market access. By its nature, a co-production is a child of two or more countries; ideally, it can claim citizenship in all of them. Your film about an American traveler and a Japanese local forming an unlikely friendship could, as a US-Japan co-production, be eligible for enhanced distribution support in both nations. You instantly broaden your potential audience. By partnering with foreign entities, you tap into new markets and diverse audiences that might have been hard to reach solo. And you get the bonus of cultural exchange: The film might resonate more globally because it's infused with multiple perspectives. We live in a connected world; stories that blend cultures or speak to universal themes across borders can punch above their weight. Look at movies like *The Farewell*, an

American-Chinese co-pro, or *Slumdog Millionaire* (UK-India) – these had crossover DNA that helped them captivate worldwide audiences.

For you, the indie hustler, an international co-pro might mean the difference between your project languishing due to lack of funds and getting a green light with support from another corner of the globe. It's also an adventure and a learning experience; you'll navigate different filmmaking cultures and practices. Yes, it can be complicated with legalities, languages, and logistics, but many have done it successfully. Some producers and lawyers specialize in stitching these deals together. Film festivals and markets like Cannes, Berlin, and Toronto are hotbeds for co-production matchmaking. Entire sections of these events are dedicated to helping filmmakers find overseas partners.

Imagine having a script set in Texas and Mexico. Instead of shooting Texas scenes in Texas and faking Mexico in your backyard, you team up with a producer in Mexico. You apply for a co-production status, which qualifies you for a grant from the Mexican Film Institute and access to a studio in Mexico City at a discounted rate. You cast a rising Mexican actor for the scenes there, boosting the film's profile in that market. Your budget stretch is insane; what was a $500k movie out-of-pocket is now easier to fund with various parties contributing. When it's done, you have a built-in premiere at a Mexican film festival through your partner, and distribution in North America is easier because, hey, two markets for the price of one. You've effectively doubled your exposure and resources by thinking internationally.

We will see more of these cross-border collaborations in the future, not fewer. Streamers and sales agents are hungry for content that appeals to multiple regions. If you can truthfully say your project has angled for North America and European and Asian territories all at once, that's a selling point. Plus, technology makes collaborating across distances easier than ever – Zoom meetings to hash out scripts with your co-writer in Paris, cloud-based post-production with editors on three continents, and digital dailies are shared instantly. The world is smaller, and that benefits you.

Ultimately, filmmaking is filmmaking; the process is the same whether your crew is from your hometown or five countries. But by venturing into co-productions, you're leveling up your hustle to a global scale. You're recognizing that great stories can come from anywhere, and your support system can too. So don't be afraid to reach out across the ocean or over a border. The future of indie film might be an international potluck, with each collaborator bringing their best to the table and everyone enjoying the feast.

Tech Is a Tool, Story Is King

Never Forget This

We've just thrown a lot at you: AI, blockchain, new platforms, TikTok, and co-productions. It's a lot of shiny new toys and evolving paradigms. It's normal if your head's spinning with excitement and confusion, but let's bring it back to a core truth that threads through every chapter of this book and should be the basis of every decision you make: Story is king. Or queen. Pick your metaphor; the point is the same. We've said it before, and we'll say it again: All the fancy tech and innovative strategies in the world won't mean a thing if you don't have a compelling story and a clear vision at the center.

It's easy to get starry-eyed about the future. You might be itching to proclaim, "I'll fund my next film with NFTs, shoot it in VR, distribute it via a blockchain streamer, and have AI aliens as co-stars!" Ambition is great, but unhinged ambition will waste your time. New tools are exactly that—*tools*. They don't *replace* the fundamentals; they *enhance* them.

Remember the chapter on knowing your market? Don't ignore it because you think some algorithm will magically find your audience. You need to define and reach your audience using tech as an assistant.

A muddled, boring film will still flop, whether on YouTube or beamed directly into people's brains via Neuralink (soon, maybe?). Conversely, a powerful story can transcend technical limitations. We've all seen a grainy, low-budget film that moved us to our core or a YouTube video shot on a phone that made us laugh harder than a $200 million studio comedy. The magic of story and human connection is that a world-changing story can be written on the back of a napkin. No algorithm can manufacture genuine heart... at least not yet, and if it ever does, we'll have bigger problems.

So, as you integrate new technology and trends into your filmmaking, do it for the story and the audience. Use AI to save money and time, then reallocate those savings to hiring a better actor or extending rehearsal time—things that improve the story. Use blockchain to engage an audience of backers, but then deliver a film that pays off their trust with quality. Use short-form content to tease and test ideas, but make sure the payoff as a feature or series delivers more than just the gimmick of being short or techy.

It's also about your brand as a filmmaker. The tools you use don't define you; *your voice does.* Don't chase a trend just because it's hot. If everyone's suddenly making interactive VR films but your passion is for classic linear storytelling, stick to your guns. Maybe incorporate a tiny interactive element if it truly adds something. Conversely, if you're a tech geek who loves this stuff, pioneer it—but keep asking, "Is the audience getting something valuable, or am I just flexing tech for tech's sake?" Hold yourself to that standard. Future audiences will be ever more media-savvy, and they can smell BS a mile away. They'll know when a film is all sizzle and no steak.

One more facet of keeping story and strategy above tech; human relationships. No AI will replace the electricity that happens when creative people brainstorm together in a room, the instinct of an experienced DP who lands a magical frame on the fly, or the emotional intelligence of a director drawing a raw performance from an actor. Those are the analog, human, almost mystical parts of filmmaking. Develop them. Cherish them. Don't let the seduction of the latest software make you skip team building, communication, and leadership—all those "soft" skills that are the bedrock of a successful production.

And when it comes to dealing with all these changes, realize once again that you don't know what you don't know. If you're not a crypto expert, consult someone before launching a token. If you've never used a specific AI tool, experiment on a smaller project before leaning on it for a big one. If a distribution avenue is foreign to you, talk to folks who have done it. Today and beyond, a filmmaker must be part artist, entrepreneur, technologist, and psychologist. It's okay if you're not all those things naturally; nobody is. But be curious enough to learn and humble enough to get help where needed.

In summary, stay grounded. Trends will come and go. Your true North should make a danged good feature, series, or short that resonates with people. Story and audience first, tech and technique second. That's how you'll navigate the future without losing your soul or sanity.

The Final Truth

It's Still a Blood Sport,

But Now the Beast Doesn't Automatically Win

Independent filmmaking has always been and always will be a blood sport. It's a gladiator arena filled with thousands of dreamers swinging their metaphorical swords of cameras and scripts, trying to make their mark. It's crowded, it's cut-throat, and it will never, *ever* be easy. This industry will test you in every way: financially, emotionally, and physically. You will face skeptics and gatekeepers, technical disasters, and eleventh-hour betrayals. You will likely pour your money into it and might not enjoy a return. You will almost certainly question your life choices at 3 AM on some awful night during post-production when nothing is working, and you're surviving on caffeine and despair.

By now, you know that we call it like it is, because tender words are for fragile minds and clueless weekend warriors. You're far above that, and now, you'll be walking into this fight with a real strategy, tools, and allies. You're not some naive kid with stars in their eyes stumbling around blindly, thinking, "Golly gee, making movies sounds fun!" We want you to hold onto the fun, but you get the drift. You, dear reader, have now armed yourself with knowledge and a plan. And that changes the game from a battleground to a playground.

After reading this book, think of everything you have going for you: You know how to approach your film as a business venture and how to plan it from concept to distribution. You know how crucial development and marketing are, so you won't be caught dead without a polished script or a budget to promote your work. You have learned the importance of a team and relationships, meaning you'll never be stranded alone. You'll have collaborators and mentors to lean on. You've accepted that you don't know everything, so you're open to learning, a true superpower. And now, on top of all that, you're hip to the future: You won't be the dinosaur cling-ing to old ways. You'll be the agile indie filmmaker who adapts, whether it's leveraging AI tools, raising money in innovative ways, or finding your audience on emerging platforms.

In short, you have a fighting chance. Your dream is still insanely hard, but now it's possible. That word "possible" is enormous. It's the difference between foolish odds and a winnable battle. A lot of people have dreams; few have a *plan*. Now, you have a plan.

By stepping into the arena with eyes wide open, you've already separat-ed yourself from the pack of delusional hopefuls who will flame out fast and drag the indie spirit down with them. Every hard day and setback adds to your origin montage in the biopic we'll someday watch about you.

You have a dream to tell stories, move people, shine a light on truths, entertain, provoke, and inspire. That dream is your fuel. Keep it front and center. The hustle makes the dream real. Protect that dream. Nurture it. It's not just about fame or money (if it is rewind to Chapter One—we need to talk). It's about the burning need inside you to create and share it with the world.

The world needs better stories. Look around—we're drowning in con-tent but starving for meaning. We have endless sequels, blockbusters, and franchises but we yearn for fresh voices that stay out of the cesspool. We need stories only you can tell with your unique perspective, background, and passion. Independent filmmakers have always pushed cinema forward, taking risks the big players won't and giving the world new eyes to see with. The future of cinema has always been written by brave souls working out-side the traditional system, innovating because they had to, and changing the whole game.

As we stand at the edge of this new era, with all its tech and turmoil, it's going to be filmmakers like you who build the future of cinema from the ground up. You have the tools, the knowledge, and the grit to do it. Whether you're creating the next great streaming series, a groundbreaking interactive film, a micro-budget genre classic, or an entirely new form of storytelling we can't even define yet, you are part of this grand evolution. And you're not doing it alone; you're joining a lineage of independent creators who refused to quit. That's inspiring.

So, here's the final rallying cry, friend: Greenlight yourself! Keep dreaming – big, wild, audacious dreams about the stories you want to tell and the impact you want to have. Keep hustling – smart, relentless hustling with all the strategies and integrity you have. And then do it all again and again. This cycle of creation and perseverance is your life now. It won't be easy, but it will be worth it.

Feeling badass yet? You should be. You got this. Go out there and show the world what *professional* independent filmmakers are made of. We'll be waiting in line to see your work—popcorn in one hand, pride in the other, saying, "We knew that storyteller back when…" Now, make it happen. The future of film is yours to shape. Films that rise above of the ocean of sunk dreams don't just happen, they're built by filmmakers who know the game and play it with purpose. The credits are about to roll on this book, but your story is just beginning.

"And they lived happily ever after,

until the end of their days."

— Bilbo Baggins.

Epilogue

By Roger Lindley

Roger v1.0 was a kid with a hammer. I knew how to build *things* but not how to build a *career path*. Later versions sent me chasing opportunity wherever it popped up—sometimes in construction, sometimes behind a camera, sometimes chasing deals that looked golden until they dissolved between my fingers.

Every crash forced an upgrade. Roger v3.0 realized *no one* cares about your dream unless you can turn it into something *they* care about. Roger v5.7 believed a single project could be the magic ticket, only to discover it lacked a solid enough foundation to build upon. Roger v8.2 discovered humility the hard way, when talent and effort weren't enough to outrun bad decisions. By the time I arrived at Roger v12.2.1, I had learned to stop waiting for that One Upgrade where I finally "arrive." The journey is the goal. Arrival is irrelevant.

With each version upgrade, I learned something essential. Construction gave me structure. Editing revealed the power of systems. Cinematography sharpened my perspective. Directing demanded organization. My entire, crazy career required patience. Together, those lessons delivered a truth I could not shortcut: Nothing great is accomplished alone, and nothing lasting is built without structure, systems, perspective, organization, and patience. You cannot greenlight yourself without the whole package. You cannot build a career on anything less and expect it to thrive.

My failures are part of the operating system just as much as my successes. Every crash, reboot, patch, and workaround built the package that sustains me now. I am not here in spite of the failures; I am here because of them.

The same will be true for you.

Maybe you're at Roger v1.0, swinging your hammer, wide-eyed and eager. Maybe you're at v4.3, fresh off your third crash, wondering if you should bother to reboot. Maybe you're closer to v9.9, well into the fight but carrying scars and running out of hard drive space. Wherever you are, your next upgrade might sting, but it will make you stronger—if you allow it.

To me, greenlighting yourself is a process. You learn. You build. You crash. And you learn again, repeating the cycle until wisdom and experience hopefully reduce mistakes to manageable nuisances. That only happens with time.

Resist perfection; *no one* has that capacity. Instead, strive for *excellence,* which carries bandwidth for mistakes (but not repeated ones). There's no final version and no upgrade that's flawlessly bug-free. There's only *iteration.* Each project, choice, risk, collaboration, patch, and bug fix adds up. Many will make you proud to be alive. A few will wreck your day. Both are necessary.

Keep upgrading. Classical computing systems are binary, ones and zeros, yes or no, on or off. But life isn't binary. It's quantum. Quantum computing isn't simply a step forward, it's countless leaps ahead, holding almost infinite possibilities until coherence locks them into reality. That's the truer metaphor for your journey. Each version draws you nearer to alignment, where coherence turns potential into form. That's quantum progression, not linear, and it resonates with who you were born to be. I have three final thoughts for you:

1- Never rest in the satisfaction of your accomplishments. The *second* you stop growing is the moment you start to die.

2- Recognize and *admit* when you don't know what you don't know—chasing in the dark after misguided expectations leads nowhere except, in hindsight, after reality slaps you around, to *clarity* hopefully, and the hard-won wisdom of experience, *if you persevere.* I've been down that road more times than I care to admit.

3- You don't need anyone's permission to unlock your future. You just need to be *ready enough.* That version might not look like much today, but neither did Roger v1.0.

By Kirk Roos

As we look ahead in media, technology, marketing, and filmmaking, it's clear that change is not just constant — it's accelerating. AI might disrupt entire workflows. Streaming platforms may rise and fall. Formats shift. Terms evolve. What was once standard — like shooting horizontal footage — becomes outdated in a vertical world of TikTok and reels. One day, you're warning your partner not to shoot vertically; the next, "verticals" are the new norm. But through every shift — from the campfire to the stage, from the stage to the screen, from the screen to the stream — one thing remains: story-telling.

Storytelling is our inheritance. It's how we make sense of the world, how we pass on wisdom, how we laugh, how we grieve, and how we heal. It predates every medium, and it will outlive every algorithm.

Sure, you need to know how to navigate budgets and pitch decks. You need to understand financing terms and legal agreements. You need to adapt when Netflix changes the rules, when technology reshapes distribution, and when new jargon like "verticals" or "compression ratios" enters the conversation. But don't let the noise distract you from the signal.

At its core, *Greenlighting Yourself* is not just about filmmaking. It's about communication—the ability to connect one human to another through intention, structure, and emotion. Whether you're writing a script, leading a crew, pitching an investor, or debating a friend, the skillset that matters most is *clear communication.*

I didn't always know this. When I was a theater student, I didn't care much for debate class or broadcast journalism. I wanted to sing, sword fight, and improvise. But years later, I realized that those communication classes—the ones I didn't take seriously—ended up preparing me to do the hardest part of indie filmmaking: explaining yourself clearly under pressure. Making a crew feel safe when the clock is ticking. Calming a financier when the market shifts. Encouraging a cast when the vision feels far away.

That's the real job. That's the real artistry. It's part mentor and part therapist and a cocktail for being a CEO, creative consultant, and guy who sleeps in the grip truck when the padlocks broke and we had no security on set... (yeah, I did that!)

Years ago, my late wife Bryn and I didn't know all the answers. But we knew enough to start. We greenlit ourselves not because we were ready, but because we had stories to tell. Over the years, I learned the hard way, too many times, that it "takes a village." And even then, you're in for a challenge.

Each project brings its own unique challenges, and the variables of those hurdles and roadblocks can build a lifetime collection of cliches for your repertoire ranging from, "the goal posts keep moving," to "dominoes kept falling" or "it was a house of cards" or "there were many ripple effects" to made up ones that will keep your crew full of belly laughs some late nights on sets. My favorite is "Producing is like herding cats." Those tend to come off a little negative, even if the truth hurts.

Long term, the "marathon, not a sprint" has worked the best for me.

I've had to make up a bunch of my own, creative and positive mantras! In fact, each year for my birthday, I give myself a new one. And often they incorporate my current business strategies, as well as my personal life goals. They've ranged from "Focus on What Matters" to "Be Here Now" to my favorite, "Trust your Heart, Walk with God." Not walk to God, or for God, but WITH. My personal journey to get to where I'm at has included a lot of self-reflection, as well as some personal hardships. When you need to declutter and filter out a lot of the "noise" in this business, it's good to check in again with what matters. Family. Friends. Your own heart.

In 1995 an actor told me, "If you want to still be doing this when you're 88, and don't mind the idea of never being rich… then you're cut out for this industry. We do it because we love it, not for the money." I remind myself of that every day. I suggest a good dose of balance as well. Go play pickleball with a friend. Take your nephew to a movie. Read. Go for a walk. Listen to music. Call a former teacher and thank them for encouraging you. Take a nap. Have a big laugh.

And that includes laughing at yourself.

OK. Now you've read twelve chapters of hard-earned lessons. That was "the tip of the iceberg," honestly. We'll have to save the lessons we left out of this book for the podcast or HBO series. I think Seth Rogen may be doing that show as we speak.

But while we shared our mistakes with tough love, we want to remind you we both have decades of beautiful experiences as well.

Coincidentally, Roger and I both worked in Kurdistan of Iraq around the same time, on different documentary films. We've both had exciting world travels, adventures, and most importantly, met some of the most amazing people you could imagine. And it's their stories that kept us in this industry. We've learned many lessons, experienced numerous failures, and achieved a few successes. But it's the people, from the crew to the audiences at film festivals to the colleagues at events, that make this so rewarding. And that's only part of what we hope you'll take away. In addition... We hope you take *action*.

We hope you meet people — *and yourself* — where they're at.

As Roger once said to a stubborn manufacturer at a film convention, sometimes you have to meet people where they are *and speak their language*. That advice applies to everyone in this business from the new writer still doubting their voice, to the seasoned producer managing a crew on fumes. The ability to bridge those gaps—to lead with clarity and heart—is your greatest asset.

The world will keep changing. Formats will evolve. AI may rewrite the rules. But your voice, your integrity, and your willingness to connect — those are timeless.

So take what you've learned.

Add your chapter to the story.

And whatever you do —

Don't wait.

Greenlight yourself.

Appendix

Comprehensive list of streaming rights, expanded from Chapter Seven:

1. Digital / Streaming Rights

Rights for distributing content via online platforms, including subscription, transactional, and ad-supported models.

- SVOD (Subscription Video on Demand): Access to content via a recurring subscription fee (e.g., Netflix, Hulu, Disney+).

- TVOD (Transactional Video on Demand): Per-transaction purchases or rentals (e.g., iTunes, Amazon, Google Play), including gifted access.

- PVOD (Premium Video on Demand): Early-window releases at a premium price (e.g., $19.99+ rentals for new films).

- AVOD (Ad-supported Video on Demand): Free content supported by advertisements (e.g., Tubi, Pluto TV).

- FAST (Free Ad-Supported Streaming Television): Linear, TV-like streaming channels (e.g., Roku Channel, Samsung TV Plus).

- EST (Electronic Sell-Through): Permanent digital ownership of content (e.g., buying a film on iTunes).

- Cloud/Digital Locker Rights: Storage of purchased content in digital lockers (e.g., Movies Anywhere).

- Social Media Rights: Content tailored for platforms like TikTok, YouTube, or Instagram (e.g., short-form promotional clips).

2. Broadcast & Cable TV Rights

Rights to distribute content via traditional television channels, including premium, free, and cable networks.

- Pay TV: Premium cable or satellite channels requiring a subscription (e.g., HBO, Showtime, Starz).

- Free TV / Linear TV: Over-the-air network television with scheduled programming (e.g., CBS, NBC, ABC).

- Cable/Satellite TV: Basic or mid-tier cable channels (e.g., Syfy, Lifetime, AMC).

- Syndication Rights: Licensing content for reruns on local or cable stations (e.g., Friends on TBS).

- International TV Rights: Licensing broadcast rights by territory (e.g., a show sold to a UK broadcaster).

- Second Window Rights: Rights for subsequent TV broadcasts after the initial airing (e.g., a film moving from HBO to basic cable).

3. Physical Media Rights

Rights to distribute content in tangible home video formats.

- DVD/Blu-ray: Domestic and international home video distribution (e.g., DVD, Blu-ray, 4K UHD).

- Sell-Through Rights: Sale of physical copies for consumer ownership.

- Rental Rights: Physical media for rental services (e.g., Redbox, historically Blockbuster).

- Collector's Editions/Special Editions: Premium physical releases (e.g., Criterion Collection box sets).

4. Theatrical Rights

Rights to exhibit content in commercial cinema settings.

- Domestic Theatrical: U.S. and Canada box office exhibitions.

- International Theatrical: Cinema exhibitions divided by territory (e.g., Germany, Japan, China).

- Festival Rights: Screenings at film festivals (e.g., Sundance, Cannes).

- IMAX/3D/Special Format Rights: Exhibitions in premium theatrical formats (e.g., IMAX, 3D, Dolby Vision).

- Re-release Rights: Rights for re-releasing films in theaters (e.g., anniversary screenings).

5. Public Performance Rights

Rights to screen content in non-commercial or institutional settings, often requiring Public Performance Rights (PPR).

- Non-Theatrical Rights: Screenings in non-commercial venues (e.g., schools, churches, libraries, prisons).

- Educational Rights: Screenings in classrooms or academic settings, often exempt under the face-to-face teaching exemption (17 U.S.C. § 110(1)).

- Military Base Rights: Screenings on military installations.

- Prison/Institutional Rights: Screenings in correctional or other institutional facilities.

- Museum/Exhibition Rights: Screenings in cultural or public institutions (e.g., museum film series).

6. Specialty Rights

Rights for niche distribution channels outside traditional cinema or institutional settings.

- Airlines (In-flight Rights): Screenings on commercial flights (e.g., via providers like Anuvu, Spafax).

- Ships/Maritime Rights: Screenings on cruise ships or other vessels.

- Hotels & Hospitality Rights: In-room entertainment systems in hotels (e.g., via LodgeNet, Vubiquity).

7. Ancillary & Derivative Rights

Rights to create new works or products derived from the original IP.

- Remake Rights: Creating a new version of a work (e.g., American remake of a foreign film like The Departed).

- Sequel/Prequel Rights: Extending the story world forward or backward (e.g., Star Wars: The Empire Strikes Back).

- Spin-off Rights: Character- or theme-based extensions (e.g., Better Call Saul from Breaking Bad).

- Merchandising Rights: Producing toys, apparel, or other products (e.g., Harry Potter merchandise).

- Novelization Rights: Adapting the story into a book or comic (e.g., Star Wars novelizations).

- Game Rights: Creating video games, mobile apps, or tabletop games (e.g., The Witcher video game).

- Stage Rights: Live theatrical adaptations, such as plays or musicals (e.g., The Lion King Broadway).

- Audio Rights: Producing podcasts, audiobooks, or radio plays (e.g., The Lord of the Rings audiobooks).

- Television Rights: Adapting a work into a TV series or miniseries (e.g., Fargo TV series).

• Theme Park/Attraction Rights: Developing rides or experiences (e.g., Harry Potter at Universal Studios).

• Serialization Rights: Adapting into serialized formats like web series or short-form content (e.g., The Mandalorian).

• Music/Sync Rights: Licensing music or songs from the IP for other uses (e.g., soundtrack licensing).

• Clip Licensing: Using excerpts in other media (e.g., trailers, documentaries).

8. Emerging Platforms

Rights for distributing or adapting content on new or evolving technologies.

• Virtual Reality (VR)/Augmented Reality (AR) Rights: Creating immersive or interactive experiences (e.g., Star Wars: Vader Immortal VR).

• NFT/Web3 Rights: Blockchain-based ownership, collectibles, or access tokens (e.g., NFT-based film tickets).

• Metaverse Rights: Content for virtual worlds (e.g., Roblox, Decentraland).

• AI-Generated Content Rights: Licensing IP for AI-driven adaptations or experiences (e.g., AI-generated story extensions).

9. Hybrid Distribution Rights

Rights that bridge traditional and digital distribution models.

• Catch-Up Rights: Allowing networks to make content available online for a limited time after airing (e.g., NBC app offering episodes for 7 days).

• Interactive Rights: Content with choose-your-own-adventure or gamified elements (e.g., Netflix's Black Mirror: Bandersnatch).

About the authors...

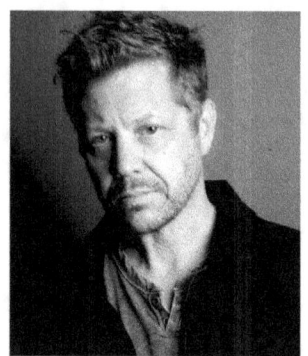

Kirk Roos, PGA

Producer

Originally from North Dakota, Kirk has worked in Hollywood for 30 years as an actor, writer, and producer. He was a founder of Northern Lights Films, Badlands Features, Heartstrings, and Profound Studios. Recent releases include: *Faith of Angels, Santa's Cousin,* and *Brothers in Blues,* the story of Jimmie and Stevie Ray Vaughan.

He recently acted in a film called *Love on Tap,* and enjoys guest speaking engagements. His other producing credits include: *The Brass Teapot, American Herro, High Road, 3 Days with Dad, Painkillers, Gold Rush: White Water,* and *Rediscover the Corps.* Kirk received his Bachelor's in Communication Arts from Minot State University and his Master's in Business from University of Mary. He has one daughter, Clarashea Roos, who recently graduated from UC Davis.

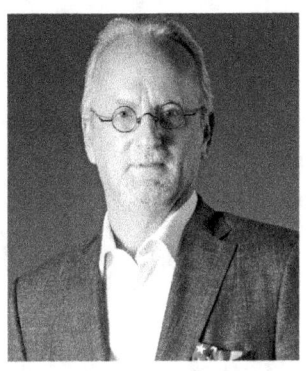

Roger Lindley
Director, Executive Producer

Roger has worked in film and television for over 40 years as a cinematographer, director, and executive producer. His camera credits include *Bollywood Beats, Meant to Be, Revelation Road: The Black Rider.* His work has appeared on CMT, CNBC, BBC, Discovery Canada, Telemundo, and The Travel Channel, among others.

As a director, he helmed the award-winning features *Taken by Grace, Revenge in Kind,* and the acclaimed *The Kurdish Factor* documentary. He continues to produce T*he American Rancher* on RFD-TV.

He is an Executive Producer for *Faith of Angels, Santa's Cousin, Brothers in Blues, Good Grief* and is co-founder of Profound Studios and its distribution brand Heartstrings. He and his wife, Shellie, live in Fort Worth, Texas. Their son, Clayton, is active in film and television production in Scottsdale, Arizona.

www.ingramcontent.com/pod-product-compliance
Lightning Source LLC
Chambersburg PA
CBHW071445220526
45472CB00003B/673